T0326310

SIR THOMAS WYATT
THE YOUNGER,
c.1521–1554
AND
WYATT'S REBELLION

Sir Thomas Wyatt the Younger, c.1521–1554

and Wyatt's Rebellion

James D. Taylor, Jr.

Algora Publishing
New York

Taylor, James D., 1958-
    Sir Thomas Wyatt the Younger and Wyatt's Rebellion / James D. Taylor, Jr.
        pages cm
    Includes bibliographical references.
    ISBN 978-1-62894-009-1 (soft cover : alk. paper) — ISBN 978-1-62894-010-
7 (hard cover : alk. paper) — ISBN 978-1-62894-011-4 (ebook)
    1. Wyatt, Thomas, 1521?–1554. 2. Insurgency—England—History—16th
century. 3. Mary I, Queen of England, 1516-1558. 4. Great Britain—History—
Mary I, 1553-1558. I. Title.
    DA347.T39 2013
    942.054092—dc23
    [B]
                                        2013027258

Printed in the United States

A little rebellion now and then...is a medicine necessary for the sound health of government.

— *Thomas Jefferson*

TABLE OF CONTENTS

PREFACE AND ACKNOWLEDGEMENTS

While working on my last book, *The Shadow of the White Rose, Edward Courtenay Earl of Devon, 1526 to 1556*, I realized that I was only telling part of a story, as there are many links between Edward Courtenay and Thomas Wyatt the Younger, son of Thomas Wyatt the Elder. Thomas Wyatt the Elder receives partial credit for introducing the sonnet into English literature, later refined by William Shakespeare. Thomas the Younger is mainly known for leading a rebellion against the advent of the Catholic Queen Mary Tudor.

This work is the product of many years of research in which I reviewed all that 600 years of history has recorded, and as when researching Edward Courtenay, I was particularly intrigued by references to missing or altered documents. The most valuable references are those from the period of Wyatt's lifetime and immediately thereafter, such as the account recorded by John Proctor, who was a schoolmaster from Tunbridge Wells and published the events of the rebellion the following year, 1554. Although Proctor's account may be slightly biased, his account is a valuable asset in comparison to those of other historians who do not offer as much detail. One additional account that is especially useful is provided by Raphael Holinshed, whose chronicles offer a rare and detailed account of a complete court trial of one of the conspirators; it is included in this edition.

Other notable historians of the period only recorded bits and pieces over the span of Wyatt's life, but when these fragments are assembled, a portrait begins to emerge of a well-educated, intelligent and disciplined man. Wyatt stood firm in his belief to the very end and discarded what could have been a comfortable life, perhaps following his father in ambassadorial duties and a comfortable and dignified retirement.

Though nothing new was discovered, this is the first complete edition about Thomas Wyatt the Younger and of the rebellion he led — which cost the lives of many who followed him — against the marriage of Queen Mary Tudor and Prince Philip of Spain. The resulting executions totaled into the many hundreds and earned Queen Mary the nickname of Bloody Mary in one of England's most violent periods of history.

The documents used in this edition are reproduced as near as may be to the way they were originally published (or the way they were originally handwritten). Due to the challenges of evolving standards of grammar, typography and orthography, some inconsistencies are unavoidable. My aim is to enable readers to see how each writer expressed himself or herself, preserving the flavor of Medieval English.

A work of this nature can only be produced with the assistance of many knowledgeable and helpful professionals. I offer a special thank-you to the staff of the Harlan Hatcher Graduate Library, the Law Library, and Angela Balla, Ph.D., of the Special Collections Library, all of the University of Michigan-Ann Arbor. My gratitude goes as well to the staff of the Purdy-Kresge Library at Wayne State University for their patience and assistance, and to the many who gave their assistance and guidance from the British Library, whose references and vast holdings helped make this book possible. Further thanks go to the Royal Historical Society University College, London, for providing copies of the original document and allowing the reproduction of the *Treatise on the Militia.* I also must thank the staff at the Pitts Theology Library at Emory University; the Bodleian Library and Ashmolean Library at Oxford; and the William Andrew Clark Memorial Library at the University of California, and the Folger Shakespeare Library; and last but most certainly not least Dr. Charlene Berry of Madonna University for her spiritual support, guidance and invaluable critiques throughout this project.

CHAPTER 1. THE WYATT FAMILY ANCESTRY

Sir Henry Wyatt

Henry Wyatt was born into a Protestant family that had lived in Yorkshire for many generations and accumulated a great deal of land. History has not recorded the early years of his life, but it is possible that he was born between 1460 and 1465, to Richard Wyatt and Margaret, daughter of William Baliff, during the reign of Edward IV. For reference, the ancestral charts of the Wyatt family are located in Appendix I. History has recorded very little about the Wyatt family prior to Henry Wyatt, as it would appear that no noteworthy circumstances attracted attention.

Henry Wyatt resisted the ascent of Richard III to the throne because of political differences and as a result was arrested and confined in the Tower for two years. One account indicated that he was restrained on a rack in Richards's presence and vinegar and mustard were forced down his throat. An apocryphal tale recounts that a cat brought Henry Wyatt a pigeon every day from a nearby dovecot while he was a prisoner in the Tower of London, preventing him from starving to death. This story is so popular that a couple of portraits are known to have survived representing Wyatt and the cat.

Richard III, last of the Plantagenets, died in battle against a distant cousin, a Lancaster, who assumed the throne as Henry VII in 1485. Richard was the last king descended from the House of York, and his demise meant the end of the War of the Roses.

Henry promptly married Elizabeth of York, uniting the bloodlines, although that was not sufficient to resolve the feud to everyone's satisfaction.

King Henry soon made new assignments in the government. The following year Henry Wyatt received a position as Clerk of the King's Jewels, and Clerk of the Mint two years later, and then he was given the assignments of Master of the Jewel House, Keeper of the Exchange and Assayer of the Coinage. Soon after, he became a member of the Privy Council and served as Esquire of the body for the King. With this very prestigious assignment he gained a great deal of recognition. For outstanding services to the King, Henry Wyatt was not only generously rewarded with annual salaries, but more importantly, the lands he received in the county of Kent and other locations were to serve as the foundation of the Wyatt's wealth. It was with these accumulations of land that the Wyatt family became more recognized and more often recorded in history.

Henry Wyatt was not only involved in administrative functions, but military also, which included leading the battle against Scottish incursions in Carlisle, most likely under the command of Richard Neville, Earl of Warwick. Wyatt then served as an agent for King Henry VII in Scotland and kept the King informed of the events there. In June 1486, England entered into negotiations with King James III of Scotland and the outcome was a treaty for a three-year truce.

Wyatt then assisted the King in Ireland during the Perkin Warbeck rebellion that began in late 1491 and lasted until Perkin surrendered six years later. It is not clear at what point Wyatt served in Perkin's suppression.

Perkin Warbeck first appeared in 1491 in Ireland, a pro-York stronghold, where opposition to king henry was strong, as a French silk seller; claims were made that he was in fact the Earl of Warwick. Rather, he claimed, he was none other than the younger son of King Edward IV, one of the princes who had been kept in the Tower, now returned from hiding and claiming a right to the English throne. Perkin Warbeck had spent some time training and learning about the family and court of Edward IV, and very interesting accounts describe his impersonations of that monarch (there have been suggestions that he made other impersonations also).

He did not get far in Ireland but was then invited to Paris by French king Charles VIII, who wanted to stop Henry VII supporting Brittany, which he was trying to take over. From there Warbeck moved to Flanders, where he was taken in by Margaret of York (sister of Richard III), now Duchesss of Burgundy, who was happy to claim him as her nephew and to to back his claim to the throne. This move led Henry VII to cut off all trade with Flanders. Warbeck tried at several more invasions, all of which failed. The Desmonds in Ireland supported Warbeck in 1495, then James IV of Scotland allowed him refuge. But when Henry VII offered James IV his daughter's hand in marriage, Warbeck was forced to flee.

The Holy Roman Emperor Maximilian then recognized Warbeck as King of England. However, the Emperor had limited authority across the empire and even less authority in English politics. Henry VII's cause was also helped by Charles VIII's loss of interest in Warbeck.

In August 1497, after one more failed attempt with an army raised in Cornwall, Warbeck gave himself up and was sentenced to remain at court under watch; as a foreigner he could not be hanged for treason. He soon learned that he could, however, be hanged for trying to escape.

The Warbeck rebellion was important as it showed the fragility of the new Tudor dynasty, but by the time Warbeck was executed and treaties were signed with Spain, Scotland and other neighbors, England was strong and stable, allowing Henry VII to arrange for his first-born son Arthur to marry Catherine of Aragon. (The marriage took place after they both came of age, in 1501, but Arthur died within months.)

In the meantime, Henry Wyatt had also served among the leaders in the fight at Blackheath against Cornish rebels who were protesting the subsidies levied to pay for the Scottish wars. During the year 1492, Wyatt purchased the estate of Allington Castle and gained other grants and properties in Yorkshire, Middlesex, Northhamptonshire, Surrey, and Berkshire. Henry Wyatt continued to serve King Henry VII in military and administrative matters until the King died of consumption at the palace of Richmond after a twenty-three year reign at the age of fifty-two.

On 23 April 1509, his son and heir, proclaimed King Henry VIII, took his place as ruler of England. King Henry VIII was now free from an oppressive and stern father and grandmother, and he stood proud with a fortune greater than that of any English king before. The kingdom rejoiced at their new king and an air of fresh hope fell upon the realm.

Among the King's first tasks was the formation of a new council and among those chosen was Sir Henry Wyatt. The new council members were familiar with the late king's method of conducting government and their knowledge would help smooth the transfer. Though this was the first mention of Henry Wyatt as "Sir," his knighthood did not come until King Henry's coronation. On 22 May, King Henry VIII made Henry Wyatt the Campsor and Assayer of the Treasury and Master and Keeper of the Jewels in the Tower of London, with a salary that came from the funds paid to Norwich castle. King Henry also awarded him the stewardships of Hatfield, Thoorne, and York that would remain in effect as long as Henry Wyatt lived.

Henry Wyatt's first mention as a member of the Privy Council is in a license the King issued on 15 June 1509 empowering him to authorize merchants to buy tin within the realm of England.

As King Henry settled into his duties, one of his first priorities was to take a wife. He had been engaged to Catherine of Aragon shortly after Arthur's death, but by the time he was old enough to marry, his father Henry VII had changed his mind. Now Henry VIII was his own man and was intent on following through; the marriage ceremony occurred at Greenwich soon after. The daughter of Queen Isabella I of Castile and King Ferdinand II of Aragon, Catherine was five years his elder. This union disappointed the Holy Roman Emperor Maximilian I, who had been pressing for a marriage with his granddaughter. The marriage entailed various controversies, but they were not publicly aired for some time.

Preparations became frantic as the day of the coronation grew closer. King Henry announced that all those who were to perform any service for him on his coronation day were to assemble at Whitehall on 20 June. On 22 June, twenty-six honorable persons were to muster in the Tower of London to serve the King at dinner, and those who were to receive a knighthood of the Bath would bear dishes to the King as a token. Among those twenty-six nobles, Henry Wyatt was one. From a tradition that dates to about AD 1127, special knighthoods were granted on royal occasions such as coronations. The name derives from the ancient ceremony where individuals participated in a vigil of fasting, prayer, and the ritual of bathing on the very day they were to receive their knighthood.

King Henry VIII's coronation ceremony took place in the palace of Westminster on 24 June where the Bishop of Canterbury anointed and crowned him. After the ceremony a banquet was held; it was described as "greater than any Caesar had known," and was followed by a tournament that lasted well into the night. Several days of jousting, feasting, and merriment followed the coronation, as King Henry spared no expense.

After the festivities settled down, King Henry began to address the issues of the realm, which included foreign affairs. The King displayed his confidence as a leader and a ruler of a land that had not been invaded in a long time. The King renewed several alliances that this father had made, including the treaty with James IV of Scotland originally formed on 24 January 1501. Henry Wyatt's name appears on the treaty with eleven other men of distinction as witnesses to its renewal, signed on 29 August 1509. Henry Wyatt's name also appears on a deed for a cancellation of debt on 22 December of the same year. This is the first mention of his title of Knight.

King Henry was not at all interested in the new prospects that Spanish explorers had discovered in the Americas but kept his interests closer, namely, in France, where English monarchs continued to feel they had a claim to the succession stemming from the days of the Plantagenet dynasty. Though an Anglo–French treaty signed in 1510 existed, King Henry met with his council to discuss war with France; but most of the council was against the idea and many gave reasons that his father would have understood. But Henry VIII was strong, backed by the fortune his father had amassed, and felt he could begin to flex his political and military muscle.

On New Year's Day 1511, Catherine gave the King a son; a cause for great rejoicing throughout the kingdom. Many festivals celebrated the arrival of Henry, Prince of Wales. However, after only seven weeks, young Henry died. The King's joy turned to grief, and from this disappointment he would devote more of himself to the prospect of war.

Thomas Wolsey, the Dean of Lincoln, was the son of a butcher who received a learned education and as he was a very able man, he quickly advanced in King Henry's administration. Wolsey won the King's admiration and advanced from a member of the Council to be the King's sole absolute minister. As preparations to invade France came together, Wolsey endorsed an outline of the King's army in April 1513 that contained several articles that shed light on the realm's strength at the time. One article indicated the budget for expenditures and another outlined the size of the King's army, which included eighty thousand well-armed fighting men, horsemen, archers, and demi-lances with complete armor and gunners.

Another article Wolsey endorsed was a description of how the army was to enter the field. This included the avant-garde consisting of thirty-two hundred; the left wing consisting of some light artillery and men to number fifteen hundred; the center consisting of several positions and about sixty-one hundred men; and the right wing, with the majority of the ordinance. Sir Henry Wyatt was one of those men.

On 26 May, Sir Henry Wyatt received the role of Treasurer of the King's jewels. This appointment earned him two yeomen and a page to assist him in his assigned duties to the King. In June of the same year, a document titled "the Middleward" was committed to history that describes the names with the retinue of the lords, knights and other noblemen who mustered with the King. This was a list of all those about the King such as the Kings guard, the grooms and pages of the Privy Chamber and Sergeant of Arms: in total, there were fourteen thousand and thirty-two assigned to assist the King. Among the names of those who oversaw the King's artillery and ordinance, Sir Henry Wyatt appears with many other great and noble men.

During the summer of 1513, King Henry and his army secured several small victories but did not push into Paris even after arriving so close to the city; instead, the King withdrew to pursue smaller victories. Early historians suggested that because of England's long period of peace, the English army had grown soft and did not make the same decisions that a seasoned army would have. Regardless, King Henry decided to return to England because the season was changing and brought less than favorable conditions to continue with any military campaign. When the King arrived home with the greater part of his army, he found the King of Scotland marching in England with a force of about fifty thousand men. Young and fresh with victories, the confidant King Henry VIII overtook the Scots in the field of Flouden and killed the King of Scotland and most of his nobles. The Queen of Scotland requested peace and King Henry readily granted her request.

The following year found King Henry again preparing for war with France but it would not occur, for within a year his sister Mary Tudor would marry the King of France. England would not go to war again with France for about eight years.

On 27 March 1514, the Lords of the Council received a report on the analysis of gold and silver made in London at the Goldsmith's Hall of English and Flemish Coin and among those present, Sir Henry Wyatt assisted in determining the differences between the various coinages. On 11 August, Henry Wyatt served as one of the five commissioners appointed by the King to review and inventory items such as tackle, apparel, ordinance, artillery, and habiliments of war that remained in a storehouse and on board six ships moored at Erith, three ships moored at Woolwich, three ships moored at

Blackwall and one ship moored at Deptford.

King Henry's sister Mary was wed to Louis XII of France in mid-October 1514 and Sir Henry Wyatt inventoried Mary's jewelry, gold and silver plate for the chapel, buffets, and kitchen and delivered all the items to two representatives of Louis' court on 10 and 11 October. Among the plate were several gilt images of St. Thomas of Canterbury, St. Katherine, and other saints, and a silver gilt mirror garnished with the initials "H" and "R" and red roses.

Henry Wyatt went on with his administrative duties for several more years, but in 1529 and 1530, he complained to the King that he was becoming too feeble to continue and requested to transfer some of his responsibilities to his son Thomas. Henry Wyatt retired to his residence of Allington and on 31 July 1536, King Henry VIII stopped to visit one last time as Wyatt's health was failing. On 10 November 1537, Henry Wyatt died and was later buried at Milton near Gravesend.

Interestingly, Henry Wyatt's life covered the span of five monarchs: the Yorkists, Edward IV (1461–83), Edward V (1483), Richard III (1483–85), and the Tudors, Henry VII (1485–1509) and Henry VIII (1509–1547). Henry Wyatt was survived by his wife Anne, daughter of John Skinner of Surrey, and his son Thomas. Thomas would receive his father's estate and possessions.

Sir Thomas Wyatt the Elder

Thomas Wyatt, the eldest son of Henry Wyatt was born in Allington about 1503. His childhood is rather obscure, but his primary education would have most likely been under the tutelage of his father and other family members and even possibly tutors who educated other members of the court. Based on his later interests in the classics, his education would have most likely included those studies and languages such as Latin, French, and possibly Spanish. His later contributions to the development of the sonnet would indicate a command and understanding of the English language based on a foundation laid during his basic education. A result of a good primary education prepared him for St. Johns College-Cambridge in 1515 where he achieved his B.A. degree in 1518 and in 1520 his master's degree. There is some speculation as to whether or not he may have passed some time in Paris after completing his studies. Shortly after graduating from college, he married Elizabeth daughter of Thomas Brooke Lord Cobham. There are suggestions that he made the acquaintance of Anne Boleyn several years before his marriage and after his marriage, there were rumors that he was her lover.

In 1524, Thomas Wyatt became the Esquire of the body of the King and appointed Clerk of the King's jewels. The following year he distinguished himself at a court tournament during Christmas and the following year 1526, he accompanied Sir Thomas Cheney to France on a diplomatic mission. In January 1527, Thomas Wyatt accompanied the ambassador Sir John Russell to the papal court in Italy. History has recorded a story that John Russell encountered Wyatt while traveling down the Thames River and Wyatt requested to accompany Russell on his journey. Russell responded "no man more welcome," and so Wyatt did accompany Russell on his assignment.

In December of the same year, Wyatt translated a work by Plutarch (46-120 A.D., Greek biographer and essayist); *Quiet of Mind*, for Queen Catherine as a New Years gift and published the following year.

During his travels, Wyatt visited Venice, Ferrara, Bologna, Florence, and Rome. While Russell was in Rome, he broke his leg and Wyatt assumed his responsibilities to negotiate on his behalf with the Venetian Republic. During his return journey to Rome, the Imperial forces captured him and a ransom demanded but Wyatt escaped to Bologna. Some early historians suggest that Wyatt's son accompanied him on this trip and developed a real hatred towards the Spanish because of his fathers' ill treatment.

In 1529 and 1530, Wyatt spent a great deal of his time in Calais where he served as High Marshal. It was also during this period that rumors continued about his relations with Anne Boleyn until King Henry VIII sought her for a wife. An early historian suggests that Wyatt confessed to the King of his past intimacies with her. There are no known ill results recorded of this confession to the King, and it appears that if there was a confession, Wyatt remained in good graces with the King.

In February 1533, Wyatt was robbed in Blofflensing, Cornwall though there are no other details known of the incident. Later the same year he became a member of the Privy Council and acted as chief 'ewerer' at Anne's coronation in place of his father and poured scented water over the Queen's hands.

The alleged past relationship Wyatt had with Anne Boleyn again caused him some turmoil when it was discovered that she was having extramarital affairs though this may have been a fabrication to justify a separation by any means of her marriage to Henry VIII because Anne had not given the King a male heir. Of course, suspicions of Wyatt grew and later confined in the Tower on 5 May 1536. History has suggested that the reason for his imprisonment was to prevent him from acting on the side of the Queen. A few early historians suggest that his arrest was because of an argument he had with the Duke of Suffolk, but there were no legal proceedings brought against him and he was released on 14 June the same year. Unfortunately, Queen Anne Boleyn would not receive the same fate, and on 19 May 1536 at about eight in the morning, Anne was escorted to the Tower Green near the White Tower and in front of a large crowd, beheaded. Her body and head buried in the chapel of the Tower.

Speculation exists about Wyatt's affection for Anne and the sorrow at her loss contained in some of his poetry. One such example is the following sonnet:

> Ye that in love find luck and sweet abundance,
> And live in lust of joyful jollity,
> Arise for shame, do way our sluggardy:
> Arise, I say, do May some observance.
> Let me in bed lie dreaming in mischance;
> Let me remember my mishaps unhappy,
> That me betide in May most commonly;
> As one whom love list little to advance.
> Stephan said true, that my nativity
> Mischanced was with the ruler of May.
> He guessed (I prove) of that the verity.
> In May my wealth, and eke my wits, I say,
> Have stond so oft in such perplexity:
> Joy; let me dream of your felicity.
> [Poetic Works of Thomas Wyatt, 5]

Because of Anne's execution in May, several attempts to implicate Wyatt in her misconduct resulted from his poetry. Another of many possible examples includes the last six lines of a sonnet:

> Who list her hunt, I put him out of doubt
> As well as I, may spend his time in vain!
> And graven with diamonds in letters plain,
> There is written her fair neck round about:
> 'Noli me tangere; for Caesar's I am,
> And wild for to hold, though I seem tame.
> [Poetic Works of Thomas Wyatt, xv]

It is possible to locate hidden meanings in this poetry such that

Wyatt had feelings for Anne, if a search is made with the intent to locate an attachment, platonic or otherwise. However, in reality, Anne and Wyatt were on different social levels and rank and above all Wyatt was at the time married and had a son from that marriage. No evidence is known to exist that could prove that Wyatt and Anne Boleyn had any type of relationship. Had any proof existed at the time, it seems logical that the King would not have released him from prison. Later that year, proof that Wyatt remained in the King's favor is clear by the command he was given against the rebels in the Northern rebellion where he supplied one hundred fifty men to serve from the county of Kent and supplied two hundred men who would be appointed to serve "upon the King's own person."

In March 1537, the King sent Thomas Wyatt to replace the sick resident ambassador with the Emperor Charles V of Spain and on 12 March, Wyatt received instructions on how to address various matters including how to address the French King's ambassador on several subjects. The main intention of his mission was to alleviate the animosities the Emperor fostered against King Henry because of his divorce from Catherine of Aragon. There are no known surviving correspondences from this mission, but it appears that the King approved of Wyatt's conduct.

There are some suggestions by early historians that Wyatt received his knighthood on Easter Day 16 April 1536, but the king addressed him as Esquire in correspondence of the period. Furthermore, on 5 September of the same year, King Henry VIII issued a grant to Sir Arthur Darcy and Thomas Wyatt, Esquire of the royal body. On 12 March 1537, Wyatt received instructions while a resident ambassador to the Emperor as Thomas Wyatt, Esquire. In two letters dated 6 June of the same year, one from Cromwell who chastised him for not writing more often and updating him with events at home (including news that the King was in high spirits because the Queen was pregnant), and the second from Wriothesely sending conduct recommendations, both address Wyatt as "Sir" and not as Esquire. Perhaps he received his knighthood just before he left England.

In late June of the same year, Wyatt and his company traveled along the borders of Spain while en route to Barcelona, where a servant of Wyatt complained in a letter to England of the rough treatment they received. The servant mentioned they were treated like Jews: their luggage searched and they were charged for everything unworn. Wyatt complained to their ill handlers and threatened to mention the incident to the Emperor, but it did not matter to the men; they replied, "If Christ or St. Francis came with all their flock, they should not escape."

King Henry VIII wrote a long letter to Wyatt in early October of the same year containing further advice on the handling of various matters and stated his approval of how Wyatt handled matters so far. Cromwell wrote also and among the topics discussed was Wyatt's mediation between the Emperor and the French King. Cromwell also mentions that he "...will see that you receive your diet and post money and to be your friend so that your enemies, if you have any, shall gain little by your absence."

On 12 October, Thomas Wyatt received instructions from England to inform the Emperor of the very good news: the Queen had given birth to a son and heir to the kingdom. Edward the Prince of Wales was born on 11 October and the King finally had an heir to the throne, but his rejoicing and celebrations soon turned to sorrow as his wife Jane Seymour died on 24 October of the same year.

It was at about this point in time during his travels abroad that Wyatt wrote a couple of letters of advice to his son upon learning of his marriage to Jane, daughter of Sir William Hawte, during the year 1537. These letters are included in the following chapter about his son.

The King continued to search for a suitable bride and he clearly indicated that he would chose a woman by himself and must be comfortable with her. Henry received intriguing information about a girl, Christina, the second daughter of the deposed Christian II of Denmark and niece of the Emperor of Spain, who at the time was sixteen. In January 1538, the King instructed Thomas Wyatt the Elder, still a resident with the Emperor, to suggest her to be his bride. However, Wyatt was to make the suggestion as his own, to motivate the Emperor to offer her to Henry, but he eventually did not choose her and remained unmarried for almost another year and a half.

In early March of 1539, King Henry VIII wrote a letter to Thomas Wyatt with instructions on topics to discuss with the Emperor, which included informing the Emperor that relations between the King and the Bishop of Rome were tense and that there could no longer be a treaty. Henry also requested that Wyatt be patient, as his return in March was deferred until April.

On 12 April, King Henry VIII wrote to Wyatt informing him that Richard Tate would be his replacement and he wrote the Emperor of the changes. On 24 April, the King wrote to inform Wyatt that Tate had departed England and he had informed the emperor of the changes. Tate may have temporarily replaced Wyatt or assumed his duties for a short period, allowing Wyatt to return to England to take care of personal matters before returning to his duties abroad.

In early June of the same year, the Emperor and the King of France had an interview with the Pope in Nice, and Wyatt was present at the event. The Emperor sent Wyatt to England to obtain Henry's instructions soon after. However, Wyatt was delayed on his arrival and unable to rejoin the Emperor within the fifteen-day allotment for his travel and had to meet up with him in Barcelona. Wyatt returned to Paris with the Emperor and wrote to his King on 2 December informing him of the meeting with the King of France and stating that peace negotiations were going well. Furthermore, the Emperor was pleased.

On 7 January 1540, Wyatt wrote a very long letter to his King. He mentioned that he and Richard Tate were together in Paris where they were attempting to question a man who escaped before they arrived at his house, and that Wyatt injured his leg but saved several letters that the man had thrown into the fire before he slipped out the back door. In the same letter, Wyatt describes an interesting conversation he had with the Emperor regarding the Inquisition and of some questions Wyatt had regarding proper English behavior; he had never seen the Emperor so vehement and imperious regarding the Inquisition.

The majority of the remaining official correspondence to or from Wyatt rarely offers any insight into Wyatt himself and only describes the events that took place. The following letter gives a rare example of one of Wyatt's attributes, his generosity. The letter was to Wyatt from Cromwell, written in the early months of 1540.

> I advise you to take patiently your abode there until April, and to send me word what money ye shall need to have sent unto you, for I shall help you. Assuring you that I could not see you that went, and hath abided there honestly furnished, to return home, and at the latter end return needy and disfurnished. I do better tender the King's honour, and do esteem you better than so to suffer you to lack. Advising you, nevertheless, that I think your gentle frank heart doth much impoverish you. When you have money, you are content to depart with it and lend it, as you did lately two hundred ducats to Mr. Hobby, the which I think had no need of them; for he had large furnishment of money at his departure hence, and likewise at his return. We accustom not to send men disprovided so far.

Take heed, therefore, how you depart of such portion as ye need. And foresee rather to be provided yourself, than for the promotion of other to leave yourself naked. Politic charity proceedeth not that way. If you shall advertise me what sums ye shall need, I shall take a way that ye shall be furnished. [Poetic Works of Thomas Wyatt, xxiv]

On 9 March of the same year, Wyatt wrote to his king from Gaunt with updates including his visit with the King of Romans and the Emperor's activities. Wyatt was still in Gaunt the following month when he wrote to Cromwell with updates and informed him that he planned to remain for an additional month to see how the hunting was and if he liked it or not.

During the last few months of the same year, the Emperor proceeded through France to the Low Countries (region of Northwest Europe now occupied by the Netherlands, Belgium and Luxembourg) and the King reappointed Wyatt as ambassador to track the Emperor's actions. They arrived in Paris in mid November and after a short stay, they departed for Blois. The interview with the King of France is described in a dispatch during the first week of December.

Wyatt left Blois and joined the Emperor at Chateaureault on 10 December then departed to Paris then to Brussels where Wyatt wrote to Cromwell on 22 January 1541 complaining of financial concerns:

"I am sorry that I have troubled your Lordship with touching my request for my revocation, seeing so small appearance of the attaining the same. I meant not even now in all my last, but that the way might by your Lordship have been framed against the expiration of my four months, to be ended at the 9th or 10th of March, for the which I have received. And here I think it not unmeet to advertise your Lordship what comfort I find at my coming for the disease I have long had. First, my house rent standeth me after the rate little lack of one hundred pounds by the year, without stabling; besides, the least fire I make to warm my shirt by stands me a groat. In my diet money I lose in the value eight shillings and eight pence every day, for that the angel is here but worth six shillings and fourpence; a barrel of beer that in England were worth twenty pence, it costs me here with the excise four shillings; a bushel of oats is worth two shillings; and other things be not unlike the rate. I beseech your Lordship take not this that I am so eager upon the King that I would augment my diet, for it is so honourable it were not honest to desire it, but for because I would another should have it. That your Lordship writeth the King's Highness to take in so good part my doings, I pray God, it may proceed of my merits as well as that doth upon his goodness; for if in the while that I would abide in this place my deeds might deserve any thing, would God my revocation and his Grace's con-tinuance of favour might be my reward." [Poetic Works of Thomas Wyatt, xxvi]

By mid April, Wyatt again indicated that he would like to re-turn to England. He also reported of a truce with Denmark and that Poland had risen against Rome. Wyatt was still in Ghent and ex-tended his time with the Emperor during the visit of the Duke of Cleves until about mid-May. Most likely, it was after this time that Wyatt did finally return to England but whether he remained for a short period before returning to his duties or simply remained in England is unclear. However, on 17 January 1541, Thomas Wyatt was arrested in his own house and taken to the Tower; his house was searched and the King's seals were placed on a chest and cup-boards protecting their contents for possible further review. Three days later the Privy Council met at Hampton Court and decided that several items were to be confiscated at Wyatt's home of Al-lington Castle including the armory, guns, jennets, and horses, and to discharge his servants with half a year's salary.

Regarded as the King's trusted ambassador, Wyatt's charges in-cluded having intelligence with Reginald Pole 9regarded as a traitor to the King) and that Wyatt treated the King with disrespect while serving as ambassador to the Emperor in 1538 and 1539. After serv-ing some time in the Tower, the Privy Council ordered him to state what had occurred during his residence at the Emperor's court. He was then indicted and brought to trial where he delivered a defense against the charges that add as much to his celebrity as his poetry. After artfully working upon the feelings of the jury by urging the jury he sustained in not being allowed counsel, he proceeded to dis-credit the charges brought against him. Furthermore, with a series of retorts and what has been described as, "...a series of satire that places his talents in the most favorable point of view" his defense brought about a complete acquittal. Many published works con-tain his defense and it is too long to be included here.

In early July, the King granted him additional lands as if to mark his conviction of his innocence and the King followed up on this act of favor the following year by appointing Wyatt the High Steward of the manor of Maidstone and gave him the estates in Dorsetshire and Somersetshire. Early historians suggest that at about this time is when Wyatt retired from his duties to his residence of Allington and composed the majority of his poetry including the seven penitential psalms that reveal the serious nature of his thoughts during that period. Furthermore, he devoted much of his leisure time to the care and education of his nephew Henry Lee and spent time improving his mansion and estate of Allington.

On 2 October 1542, Wyatt was recalled to the duties of ambassador even after turning over some of his duties to his son. Thomas Wyatt the Elder was to meet Mr. De Courrieres when he arrived at Falmouth. When Thomas Wyatt traveled about eighty miles from London he fell ill, believed to be the result of the very hot weather and the fatigue of the journey. Wyatt remained confined to his bed and later died on 10 or 11 October 1542 at Sherborne in Dorsetshire and buried in the church of Sherborne, but no inscription marked the spot.

Thomas Wyatt the Elder belonged to the cultivated circle of Henry VIII's court. He studied foreign literature and is perhaps best known for introducing the sonnet into English literature with Henry Howard the Earl of Surrey. The sonnet is described as a poem of fourteen lines usually rhymed and written in iambic pentameter. The sonnet takes its roots from the Sicilian court of Frederick II of about 1220 to 1230. Wyatt wrote both secular and sacred verse but none of his compositions were published in his lifetime. William Shakespeare was to later refine the sonnet and popularize it.

Wyatt is known to have excelled in playing the lute and was well known for his conversational powers, but the agreeable qualities of his private character excel above all others. He has been described as eminently handsome, tall and of a commanding presence, elegantly formed, and gifted with a noteworthy countenance.

History has recorded many of his witticisms such as when the King once urged him to dance at one of the splendid midnight masquerades with which the King so often indulged the court. Wyatt with great modesty excused himself and when Henry pressed him for his reason, he replied, "Sir, he who would be thought a wise man in the daytime, must not play the fool at night."

It was not until 1557 that thirty-eight of his sonnets appeared in Richard Tottel's *Songs and Sonnets*, often regarded simply as *Tottel's Miscellany*. The following is one example of Thomas Wyatt's compositions.

The longe loue, that in my thought I harber,

And in my hart doth kepe his residence,
Into my face presseth with bold pretence,
And there campeth, displaying his banner.
She that me learns to loue, and to suffer,
And willes that my trust, and lustes negligence
Be reined by reason, shame, and reuerence,
With his hardinesse takes displeasure.
Wherwith loue to the hartes forest he fleeth,
Leauyng his enterprise with paine and crye,
And there him hideth and not appeareth.
What may I do? when my maister seareth,
But in the field with him to liue and dye,
For good is the life, endyng faithfully. [Arber, 33]

The Earl of Surrey composed the following poem in honor of his friend:

An Epitaph on Sir Thomas Wyatt the Elder.

WYATT resteth here, that quick could never rest;
Whose heavenly gifts increased by disdain;
And virtue sank the deeper in his breast:
Such profit he by envy could obtain.
A head, where wisdom mysteries did frame;
Whose hammers beat still in that lively brain,
As on a stithy, where some work of fame
Was daily wrought, to turn to Britain's.gain.
A visage stern, and mild; where both did grow
Vice to contemn, in virtue to rejoice:
Amid great storms whom grace assured so,
To live upright, and smile at fortune's choice.
A hand, that taught what might be said in rhyme;
That reft Chaucer the glory of his wit.
A mark, the which (unperfected for time),
Some may approach, but never none shall hit.
A tongue, that serv'd in foreign realms his king;
Whose courteous talk to virtue did inflame
Each noble heart; a worthy guide to bring
Our English youth, by travail unto fame.
An eye, whose judgment no effect could blind,
Friends to allure, and foes to reconcile;
Whose piercing look did represent a mind
With virtue fraught, reposed, void of guile.
A heart, where dread was never so imprest

To hide the thought that might the truth advance;
In neither fortune lost, nor yet represt,
To swell in wealth, or yield unto mischance.
A valiant corpse, where force and beauty met;
Happy, alas! too happy, but for foes,
Lived, and ran the race, that nature set;
Of manhood's shape, where she the mould did lose.
But to the heavens that simple soul is fled,
Which left, with such as covet Christ to know,
Witness of faith, that never shall be dead;
Sent for our health, but not received so.
Thus for our guilt, this jewel have we lost;
The earth his bones, the heavens possess his ghost.
[Nott, volume II, CXI-CXII]

Thomas Wyatt the Elder was survived by his wife, and by her had a son, Thomas, often referred to as Thomas Wyatt the Younger, the subject of this book.

CHAPTER 2. THOMAS WYATT THE YOUNGER, 1520 TO OCTOBER 1553

There are no known surviving documents indicating the year Thomas Wyatt the Younger was born. He is described as being "twenty-one years and upwards" in the "inquisitio post mortem" of his father dated 8 January 1543 and another piece of evidence indicates that he was fifteen when his father wrote him giving moral advice in 1537. Both could place his birth at about 1521 or 1522 and would have most likely occurred at his father's residence of Allington Castle located a couple of miles north of Maidstone in the county of Kent. The Duke of Norfolk was his godfather.

History has not recorded the early years of the life of the son of a famous poet. He would have most certainly received a proper primary education possibly with one or even several tutors, and possibly from the court as his father's position could have afforded such. Other contributors to his education would have most certainly included his father and other members of his family. Along with the fundamental skills of reading, writing, and arithmetic, his studies would have likely included the languages of French and Latin, as Latin would have been secondary to English and fundamental in understanding the classic texts to which his father would have ensured his exposure. Certainly, he would have an exposure to the arts and possibly was able to perform on a musical instrument such as the guitar or lute. As the son of a poet, he possibly wrote poetry as his father had and furthermore would have had a great deal of exposure to the literary world.

Because of his father's frequent involvement in the court of King Henry VIII, his education would have also included exposure to the many aspects and tools required to act properly during those interactions of court with his father acting as chief instructor in those matters. There are no known documents to indicate or suggest that Thomas Wyatt the Younger attended college, but if his father had any influence over him, he would have.

Early historians suggest that Thomas Wyatt the Younger accompanied his father on an ambassadorial assignment while he was a boy when the ambassador John Russell broke his leg and Wyatt's father assumed his duties and was captured outside of Rome in January of 1527 and threatened by the Inquisition. The Inquisition was a court set up by the Roman Catholic Church in the Middle Ages to seek out and punish heresy and the accused were sometimes interrogated by torture. Punishments ranged from penance to banishments to horrible death by various means such as being burned at the stake and beheaded. Possibly, because of his father's treatment during his capture, Thomas Wyatt the Younger developed a permanent hatred of the Spanish government that he would maintain for the remainder of his life.

At some point in the year 1536, Henry Wyatt wrote a letter to King Henry VIII thanking him for not chastising his son and apologized to the King because due to health problems he was experiencing, he must turn his duties over to his son Thomas Wyatt the Elder. Thomas Wyatt the Elder was appointed as resident ambassador to the Emperor Charles V of Spain in early March 1537 and shortly after his arrival in Spain, he found time to write his son a couple of letters giving moral advice as he had received information of his son's marriage to Jane, daughter of Sir William Hawte.

Letter 1:

In as much as now ye are come to some years of understanding, and that you should gather within yourself some frame of Honesty, I thought that I should not lose my labour wholly if now I did something advertise you to take the sure foundations and stablished opinions that leadeth to Honesty.

And here, I call not Honesty that, men commonly call Honesty, as reputation for riches, for authority, or some like thing; but that Honesty, that I dare well say your grandfather, (whose soul God pardon,) had rather left to me than all the lands he did leave me; that was, Wisdom,

Gentleness, Soberness, desire to do Good, Friendliness to get the love of many, and Truth above all the rest. A great part to have all these things is to desire to have them. And although glory and honest name are not the very ends wherefore these things are to be followed, yet surely they must needs follow them as light followeth fire, though it were kindled for warmth.

Out of these things the chiefest and infallible ground is the dread and reverence of God, whereupon shall ensue the eschewing of the contraries of these said virtues; that is to say, ignorance, unkindness, rashness, desire of harm, unquiet enmity, hatred, many and crafty falsehood, the very root of all shame and dishonesty. I say, the only dread and reverence of God, that seeth all things, is the defence of the creeping in of all these mischiefs' into you. And for my part, although I do well say there is no man that would his son better than I, yet on my faith I had rather have you lifeless, than subject to these vices.

Think and imagine always that you are in presence of some honest man that you know; as Sir John Russell, your Father-in-law, your Uncle Parson, or some other such, and ye shall, if at any time you find a pleasure in naughty touches, remember what shame it were afore these men to do naughtily. And sure this imagination shall cause you re-member, that the pleasure of a naughty deed is soon past, and the rebuke, shame, and the note thereof shall remain ever. Then, if these things ye take for vain imaginations, yet remember that it is certain, and no imagination, that ye are always in the presence and sight of God: and though you see him not, so much is the reverence the more to be had for that He seeth, and is not seen.

Men punish with shame as greatest punishment on earth, yea! greater than death; but His punishment is, first, the withdrawing of his favour, and grace, and in leaving his hand to rule the stern to let the ship run without guide to its own destruction; and suffereth so the man that he forsaketh to run headlong as subject to all mishaps, and at last with shameful end to everlasting shame and death. Ye may see continual examples both of the one sort, and of the other; and the better, if ye mark them well that your-self are come of; and consider well your good grandfather, what things there were in him, and his end. And they that knew him noted him thus; first, and chiefly to have a great reverence of God and good opinion of godly things. Next that, there was no man more pitiful; no man more true of his word; no man faster to his friend; no man diligenter nor more circumspect, which thing, both the Kings his masters noted in him greatly. And if these things, and specially the grace of God that the fear of God alway kept with him, had not been, the chances of this troublesome world that he was in had long ago overwhelmed him. This preserved him in prison from the hands of the tyrant that could find in his heart to see him racked; from two years and more prisonment in Scotland in irons and stocks; from the danger of sudden changes and commotions divers, till that well beloved of many, hated of none, in his fair age, and good reputation, godly and christianly he went to Him that loved him, for that he always had Him in reverence.

And of myself, I may be a near example unto you of my folly and unthriftness, that hath, as I well deserved, brought me into a thousand dangers and hazards, enmities, hatreds, prisonments, despites, and indignations; but that God hath of his goodness chastised me, and not cast me clean out of his favour; which thing I can impute to noth-ing but to the goodness of my good father, that, I dare well say purchased with continual request of God his Grace to-wards me more than I regarded, or considered myself; and a little part to the small fear that I had of God in the most of my rage, and the little delight that I had in mischief. You therefore if ye be sure, and have God in your sleeve to call you to his grace at last, venture hardily by mine example upon naughty unthriftiness, in trust of his goodness; and besides the shame, I dare lay ten to one ye shall perish in the adventure; for trust me, that my wish or desire of God for you shall not stand you in as much effect, as I think my father's did for me: we are not all accepted of Him.

Begin therefore betimes. Make God and good-'ness your foundations. Make your examples of wise and honest men: shoot at that mark: be no mocker: mocks follow them that delight therein. He shall be sure of shame that feeleth no grief in other men's shames. Have your friends in a rev-erence; and think unkindness to be the greatest offence, and least punished amongst men; but so much the more to be dread, for God is justiser upon that alone.

Love well, and agree with your wife; for where is noise and debate in the house there is unquiet dwelling; and much more, where it is in one bed. Frame well yourself to love and rule well and honestly your wife as your fellow, and she shall love and reverence you as her head. Such as you are unto her, such shall she be unto you. Obey and reverence your father-in-law, as you would me; and remember that long life followeth them that reverence their fathers and elders; and the blessing of God, for good agreement between the wife and husband, is fruit of many children.

Read oft this my letter, and it shall be as though I had often written to you; and think that I have herein printed a fatherly affection to you. If I may see that I have not lost my pain, mine shall be the contentation, and yours the profit; and, upon condition that you follow my advertisement, I send you God's blessing and mine, and as well to come to honesty, as to increase of years. [The Poetical Works of Sir Thomas Wyatt, xxxviii-xlii]

Royall Tyler, editor of *The Calendar of Letters, Despatches, and State Papers relating to the negotiations between England and Spain* has the following footnote preceding the first letter: "later copy, headed 'From him out of Spain to his son, then xv years old.'" Tyler indicates, "the figure 'xv' had been altered by the writer who apparently had written 'iii' meaning perhaps to have added a final 'j', but afterward wrote a 'v' across." The 'j' was often used to replace the 'i' in final position, though its use is rare in modern use of Roman numerals. (The *Calendar of Letters* is similar to an index or record of documents, only listing the type or title of a document. Royall Tyler reviewed the original letters but did not include them in their entirety.)

Letter 2:

I Doubt not but long ere this time my letters are come to you. I remember I wrote to you in them, that if you read them often it shall be as though I had written often to you. For all that, I cannot so content me but still to call upon you with my letters. I would not for all that, that if any thing be well warned in the other that you should leave to remember it because of this new. For it is not like with advertisements as it is with apparel that with long wearing a man casteth away, when he hath new. Honest teachings never wear; unless they wear out of his remembrance that should keep and follow them, to the shame and hurt of himself. Think not also that I have any new or change of advertisements to send you; but still it is one that I would. I have nothing to cry and call upon you for but Honesty, Honesty. It may be diversely named, but alway it tendeth to one end; and as I wrote to you last, I mean not that Honesty that the common sort calleth an honest man. Trust me, that honest man is as common a name as the name of a good fellow; that is to say, a drunkard, a tavern haunter, a rioter, a gamer, a waster. So are among the common sort all men honest men that are not known for manifest naughty knaves.

Seek not I pray thee, my Son, that Honesty which appeareth, and is not indeed. Be well assured it is no common thing, nor no common man's judgment to judge well of Honesty; nor it is no common thing to come by; but so much it is the more goodly, for that it is so rare and strange.

Follow not therefore the common reputation of Honesty. If you will seem honest, be honest; or else seem as you are. Seek not the name without the thing; nor let not the name be the only mark you shoot at: that will follow though you regard it not; yea! and the more you regard it, the less. I mean not by regard it not, esteem it not; for well I wot honest name is goodly. But he that hunteth only for that, is like him that had rather seem warm than be warm, and edgeth a single coat about with a fur. Honest name is to be kept, preserved, and defended, and not to employ all a man's wit about the study of it; for that smelleth of a glorious and ambitious fool. I say, as I wrote unto you in my last letters, get the thing, and the other must of necessity follow, as the shadow followeth the thing that it is of; and even so much is the very Honesty better than the name, as the thing is better than the shadow.

The coming to this point that I would so fain have you have, is to consider a man's own self what he is, and wherefore he is; and herein let him think verily that so goodly a work as man is, for whom all other things were wrought, was not wrought but for goodly things. After a man hath gotten a will and desire to them, is first to avoid evil, and learn that point alone: 'Never to do that, that within yourself you find a certain grudging against.' No doubt in any thing you do, if you ask yourself, or examine the thing in yourself afore you do it, you shall find, if it be evil, a repining against it. My Son! for our Lord's love keep well that repining; suffer it not to be darked and corrupted by naughty example, as though any thing were to you excusable because other men do the same. That same repining, if it did punish as he doth judge, there were no such justicer; and of truth, so doth it punish; but not so apparently. Here however it is no small grief, of a conscience that condemneth itself; but be well assured, after this life it is a continual gnawing.

When there is a custom gotten of avoiding to do evil, then cometh a gentle courage. Be content to be idle, and to rest without doing any thing. Then too had ye need to gather an heap of good opinions and to get them perfectly, as it were on your fingers' ends. Rest not greatly upon the approving of them; take them as already approved, because they were of honest men's leavings. Of them of God, there is no question; and it is no small help to them, the good opinion of moral philosophers, among whom I would Seneca [in] your study; and Epictetus, because it is little, to be ever in bosom.

These things shall lead you to know goodly [things]; which when a man knoweth and taketh pleasure in them, he is a beast that followeth not them: no, nor he cannot but follow them. But take this for conclusion and sum of all; that if God and his Grace be not the foundation, neither can ye avoid evil, nor judge well, nor do any goodly thing. Let Him be foundation of all. Will these things; desire them earnestly, and seek them at his hands, and knowledge them to come of Him, and questionless He will both give you the use and pleasure in using them, and also reward you for them that come of Him; so liberal and good is He.

I would fain see that my letters might work to frame you honest. And think that without that, I esteem nothing of you: no! not that you are my son. For I reckon it no small dishonesty to myself to have an unhonest taught child: but the fault shall not be in me. I shall do the part of a father: and if you answer not to that I look for at your hands, I shall as well study with that that I shall leave, to make such [some] honest man, as you. [The Poetical Works of Sir Thomas Wyatt, xlii-xlvi]

History has not recorded any events involving Thomas Wyatt the Younger after his marriage but five years later in October 1542 when his father died at Sherborne, Thomas Wyatt would have certainly attended his funeral and burial in the church of Sherborne. Furthermore, at about the same time, there is mention that Thomas Wyatt the Younger received a pardon for robbery but no further information is given.

The following year, several members of the Council questioned Milsent Arundel, wife of the Duke of Arundel, on 28 March 1543 regarding her husband and several others who ate meat during Lent in her house, also about her husband and several others, including Thomas Wyatt the Younger, who ate meat on Fridays and Fast days: these were serious allegations. Furthermore, questioning included her knowledge of the activities of Henry Howard the Earl of Surrey and his servant Thomas Clere, as well as Thomas Wyatt the Younger and young Pickering with their servants. They had left her house at 9:00 pm with four stone bows (a kind of light cross bow or catapult used for shooting small stones or pellets) and did not return until about midnight on Candlemas Day (2 February, the Feast of Purification of the Virgin Mary and the presentation of Jesus in the Temple, when candles are blessed). She was also questioned about the activities of the same group who were involved in breaking glass windows in several houses of prominent citizens and churches while some men were shot at with stones in the streets. Apparently, a Mr. Birche received the most injuries from the stones and Sir Richard Gressam's windows received the most damage. Prior to questioning, Milsent instructed her household to say nothing of their activities and denied any knowledge of it when asked by her neighbors. During the questioning, she indicated that she had heard Surrey say:

> "...the night after, when Mr. Blage rebuked him for it, say that he had liever than all the good in the world it were undone, for he was sure it should come before the King and his council; but we shall have a madding time in our youth, and therefore I am very sorry for it" [Calendar of Letters and Papers, Foreign and Domestic, Henry VIII, Vol. xviii, 185]

During her questioning, Milsent also mentioned that on that same night or perhaps the night before, Thomas Clere told her that the same group had, while rowing along the Thames, shot at the "queens at the bank." This is probably referring to shooting at the Queen's gate entrance to the Tower while they were on the Thames River.

As a result of Milsent's information, arrests were made of Surrey, Thomas Wyatt the Younger, and the others for having eaten meat during Lent and breaking windows at night with stone bows. Thomas Wyatt admitted to the first charge but denied the second. The Privy Council recorded their meeting of 1 April at St. James in which their business was to discuss punishment. The Earl of Surrey was charged with eating flesh and breaking windows with a stone bow and Surrey alleged his license for the first and as for the stone bows, admitted that he participated in the activity. Surrey is quoted as saying:

> "My motive," he said, "was a religious one, though I confess that it lies open to misconstruction. It grieved me, my Lords, to see the licentious manners of the citizens of London. They resembled the manners of Papal Rome in her corruptest state, and not those of a Christian communion. Was I to suffer these unhappy men to perish Avithout warning? That common charity forbade. The remonstrances' of their Spiritual pastors had been urged, I knew, in vain. I therefore went at midnight through the streets, and shot from my cross-bow at their windows, that the stones passing noiseless through the air, and breaking in suddenly upon their guilty secrecy, might remind them of the suddenness of that punishment which the Scriptures tell us Divine Justice will inflict on impenitent sinners; and so lead them to a reformation of manners." [Nott, Volume 1, liii]

Henry Howard the Earl of Surrey was committed to the Fleet Street prison for his punishment. Pickering sent to the Porters Lodge and Thomas Wyatt the Younger sent to the Tower, where he remained until 3 May, then released at the King's request.

Though only spending a short time in the Tower, Wyatt would have a great deal of quiet time to reflect upon his life and those actions that had placed him in confinement. As soon as he was released, Wyatt redirected his energies by joining the service of the King's army. In July of the same year, an army was formed which would defend the Emperor's Low Countries against the common enemy, the French King. The principal leader of this army was Sir John Wallop, who directed his men as required by the Emperor's chief captains. All would serve in the army for a period of one hundred twelve days from the day of their entry, either defending against the enemy or invading his dominions. Wallop was also to see that all the artillery and munitions were well stocked and manned and to maintain order and discipline within the ranks. Among the men serving from the various counties in England were the Archbishop of Canterbury, who would supply ten horsemen and one hundred foot soldiers; Sir Henry Isle would supply thirty-eight foot soldiers; Thomas Wyatt would supply one hundred foot soldiers and the largest supply of men from Kent, and Nicholas Throckmorton commanded a troop of unknown size. Thomas Churchyard, who also served in the King's army during that same period, noted in his *A pleasant discourse of Court of wars, with a replication to them both, and a commendation of all those that truly serve Prince and Country,* published in 1596, that Wyatt began to distinguish himself as a worthy military commander during that campaign and several other campaigns in a period of about one year.

Based on information extracted from a record in the Augmentation Office dated the last part of November 1543, we see that Thomas Wyatt sold his estates of "the manor of Combe, the hundred of Howe, with the advowson of the church of St. Mary, the manors of Hooe Little and Hooe Windehill, with the advowson of the church at Halstowe." Wyatt sold these estates to alleviate the debts to the King left by his father when he died. These sales amount to 3669*l*, eight, and 2d.

In the third week of July 1544, King Henry VIII arrived at Calais and the Duke of Suffolk quickly began to survey the land around the French town of Boulogne with the purpose of determining the best way to take the town. A week later the siege began with the King's army split in two, one side under the command of the Duke of Norfolk whose campaign would take place outside of Montreuil and the other under the command of the Duke of Suffolk whose campaign would take place about twenty-five miles to the north and take Boulogne. In this campaign, Thomas Wyatt again supplied one hundred foot soldiers and Henry Isley supplied thirty-eight foot soldiers among others from Kent as part of the Duke of Norfolk's "vanguard" forces.

Hindered by bad weather and a shortage of gunpowder until early August, King Henry's forces opened up with a full battery of artillery against Boulogne. After the castle sustained a considerable amount of damage on 11 September, the terms of surrender were given and on 18 September, King Henry VIII entered Boulogne in triumph. Though described as a rather dismal campaign that hardly justified the large expenditure of money and men, King Henry did enjoy his triumph unaware that the Emperor had come to terms with the French at Creps.

Problems soon arose as the dauphin moved quickly to relieve Montreuil and threaten the Duke of Norfolk who was experiencing an array of problems himself. Hearing of the dauphin's advances, the Duke of Norfolk quickly gathered his forces and left Montreuil for Boulogne. Soon after King Henry arrived back in England, he received word that Suffolk and Norfolk disobeyed orders by withdrawing their forces from Boulogne to Calais. The King quickly dispatched an order to them to return to their posts, but it was too late and the dauphin regained control and Suffolk and Norfolk began to send their forces home, leaving some in Boulogne. The King and the Council severely criticized their actions.

On 5 October of the same year, the Duke of Norfolk reported to King Henry VIII that the Lord Admiral requested that the number of men who were left in Boulogne be increased by five hundred and would be under the command of Thomas Poynings and Thomas Wyatt, which would give them a total of three thousand three hundred men. The Privy Council responded by indicating that the King was pleased with his advice to appoint and promote Poynings to Captain of those stationed in Base Boulogne and Thomas Wyatt to Captain of those stationed in the Old Man (an English fortress of importance at the entrance to the harbor of Boulogne). The Earl of Surrey drew a map of this fortress included in his correspondence. This map is included in appendix VI as map 3.

In late January 1545, a report was given about the towns of Guisnes and Boulogne which mentioned several military appointments including the King's choice for Wyatt to be Captain of "Basseboulloyn," and Thomas Palmer to be Captain of the Old Man with each to receive wages of 26s 8d per day that they served as captains.

On 11 May of the same year, Lord Thomas Poynings updated King Henry with the events across the channel in France. Poynings had given Wyatt charge of three hundred hackbuttiers (a soldier armed with a firearm).

> "[C]oming to a gate on the first bridge he went into the door, which he (Wyatt) brake open and himself being the first man that entered, slew one of their watchmen upon the said bridge, took other twain of them and set his hackbutters in the braye about the castle." [Nott, 188]

Poynings placed artillery in front of the gates then summoned the captain stationed inside to surrender but a lieutenant responded that he would not do so. Poynings then fired two shots from the cannons that prompted the lieutenant to give up the castle with the conditions that his men of war, women, and children be allowed to depart with their weapons and baggage. These terms were agreeable and they vacated the castle. Wyatt then stationed his lieutenant and one hundred men inside the castle to watch after their prize.

In recognition for his service, the Earl of Surrey received the appointment as governor of Boulogne in September of the same year. Thomas Wyatt received an appointment as one of the Council members in part for recognition of his outstanding service and his name appears on several pieces of correspondence from that period.

Even though the English had secured the fortress of Boulogne, the French continued to dominate the waters off the coast. As read in the following two letters, their presence prevented much needed supplies from reaching Surrey's men holding the fort.

> From the Council at Boulogne to the Privy Council
>
> After our right hearty commendations to your good Lordships: The same shall understand that the ninth of this present, Thomas Norwick of London, bearer hereof, brought hither a crayer of the burthen of twenty-five ton, laden with victuals for the better furniture of the King's Majesty's garrison here and after that he had discharged the most part of the same victuals, behind th' Old Man, there came certain French gallies and forced the mariners for safeguard of themselves to run the vessel on ground; which afterwards was carried away by the Frenchmen, having in her six barrels [of] butter, eight barrels of beer, and two double barrels. In consideration whereof we have thought good to desire your Lordships to be mean unto the King's Majesty, that the poor man may have some reasonable recompence for his said crayer; which shall not only be a great comfort to him; but also encourage others more willingly to adventure themselves, and their goods for the relief of his Highness's garrison hereafter. And thus we commit your honourable Lordships to Almighty God. From Boulogne, the 14th of September, 1545.
>
> Your good Lordship's to command,
>
> H. Surrey, John Bryggys, Rauf Ellerkar, Thomas Palmer, Thomas Wyatt.
>
> To the Right Honourable, and our very good lords, the Lords of the King's Majesty Privy Council [Nott, 172-173]

Letter 2:

From the Council of Boulogne to the Privy Council

After our right hearty commendations to your good Lordships: The same shall understand that the ninth of this present, this bearer, Richard Songar of Dover, brought hither a pinnace of the burthen of twenty-five ton, fraughted with muttons, and other provision, for the better furniture of this, the King's Majesty's garrison: and the same being discharged behind th Old Man; it fortuned the vessel to be driven on land by certain French gallies, which afterwards took it away with them. In consideration whereof we have thought to desire your Lordships to be mean unto the King's Majesty, that this poor man may have such recompence for his boat and ordinance, as both he and others may thereby be encouraged more willingly to adventure themselves and their goods for the relief of his Highness's said garrison hereafter. And thus we commit your honourable Lordships to Almighty God. From Boulogne, the 14th of September, 1545.

Your good Lordship's to command,

H. Surrey, John Bryggys, Thomas Wiatt, Hugh Poulett, Thomas Palmer.

To the Right Honourable, and our very good Lords, the Lords of the King's Majesty's Privy Council. [Nott, 174]

Many of the letters wrote by and addressed to the Earl of Surrey during the campaign in France have been preserved in *The Works of Henry Howard Earl of Surrey and of Sir Thomas Wyatt the Elder*, by George Frederick Nott. I have chosen to include the following three letters the Earl of Surrey wrote to King Henry VIII not only because of his mention of Thomas Wyatt, but to portray the events across the channel as Surrey described them which paints a vivid portrait of that turbulent period in which Wyatt was involved.

Letter 1:

To the King's most excellent Majesty.

Pleaseth it your most excellent Majesty; that since the revictualment made by Monsieur De Tays, declared in my last letters, which upon a more certain intelligence, besides the sheep and oxen, were but sixteen carts laden with thirty pieces of wine; the rest all returned to Montreuil for fear. Whereupon the enemy were constrained with a great force to intend a new re-victualment. Whereof I having certain espial (spies) that this morning they would come with six or seven hundred horse at the full sea, to put in a great number of carts; and that the Almains (had) marched from Aussie Chateau, and would within a day or twain come to Port hill, to land there such munition as should come hither from Dieppe and Estaples, for lack of carriages to convey the same by land; I first gave in charge to your Majesty's ships to keep upon this shore: and this morning, three hours before day, sent forth Mr. Wyat and Mr. Palmer, with a thousand footmen, to embush themselves under the hill side where the church of St. Etinenne stood. Which church because the enemy always kept, (to have espial [spies] upon us when we would pass the river as at the last journey we made into Boulonnois, when Mr. Bridges burned Sammer Town and all the country there about, and spoiled the cattle of the same). Mr. Wyatt, accompanied with the Master of the ordnance and Mr. Flammock also, overthrew, with twelve Gascoigns which would not yield the same.

And I, with Mr. Marshall, this morning at the opening of the gates with th' ordinary horsemen of this town, to th' intent th' enemy should not discover our embush, if he should send for the same purpose. And so tarrying there looking for them coming, sending the northern men to scout towards Hardelot, which were all the night before to watch the same, I sent Mr. Palmer and Mr. Wyatt with a few horsemen towards the fortress, to seek out the ground of most advantage for your Majesty's camp, if it should be your pleasure to come to the field the next year.

They took the way towards Port hill, where by chance they found all their sheep; which, fearing lest the victuals would not have come that day, Mr. Palmer having taken a prisoner of the fortress with his own hands, took occasion to drive him and the sheep towards us, to train the footmen to the embush. Which indeed took such effect, that above seven hundred followed the sheep, and were come more than a mile towards us; so that they could not have escaped us, peradventure with some danger of their fortress, had not the troop of seven hundred horsemen between us and Hardelot been discovered at the same moment.

Then left we the sheep, and assembled our horsemen upon the hill, and drew our footmen upon the scantling of the hill as high as we could, not to be discovered; and Mr. Marshall and the cavalry offered the charge upon them. Th' enemy seeing but our ordinary horsemen, the flood increase; and having no advertisement from the fort of any footmen that were issued, gave without fear the charge upon our men. Our horsemen seeming to fly, made down to the passage, leaving our footmen upon the left hand. So that th' enemy being upon the spur followed lower to the river than our footmen, and then discovering our footmen would have returned, and could not, so that there were taken seven men at arms, which our men would never suffer to recover the hill again. At the which charge Mr. Marshall very honestly and hardily brake his mace upon a Frenchman; Mr. Shelly brake his staff upon a tall young gentleman of Monsieur De Botyer's band, and took him prisoner: and in effect, all the men at arms of this town brake their staves.

The Frenchmen having then discovered our footmen, made an offer as though they would charge upon the same; amongst whom, for fear our own horsemen, being weak, might make some disorder, I made all our footmen take the trench upon the top of the hill, which the enemy had made this year when their camp lay there (a very strong plat of ground) which I determined, and might well have kept if their footmen had marched, till our succour had come from the town, which also I sent for. And then I sent Mr. Dudley, this bearer, his brother and Captain Clement of the Italians, who most honestly offered themselves to take the hedges near unto the troop; which was then stronger and nearer unto us, as me seemed, than I saw them this year. Our horsemen stood where they might back the footmen; which in regard of them God wot! were right weak. When the Frenchmen saw the harquibutters shoot off they began to retire; and so reinforcing our skirmish, giving Sir Thomas Palmer the charge of the same, we drove them from place to place to the Sandhills, and so from hill to hill to Hardelot.

By that time our succours were come from the town; so that we were within the trenches upon the hill, a fifteen hundred men in squadre, and five hundred at the passage to keep the same on the other side. We might also discern all the carts swarm up the hill again towards Montreuil, which as I guess had never passed Neuf-Chateau; and might discover five ensigns of footmen coming out of the wood. Whereupon being then three o'clock, and we four miles from home, judging by the fires that we saw in the woods, that the Almains were come; and that also one of our men did discover nine ensigns of footmen; having empeched the thing wherefore we same, by the advice of the rest I thought it meet to return to my charge where I had left Mr. Bridges, Mr. Under Marshall, the Master of the Ordnance, and Mr. Porter; assuring your Majesty that I think at the retire their houses were well dagged with arrows, and that they were for one day right well affrayed; albeit when they saw our small power of horsemen, they might retire against our will: wishing to God that your Majesty, with the surety of the same, had seen the willing hearts as well of the gentleman and strangers of this town, as also of the poor soldiers.

This day I think, if the Almains be some, they shall put in their carts against our will. Yet sent I yesterday of my Lord Gray with his horsemen, with whom, if he come, we shall devise what is devise what is further to be done; trusting that the bitterness of this weather will soon make them weary, and the Almains shall lose the intent of their journey, by the reason of your Majesty's ships, which shall let their revictualment by Port hill; and as I hear they have already taken divers sails laden with herring and coals; assuring your Majesty, that if we had any number of horsemen here, and meat for the same, and certain pinnaces that would do their duty to keep upon this shore, I would hope the revicualling of this fortress should cost the French king dear.

Beseeching your Majesty, that your Council present at this journay, the Colonels of the Albanois, and Italians, with the other Captains and Gentlemen of this town, may receive thanks for their good service. Amongst whom I beseech your Highness to be good and gracious Lord to this bearer, Mr. Dudley; who for his towardness and good will to serve hath few fellows in this town: and hath a brother in the Old Man, a gentleman of as good a sort, and as serviceable as I have much seen. Mr. Arden also, both now and at sundry times for his service hath deserved to be humbly commended by me unto your Majesty. Mr. Adrain Poynings, I assure your Majesty, is a man for his discretion and hardiness of great service. Francis Aslebye, that hurt Mons. D'Aumale, break his staff very honestly. Trusting that as this ground hath been now, and in my Lord Admiral's time, happy to your Majesty's service, it shall always so continue. Not doubting but when your pleasure shall be such to keep the field, it shall be seen how the French King hath [?] his fortress; as your Majesty would have said, if the same had seen us in the field, and how easy it is to keep the strait.

And thus leaving to trouble your Majesty with the circumstances of this Journay, I shall leave the same to the declaration of this said Bearer; to whom it may please your Majesty to give credit. I pray God to preserve your most excellent Majesty.

Your Majesty's most humble and obedient servant, and subject, H. Surrey.

From your Majesty's Town of Boulogne,
This fourth of December 1545. [Nott, 181-186]

Letter 2:
From the Earl of Surrey to the King.

It may like your most excellent Majesty: that according to my formal advertisement, my Lord Gray having received my message, assembling together such number of horsemen as so short warning would suffer, to the number of three hundred, arrived here with Mr. Pollard upon Saturday night at eleven o'clock, having made a right painful journey; as well for the bitterness of the weather as for lack of meat for his horses here; which he regarded not, in respect of your Majesty's service: for the which I beseech your Highness he may receive his thanks accordingly.

We then jointly resolved to attempt nothing till a further advantage were seen; considering that their horsemen were increased, being no fewer in number than a thousand; their Almains all encamped upon the border in the wood, beyond Hardelot; and those carts of victuals that they had brought, and could spare from themselves, put into the fortress upon Friday at the full sea. Upon Saturday, at night, they laid a thousand men at Porthill by night, to receive the victuals that should come from Dieppe, which was the only intent of their journey. But Mr. Cotton, Vice Admiral of your Majesty's fleet, (according to the direction given him from hence by the advertisement of mine espial(spies)) lay for them a sea board Somme head, so that in the morning he might descry them a forty sail: and making with them, the men of war that were their conductors fled first; the victuallers escaped into Somme, saving seven that were passed by, which were taken; whereof six laden with meal and salt beef, and the other with wine. These boats were wonderfully well devised only for the revictualment of this fortress by Porthill; of great stowage, and drawing but three feet water. Beseeching your Majesty that Mr. Cotton may receive his thanks accordingly; referring unto your Highness's most prudent consideration of what importance this service is. Whereby, besides the ruin of their horsemen and footmen by the extremity of the weather, their whole purpose is for this present disappointed.

On Sunday, at night, fearing lest they had returned their carts to Montreuil for more victuals, we resolved, this morning before day to lay our whole ambush of horsemen and footmen at St. Etienne, and towards Hardelot, to see whether by any alarm in the break of the day we could train them out; and the rest of the day to have kept our trenches with some field pieces: and with our horsemen to have done our best to let their revictualment; sending afore night a few horsemen to dodge them to their lodging. But upon the news of the taking of their ships, as I think, the whole camp retired towards Montreuil, chafed for choler, and yet I think right well a-cold.

The prizes, saving that of wine, I have been so bold to retain here for the revictualling of this town; for that I trust if these sails attempt to come again, to do some service with the same. Considering that I might put in each of them seven score men; and think it not unmeet that your majesty saw them; to the intent the same might provide such like for the revictualling of this town from Calais, to steal along the shore; for the which purpose only they were made. Thus may your majesty perceive with what difficulty this fortress may be victualled; and that they shall be driven to make an army by sea and by land to discharge the same at Porthill.

Finally; whereas Sir Thomas Palmer and Sir Thomas Wyatt (whom your majesty of ignorant men hath framed to such towardness and knowledge in the war, that as I am able to judge of that I understand not myself, none other dispraised, your majesty hath not of their behavior and youth many the like within your realm, both for their hardiness, painfulness, circumspection, and natural disposition to war) have desired license to repair into England in this time of least service, to settle their private affairs; which for their zeal to your Majesty's service they have long neglected; I have thought it good to beseech your Majesty to give them credit for the declaration of such conferences and discourses as we have had together concerning the order of your Majesty's wars on this side of the sea. Which hath proceeded, I take God to witness, rather of a care beyond all other affections to your Majesty's service, than to any presumptions of knowledge: and that I hope your Majesty will at least take in good part upon the sight of things, the humble advertisement from time to time of him, whom most unworthy, your Majesty hath placed here. Neither do I think it my duty to use any other mean for the declaration of the discourse of any service to be done here, than to your Majesty. Beseeching your Highness that these Gentlemen may know that I have not unremembered to your Majesty their divers and sundry good services done the same.

And thus I pray God to preserve your most excellent Majesty. Your Majesty's most humble, and obedient servant, and subject, H. Surrey. From your Majesty's Town of Boulogne this seventh of December, 1545. [Nott, 186-189]

Letter 3:

From the Earl of Surrey to the King

Pleaseth it your most excellent Majesty;

WHEREAS of late I was so bold to dispatch unto your Highness Sir Thomas Palmer and Sir Thomas Wyatt, to declare my poor opinion by what mean this new fortress might be best attempted, the overture whereof it pleased your Majesty to command them then to differ, until it were seen what success the treatise of peace, then in hand, were like to have; having received commandment from your Highness by Mr. Secretary to give order for the war in all your Majesty's pieces here; I was so bold, after that I had in the company of Mr. Marshall, Sir Thomas Wyatt, and Sir Thomas Palmer, which jointly have consented to this devise, revisited the grounds of most advantage, to cause Giles your Highness's servant to draw a plat, and send the same by Rogers unto your Majesty: and then having lately received letters and credit from your Highness by Mr. Bellingham, that I, and the rest of your Majesty's council here should with him, and Tomazo, (who is not yet arrived here,) consult by what means and with what numbers this fortress might be won; I have not thought it yet good to stay the dispatch of Rogers, to the which I have made only privy Mr. Bellingham, Mr. Marshall, Mr. Wyatt, and Sir Thomas Palmer; and in the mean while, till your Majesty have returned your pleasure; to consult with the rest of your Highness' Council here, and to advertise the general opinion of us all. Beseeching your Majesty to give credit to Rogers in that, he hath to declare in my behalf, touching as well my fore said opinion, as the misery that the fortress now standeth in; which is such, that if the great revictualment now prepared might be empeched, your Majesty should never need to besiege the same. Whereby your Highness shall perceive your garrison here hath done their duty to keep the fortress so short, as the enemy is driven, with half a camp to revictual the same. The power that they have assembled, as I hear, is their old band of Almains, which be not now much above two thousand; and as many Picards or more, with a five hundred men at arms.

For as much as this new fortress is an annoyful neighbour to your Majesty's town of Boulogne, and county of the same; and that if the enemy have commodity the next year to finish the same, the difficulty to win it will increase, I would wish that your Majesty should besiege the same as timely as all necessaries may be prepared; and the time of the year meet for men to lie in the field. The only difficulty wherein, that I see, is the conveyance of victual hither; which, after the French King hath put his ships into the seas, without a navy cannot be done. Your Majesty's only mean to win the fort, as me seemeth, is to prevent the enemy in the field, and to encamp so, strongly in the strait in, divers places trenched the one from the other, as no relief of victuals may pass: with a determination to famish the same, and in our strength to abide the enemy, and not, to fight. Which, with trenches and a mount in every camp, the nature of the ground considered, seemeth unto me feasable.

The great difficulty in all your Majesty's wars [hath ever been] of horsemen; the service of whom is either in battle to encounter the like, or to convey the victual. In this case a small number may serve, considering that in my devise, as it appeareth by my plat, our victual once landed is conveyed to us within the precinct of our camp, without the danger of any other enemy but the fortress: and, if the French King's navy be not upon the seas, the victual may be landed with boats within the creek of Portet; which is also within our camp. And if your Majesty shall prevent the enemy in the field (and considering the ruin of his country, and the small number of men that he hath already assembled, unless lie were advertised of your "Majesty's enterprise, he cannot be prepared for the field so timely) so shall it not be possible for him to refresh the fort with any great mass of victual by land, if your Majesty would betimes give order by sea. So that I think the fortress would be starved before the season of the year would serve the enemy to put his gallies to the sea.

For the numbers of men, and all other things necessary for this enterprise, I remit the same most humbly to your Majesty's consideration. And albeit a great number of pioneers is requisite, yet, for th' expedition of the fortifying of the camp, wherein consisteth the surety of the whole enterprise, there is no doubt but every soldier will set his hands thereto.

Which done, if seemeth to me that what by the camp, the sea, the river, and your Majesty's pieces on the other side, there was never fortress more straitlier besieged, and more desperate of succour: and that the army of the enemy, be it never so great, shall not be able to levy us, being strongly entrenched, and having taken already the advantage of the highest grounds: enterlacing with trenches, the one hill to the other, and receiving our victuals always in surety: when also, in your Majesty's pieces a small garrison may serve.

Which devise, if it shall seem good unto your Highness, it shall be meet that in the mean time were placed here, a good number of horsemen to put by the small revictual-ments, to make the fortress the meeter for the other enter-prise; wherein the secret and diligent preparation in time for necessaries is most requisite; but chiefy your Majesty's navy by sea importeth the whole success of the enterprise,

And whereas your Majesty, for lack of answer to the dispatch of the Clerk of the Council of this town, hath in wages still as many Captains, and double-pays, for the number that here now remaineth, as when there were here the whole eight thousand; it may please your High-ness, remembering your charge, to return your resolution: and if the same mind to reduce the companies of footmen to three hundred, then, out of such captains as shall be cassed, it might please your Majesty, besides them that shall serve for the ordinary garrison, to choose some of the most experience and service, and to entertain them with-out men, after the wages of a Captain. So shall they be here occupied in place of service. And when your Highness shall amass more foot-men, those captains be in a readiness to take the leading of them; and the men by this means sooner equeried than when the men and captains both are with-out experience. The charge whereof shall not be great, and the comfort to your subjects here much, when they shall see that your Majesty will entertain them still for their passed service. Beseeching the same to remember them generally with some letter of comfort, which shall afresh encourage them most willingly to adventure their lives, according to their most bounden duty, in your Majesty's service. So shall the same wipe out of their hearts the fear that they gave conceived that your Highness should gather some suspicion of them, concerning the excessive allow-ance before the time made. Assuring your Majesty, upon my most bounden duty to the same, that as I cannot speak but sith my coming hither, I dare say at this present there was never Prince more truly served in that behalf: and that with the advice of your Highness's Council there is set so direct and certain orders for the payment of the garrison, that there is in effect no gate left open to deceit, as I think.

Mr. Southwell will inform your Majesty, at his return,

that he findeth at this present that your Highness's affairs go directly. And if there were any fault before time, on my faith I think the foreign trouble of the enemy was rather the cause, than any spot or lack of duty to your Majesty.

On the contrary part, if your Majesty shall determine on war defensive, the same shall do well to resolve in what order your fortifications shall proceed, and upon your pleasure known, every way I shall travail to my power to your Majesty's contentation.

[There is a portion of the document missing at this point]

which I assure your Majesty I cannot yet see how they can bring to pass, if this weather continue; so that your Highness would give order that your ships might keep upon this shore, when the weather would serve: assuring your Majesty that these six days their whole garrison hath lived with biscuit and water; having neither wood, nor coal. Whereupon I have sent for the horsemen of Guisnes to bring hay with them by land, if the weather will suffer; for we had none here these ten days; and if they come, there shall be nothing left undone that shall be thought meet with the surety of your Majesty's pieces.

Finally, it may please your Majesty to receive herein enclosed my simple discourse concerning the attempting of the fortress; and, pardoning my folly, to accept my good intent; beseeching your Highness that this bearer may know I have most humbly commended his honest service here unto your Majesty. And that Giles may perceive the same taketh in good part his honest travail; who desireth your Highness to pardon this plat made in haste, and promiseth to present your majesty with another shortly to the full perfection; who, coming hither for his own affairs, hath been stayed here by me for this purpose. And thus I pray God to preserve your most excellent Majesty.

Your Majesty's most humble
and obedient servant,
and subject,
H. Surrey.

From your Majesty's town of Boulogne,
this 5th of January, 1546 [Nott, 191-196]

On 8 January 1546, the Earl of Surrey reported to the King that they detected the enemy's movement of about six hundred horses and three hundred foot soldiers by the abandoned fires they left behind and they had in fact moved about six miles from Montreuil. As Surrey's forces passed the town of Hardelot in pursuit, a gentleman was shot in the knee and later died. Surrey ordered Wyatt, Palmer, Bridges, and two thousand foot soldiers to give chase to the moving enemy leaving behind two thousand foot soldiers and remaining members of the Council.

As soon as Surrey had his forces in place near the town of St. Etienne, the enemy had also prepared themselves for battle with about five hundred horsemen and about four thousand foot soldiers outside Hardelot. The Earl of Surrey described the events to the King:

> From the Earl of Surrey to the King.
>
> It may like your most excellent Majesty; that having certain espial (spies) that Monsieur Du Biez was set fort [forth] of Montreuil with six hundred horse, and three thousand footmen, to relieve the great necessity of the fortress, mentioned in our former letters; we took yesterday before day the trenches at St. Etienne, with six hundred footmen, and sent out Mr. Ellerkar with all the horsemen of this town; and Mr. Pollard with two hundred that he brought the night before from Guisnes, to discover whither their camp marched, which he had discovered by their fires at Nouclier over night, six miles on this side Montreuil. And as they passed by Hardelot, Mr. Pollard was hurt with a culverin in the knee, and died thereof the night following; of whom your Majesty had a notable loss.
>
> Our horsemen discovered their march beyond Hardelot, whereupon I th' Earl of Surrey being advertised, according to the order agreed upon amongst us, issued out with Mr. Bridges, Sir Henry Palmer, Thomas Palmer, Sir Thomas Wyatt, and two thousand footmen, leaving within your Majesty's pieces two thousand footmen, and the rest of the Council here, divided in the pieces. And by that time that we had set our horsemen and footmen in order of battle without the trench of St. Etienne, the enemy was also in order of battle on this side Hardelot, and had put on their carriages by the sea's side towards the fortress. Whereupon, having discovered their horsemen not above five hundred, and footmen about four thousand, ponder-

ing the weight of the service, which might have imported no less success than the wining of the fortress; and the courage and good will that seemed in our men (the surety of your Majesty's pieces being provided for) upon a consultation we presented them the fight with a squadre of pikes and bills, about three score in file, and two of harquebussiers, and one of bows; and our horsemen on the right wing. Many of the Captains and Gentlemen were in the first rank by their desire; for because they were well armed in corselets. The battle of the Almains came towards us likewise with two wings of harquebussiers, and two troops of horsemen.

Mr. Marshall, Mr. Bellingham, Mr. Porter, Mr. Shelley, and Mr. Granado, with all the horsemen of this town, and Guisnes, gave the charge upon their right flank, and brake their harquebussiers. Their horsemen fled and ours followed the victory, and killed and slew till they came to the carriages, where they brake four score and ten, accomped by tale this morning. Our squadre then joined with th' Almains; with a cry of as great courage, and in as good order as we could wish. And by that time our first rank and the second were come to the push of the pike, there grew a disorder in our men, and without cause fled; at which time many of our gentlemen were slain, which gave as hardy an onset as hath been seen, and could but have had good success, if they had been followed. So, stinted they never for any devise, that we could use, till they came to the trenches: and being well settled there; which is such a place as may be kept against all their camp, they forsook that and took the river; which gave th' enemy courage to follow them: albeit the night drawing then on, they followed not far beyond. Assuring your Majesty that the fury of their flight was such, that it booted, little the travail that was taken upon every strait to stay them. And so seeing it not possible to stop them, we suffered them: to retire to the town. In the meanwhile, our horsemen thinking all won, finding the disorder, were fain to pass over at a passage a mile beneath Pont de Britque, without any loss, having slain a great number of the enemies; whereof we have yet no certain advertisement.

Thus was there loss and victory on both sides. And this morning we sent over afore day to number the dead. There was slain of our side two hundred and five; whereof Captains Mr. Edward Poynings; Captain Story, Captain Jones, Spencer, Roberts, Basford, Wourth, Wynchcombe, Mr. Vawse, and a man at arms called Harvy. Captain Crayford and Mr. John Palmer, and Captain Shelley, and Captain Cobham, missed but not found. All these were slain in the first rank. Other there were that escaped. Among whom Mr. Wyatt was one; assuring your Majesty that there were never gentlemen served more hardily, if it had chanced and saving the disorder of our footmen that fled without cause, when all things almost seemed won.

The enemy took more loss than we, but for the gentlemen; whose loss was much to be lamented. And this day we have kept the field from the break of day; and the enemy retired to Montreuil immediately after the fight, and left their carriages distressed behind them. And not twenty carts entered into the fortress; and that biscuit.

Beseeching your Majesty, though the success hath not been such as we wished, to accept the good intent of us all; considering that it seemed to us, in a matter of such importance, a necessary thing to present the fight. And that Mr. Ellerkar may know we have humbly recommended his good service unto your Highness; which was such, as if all the rest had answered to the same, the enemy had been utterly discomforted; and that it may please your Majesty to give him credit for the declaration thereof more at large.

Further; whereas Mr. Henry Dudley was one of those of the first rank that gave the onset upon the enemy, and is a man [to be esteemed] for his knowledge, heart, and of good service, it may like your Highness to be his good and gracious Lord; that whereas Mr. Poynings, late Captain of your Majesty's guard here is deceased, if your Highness shall think him able to succeed him in that room, at our humble intercession to admit him thereto; if it may so stand with your most gracious pleasure.

And thus beseeching your Highness to accept our poor service, albeit the success in all things was not such as we wished, yet was th' enemies enterprise disappointed; which could not have been otherwise done, and mo' of their part slain than of ours; and the fortress in as great misery as before; and a sudden flight the let of a full victory. And, if any disorder there were, we assure your Majesty there was no default in the rulers, nor lack of courage to be given them, but a humour that sometime reigneth in Englishmen: most humbly thanking your Majesty that it hath pleased the same to consider their payment; which shall much revive their hearts to adventure most willingly their lives, according to their most bounden duty, in your Majesty's service, to make recompence for the disorder that now they have made.

And thus we pray to God to preserve your most excellent Majesty, from your Highness's Town of Boulogne, this 8th of January, 1546.

Your Majesty's most humble and obedient servants,

H. Surrey, Hugh Poulet, Henry Palmer, Richard Cavindish, John Bryggys, Richard Wyndebancke.

Postscript. Whereas we think that this victual can serve for no long time, that they have put into the fortress; wherefore it is to be thought th' enemy will attempt the like again shortly: it may please your Majesty to resolve what is further to be done by us; and for the declaration of our poor opinions therein, we have sent Mr. Ellerker to your Majesty, to whom may it please your Highness to give credit in that behalf, and the present tempest being such, we have thought it meet to send these before, and stay him for a better passage.

To the King's most excellent Majesty. [Nott, 198-201]

Two days later the Earl of Surrey dispatched a letter to the Privy Council:

From the Council at Boulogne to the Privy Council.

After our hearty commendations to your good Lordships; whereas, having matters of importance to impart with you concerning the service of the King's Majesty, we have addressed Sir Thomas Wyatt for the declaration thereof in our behalfs unto you; desiring you therefore to give credit unto him, and with expedition to give order for the same accordingly.

Thus we bid your Lordships most heartily farewell. From Boulogne, this tenth day of January, 1546.

Your Lordships assured loving Friends,

H. Surrey, John Bryggys, Richard Cavendish, Hugh Jowler, Thomas Palmer.

To our very good Lords, my Lord Cobham,
Deputy of Calais; and my Lord Gray, General of all the
King's Crews at Calais and Guisnes. [Nott, 203]

Eventually the events in France calmed down with really no
opposition by the French. Wyatt was still in Boulogne in about
late May to early April. It was at this time when King Henry announced changes in command and in early April, Surrey received
orders to return to England so the King could confer with him on
those changes in Boulogne; then he would return to his command,
or so was promised. History is rather vague on the reason(s) for the
changes and the only real clue from the following letter to the Earl
of Surrey from Secretary Paget:

> From Mr. Secretary Paget to the Earl of Surrey:
> My very good Lord,
> With most hearty commendations, it may like you to
> understand that I have received your letter of the sixteenth
> of this present, and communicated the same to the King's
> Majesty for answer; whereunto his Highness requireth
> your Lordship to depeche from thence all such captains
> with their officers as you wrote be cassed: for his Majesty
> knoweth not how to employ the same. Nevertheless, if
> there be any captain of the cassed which is a special man
> of service, his Majesty would, ere your Lordship discharge
> him, be advertised of him to th' intent further order may be
> given for him, as his Majesty shall think good. As touching
> the want in th' Old Man, [it] shall be supplied as soon as
> may be conveniently.
> My Lord, the latter part of your letter, touching th'
> intended enterprize of th' enemy, giveth me occasion to
> write unto you frankly my poor opinion; trusting your
> Lordship will take the same in no worse part than I mean
> it. As your Lordship wisheth, so his Majesty mindeth to
> do somewhat for the endommaging of the enemy: and for
> that purpose hath appointed to send an army over shortly,
> and that my Lord of Hertford shall be his Highness's Lieu-
> tenant General at his being in Boulonnois. Whereby I fear
> your authority of Lieutenant shall, be touched: for I believe
> that the later ordering of a Lieutenant taketh away the
> commission of him that was there before.
> Now, my Lord, because you have been pleased I should
> write mine advice to your Lordship in things concerning

your honour and benefit, I could no less do than put you in remembrance how much in mine opinion this shall touch your honour, if you should pass the thing over in silence until the very time of my Lord of Hertford's coming over thither; for so should both your authority be taken away, as I fear in Boulonnois, and also it should fortune ye to come abroad without any place of estimation in the field; which the world would much muse at, and, though there be no such matter, think you were rejected upon occasion of some either negligence, inexperience, or such other like fault; for so many heads so many judgments. Wherefore, my Lord, in my opinion, you should do well to make sure by times to his Majesty to appoint you to some place of service in th' army; as to the captainship of the Foreward, or Rearward; or to such other place of honour as should be meet for you; for so should you be where knowledge and experience may be gotten. Whereby you should the better be able hereafter to serve, and also to have peradventure occasion to do some notable service in revenge of your men, at the last encounter with th' enemies, which should be to your reputation in the world. Whereas, being hither-to noted as you are a man of a noble courage, and of a desire to shew the same to the face of your enemies, if you should now tarry at home within a wall, having I doubt a shew of your authority touched, it would be thought abroad I fear, that either you were desirous to tarry in a sure place of rest, or else that the credit of your courage and forward-ness to serve were diminished; and that you were taken here for a man of [little] activity or service.

Wherefore, in my opinion, you shall do well, and pro-vide wisely for the conservation of your reputation, to sue to his Majesty for a place of service in the field. Wherein if it shall please you to use me as a mean to his Majesty, I trust so to set forth the matter to his Majesty, as he shall take the same in gracious part, and be content to appoint you to such a place as may best stand with your honour. And this counsel I write unto you as one that would do you well; trusting that your Lordship will even so inter-pret the same, and let me know your mind herein betimes.

Whereas your Lordship, with the rest of the Council there, wrote in the favour of Croft to be Lieutenant of th' Old Man, it may like you t' understand that his Highness had before appointed Thomas Awdley to have the place; the same being indeed a very meet man t' occupy the same, as your Lordship knoweth right well. And also hath appointed Adrian Poynings to be Lieutenant to Mr. Wyatt in the citadel; whereof his Majesty hath willed me to advertise your Lordship; for the same shall resort thither to their charge shortly.

Finally, I shall desire your Lordship to send unto me the testament of Mr. Rous, with his seal, his keys, and such books of reckonings, or accounts as he hath there: until which time such as be hath ordained, his executors wot not how to procede in his things.

To the Right Honourable and my special good Lord th' Earl of Surrey, the King's Majesty's Lieutenant General of Boulogne and county of Boullonoys. [Nott, 224-227]

On 9 April 1546, Lord Grey relieved the Earl of Surrey of his command then Surrey returned to England to assume his duties there. Several months passed without further incident by the French and Thomas Wyatt wrote to Lord William Paget on 15 June indicating his desire to return home as the King gave Lord Sturton his command:

"I would have used no other help but my lord of Hartford's in discharging me from Base Bolleyn, as though he had afore so done when he placed me in this fort, had I not thought that those that have, by bringing this to pass, made reckoning to have done me a foul displeasure, will now, when they shall perceive how little I esteem that, work me to tarry where they may do me displeasure indeed. Wherefore, gentle Mr. Secretary, help me herein, knowing that, though I should less have troubled you the other way, yet I should not have been so assured to obtain that so greatly I do desire, nor have had any thank at your hand for not using your friendship, which hath been more a great deal than I have deserved or am able to recompense." [Calendar of Letters, Despatches and State Papers, 530]

It is unclear how long Thomas Wyatt remained at his post in Boulogne, but there are indications that he returned home possibly within a year from the time that he wrote the letter to William Paget. There have been suggestions that the Earl of Surrey maintained communications with Wyatt but no correspondence has been located from that period.

Trouble began for the Earl of Surrey shortly after he arrived back in England. Though history records several conflicting reasons, it appears to have been religious in nature and as a result, he spent some time confined in Windsor Castle but only for a short period. Many of the poems he wrote while in confinement are preserved and show the pain he was experiencing at that point in life. Perhaps the most notable is his last known letter of 14 July 1546 in which the location from which he sent the letter is unknown.

Surrey did not enjoy his freedom long. He was arrested on 12 December while sitting for a painter of his portrait. Following his arrest, several individuals appeared before the Council and though none of those depositions given constituted any legal or moral offence, Surrey was indicted for high treason and was quickly sent to trial on 13 January 1547. History records that Surrey defended the frivolous charges alleged against him with great skill but the jury found him guilty and he was beheaded on 19 or 20 January on Tower Hill. His body was buried in the church of All Hallows, Barking, and later moved by his son to the church at Framlingham, Suffolk.

In early January 1547, King Henry VIII had fallen gravely ill though he recovered enough to meet with the Imperial and French ambassadors on 16 January and was able to discuss several issues with them. Nevertheless, about ten days later the King relapsed and several, including his own doctors admitted that the King's death was near. Henry himself must have known this as he prepared, requested forgiveness for his sins, and made reflections of his own life and in the early hours of 28 January, King Henry VIII died at the age of fifty-six and in his thirty-seventh year reigning. For several days the King's death was kept a secret and on 8 February every parish church rang its bells and the following day Mass was held. Henry was buried in St. George's chapel in Windsor next to his wife Jane Seymour's grave. There are several stories that suggest that his grave was disturbed several times and his body moved.

His only son and heir Edward VI was crowned on 20 February 1547 in the richly decorated Westminster Abbey at the tender age of ten years old. Though Edward was officially the King, he was only a minor and unable to fully undertake the responsibilities and make decisions as King until he was eighteen. His father had seen to it that sixteen executers were to assume the responsibilities of the government and to those executers; twelve counselors were assigned and though they possessed no real power, they could lend advice if required. Among the issues these bodies were to address was to appoint a protector to act on the King's behalf.

On 26 May of the same year, commissioners were assigned to keep the King's peace and enforce the statutes and ordinances made for its preservation. Among those commissioned from the county of Kent were Sir Thomas Wyatt, Henry Isley, the Duke of Somerset and the Archbishop of Canterbury. They were sworn by oath as justices to follow up on reports about all felonies, trespasses, or other illegal or suspicious activities. They were to immediately act on reports about those who rode armed in assemblies against the King's peace and in disturbance of his people and to immediately act on those who laid in wait to maim or kill people and who would falsely wear caps or other clothing to impersonate sheriffs, knights or other important persons.

On 12 November 1549, Thomas Wyatt, Thomas Culpeper, and Henry Isley were appointed as sheriffs of Kent. For his services rendered to the King during the various campaigns in France, the King awarded Thomas Wyatt on 13 June 1550 the lordships and manors of Maydeston and Oldborowes in Kent, the lands called "oldeborowes" in Maydeston, Maydeston Parke, and the fulling mill called Paddesmyll in the parish of Maydeston, which had formerly belonged to the Archbishop of Canterbury. Thomas Wyatt also received the message and a great barn, stable, dove house, orchard, garden, and the lands called Fuller Meade, Upper Saltelande, Nether Saltelande, Bullock Field, Uppercombe, and Nethercombe, and a parcel of meadow (one acre) adjacent to Nethercombe, a parcel of meadow at the end of the bridge of Maydeston, and a barn in Bower Streate. Furthermore, Wyatt received a messuage (dwelling house) and orchard, two little gardens (two acres) and some land at Fant in Maydeston, the messuage and garden at Newarkegate in Maydeston, the rectory of Maydeston, and chapels of Loose and Detlyng in the county of Kent.

On 11 November 1550, Thomas Wyatt, Henry Isley, and Reynold Scott were again chosen by the King to serve as sheriffs in the county of Kent. During the same month, Thomas Wyatt was named as a commissioner to delimit the English frontier in France, but he was unable to fulfill this obligation due to an illness.

With King Edward VI now firmly seated on the throne, the protector was faced with the possibility of war with Scotland. Despite his efforts to prevent it, war did occur late in the year. It is not clear if Thomas Wyatt served under the Protector Somerset in the battle of Musselburgh or called the battle of Pinkey by modern historians, because his name does not appear on any rosters of the period and he most likely fulfilled his obligations to the King and was not required to serve any additional time. Accounts of the Battle of Pinkey mention ten thousand Scottish fatalities; fifteen hundred taken prisoner and only five hundred English soldiers were lost in the battle. The only correspondence recorded was from the Protector who dispatched news of the battle to London and recommended Nicholas Throckmorton for commendation because of his conduct. Throckmorton was later knighted and obtained a place in the Privy Chamber and is noted as being taken in special favor by King Edward.

As the result of the Protectors' mishandling of several other situations, he was relieved of his position and John Dudley the Earl of Warwick replaced him. Eventually peace with Scotland and France allowed for other ambitions to be pursued and the Earl of Warwick won the favor of King Edward and was soon after made the Duke of Northumberland.

King Edward was soon burdened by the increasing debts of the kingdom that several military campaigns had contributed to and of his own declining health. The young King was at first overtaken by the measles, which he overcame, but was soon afflicted with an obstinate cough that he could not overcome even with the use of medicine and the signs of consumption began to appear. In February 1553, the King contracted a feverish cold that he was unable to overcome and he opened a session of Parliament in the great chamber of Whitehall instead of at Westminster; he was also unable to go to Greenwich for Easter as his symptoms continued to worsen. Rumors began to spread that the King would not live long.

On 3 March, the King commissioned individuals from various counties to inventory and deal with items belonging to the churches and Thomas Wyatt, George Harper, and Henry Isley received their commissions for the county of Kent.

In June of the same year, the overambitious Duke of Northumberland devised a plan in which he could attain a higher level of social status that included manipulating the young and dying King Edward VI into changing his father's will and the order of succession to the throne. Edward was at first reluctant to change his fathers' will, but the skillful Duke was able to alleviate the concerns the King had expressed. Northumberland based his plan on a decision that Parliament made declaring Mary and Elizabeth bastards and without claim to the throne. Next, Northumberland convinced Edward that Mary, be overlooked because of her foreign affairs and Frances Brandon because of her age. Finally, Northumberland was able to convince Edward that Lady Jane Grey was a worthy heir to the throne and Edward was content with the changes. In late May, Northumberland's only unwed son Guildford wed Lady Jane Grey and now with Edward's devise in hand, Northumberland would soon be the father of the King of England when Edward died and Jane ascended the throne.

King Edward signed the devise and Northumberland had yet another obstacle to overcome, the Council, and after intimidating several members who were reluctant to sign and rewarding those who did, Northumberland was able to push the King's devise through, thus placing it into effect. He was one step closer to being the father of the King of England. As Edward's illness grew worse, Northumberland was relieved that the changes were in place and Northumberland did not have to wait long as Edward died between eight and nine o'clock on the evening of 6 July in the arms of Doctor Sidney. England lost the last Tudor King.

There were strong suspicions about the use of poison to quicken the death of the young King. Shortly before the King died, the Duke of Northumberland dismissed Edward's own physicians, replaced them with a schoolmistress who promised to restore the King's health to normal. She administered small amounts of formaldehyde in her medications. When Edward's skin color changed and his health worsened, her methods were severely questioned, then she was dismissed, never to be heard from again. Edward's physicians were brought back, but it was too late. Edward's death was kept a secret, which allowed preparations to be made for the change in succession and for Jane to take her place on the throne. It has been suggested that schoolmistress was murdered to prevent her from mentioning anything.

Early historians suggest that the Duke of Northumberland faced yet another problem: what to do with Edward's body. An autopsy preceding the embalming might reveal symptoms confirming the use of poison (formaldehyde in his blood). Some early historians suggest that the bones now lying beneath the altar of the Chapel of Henry VIII in Westminster Abbey are not Edward's, but in fact, those of a young boy who looked like him. No evidence substantiates this claim and without a statement by someone near Edward's death, the fate of his body remains a mystery.

It did not take long for Lady Jane Grey to be proclaimed Queen, despite Mary strongly disputing what she felt was rightfully hers as her father Henry VIII had indicated in his will. As Lady Jane settled into her new duties as Queen, Mary Tudor was gaining support as many in the realm felt that she was the rightful heir and many including noblemen, were abandoning Jane. After only nine days, Mary gained enough support to take the throne from Jane Grey then was immediately proclaimed Queen. Jane and her husband were placed in the Tower.

It was about this point in time that Thomas Wyatt, as indicated in his later trial, served with the Earl of Arundel to locate the traitorous Duke of Northumberland and bring him to justice and eventually Northumberland and his party surrendered at Cambridge to the Earl of Arundel on 24 July. The following day, they arrived in London at dusk to find large crowds gathered along the streets that threw stones, rotten eggs, and filth from the gutters and one witness indicated that a dead cat was hurled at the Duke. The crowd attempted to rush the Duke, shouting, "Death! Death to the traitor!" The once confident, powerful, and arrogant Duke of Northumberland was at last humbled and witnesses noted that as they entered London, the Duke held his head down in shame and tears flowed from his face. The Duke of Northumberland was later tried, convicted of treason then beheaded on Tower Hill.

As Mary began to settle into her duties as Queen, talk soon spread about whom she would marry, as many felt that she would not attempt to rule without the guidance of a husband. Several candidates were considered, including the recently released Earl of Devonshire and Cardinal Pole. As those around the Queen discussed who would be her husband, others were frantic with the preparations for her coronation on 27 September. Her sister Elizabeth and their attendants accompanied Mary as they traveled down the Thames River to the Tower where they were greeted with a magnificent display of light and thunder as the cannons came to life.

On 1 October 1553, Mary rode in a chariot richly adorned with cloth tissue drawn by six horses draped with similar tissue. Mary wore a lavish gown made of purple velvet draped with powdered furs of ermine. She wore a headdress in the shape of a ball of cloth of tinsel inset adorned with pearl and precious jewels. Her headdress was so tall that she had to support her head with one hand and the canopy was raised to accommodate the additional height. Riding ahead of Mary's chariot were several gentlemen and knights and it is quite possible that Thomas Wyatt would have been with that group. They were followed by doctors of divinity, bishops, lords, members of the Privy Council and the Knights of the Bath wearing their robes. The Bishop of Winchester, the Marques of Winchester, the Lord High Treasurer, and the Earl of Oxford who was carrying a sword just ahead of Mary's chariot had followed them. Following the procession of noblemen was Mary's chariot led by Sir Edward Hastings holding the reigns of the horses. Another chariot followed the Queen with Princess Elizabeth and Anne of Cleves. Their chariot was covered in a silver and white cloth. Elizabeth's chariot was followed by a long procession of forty-six gentlemen and ladies all wearing gowns of red velvet.

The Bishop of Winchester crowned Mary in the magnificently adorned Westminster Abbey. Edward Courtenay carried a sword during the procession as did the Earl of Westmoreland and the Earl of Shrewsbury carried the crown. The Duke of Norfolk served as Marshal and the Earl of Arundel was Lord Steward. Following the oath of allegiance and ceremonies was a lavish feast where Mary was offered 312 dishes. Over seven thousand dishes were offered to all those in attendance of which 4900 were declared waste and offered to the poor citizens following the banquet.

As the Queen settled into her duties, she was plagued with ever-increasing debts that forced her to look outside her realm for sources of money. Mary was advised that no such man in the kingdom could offer assistance but Prince Philip of Spain could; and by late October, Mary strongly considered a union with Spain, though many in her Council indicated that the kingdom would not support such a marriage with a "stranger." Regardless of her Council's concerns, Mary instructed her ambassador to request the conditions for an alliance from the Emperor on 31 October. By now, it was clear that Mary's choice for a husband was Philip and not the others for which many had hoped.

By now, Edward Courtenay fell out of the Queen's favor as reports spread that he was seen more with Princess Elizabeth for reasons that were not known. Very soon after, those close to Mary recommended that Edward Courtenay should marry Elizabeth despite reports that she had been lending an ear to certain French heretics. Reports also increased regarding the frequency of visits by Nicholas Throckmorton with the Princess though the reasons were unknown. Mary was faced with many pressures and withdrew from court for a couple of days pretending to be sick so she could consider all her options without outside disturbances. History has recorded that she made her decision not based on her own emotions, but only considered the well being of her kingdom as some began to worry about the union of the half Spanish Queen with Spain, but kept quiet about their concerns.

On 13 November Lady Jane Grey and her husband Guildford were brought to trial and though no actual transcript is known to have survived, there are a couple of accounts, with the following being perhaps the most vivid:

> Lady Jane appeared before her judges in all her wonted loveliness: her fortitude and composure never forsook her; nor did the throng and bustle of the court, the awful appearance of the seat of judgment, or the passing of the solemn sentence of the law, seem to disturb her mind: of their native bloom her cheeks were never robbed, nor did her voice seem once to falter: on the beauteous traitress every eye was fixed; and the grief that reigned throughout the whole assembly bespoke a general interest in her fate: indeed,

> > Her very judges wrung their hands for pity:
> > Their old hearts melted in 'em as she spoke,
> > And tears ran down upon their silver beards.
> > E'en her enemies were moved, and for a moment
> > Felt wrath suspended in their doubtful breasts,
> > And questioned if the voice they heard were mortal.

> [Bayley 428]

Lady Jane and Guildford were found guilty of treason and sentenced to death, though at the time they believed Mary would forgive them and release them to lead a private life after serving some term of imprisonment; but this was not to be, as Mary would not take a chance that Jane could be placed back on the throne.

Regardless of the attempts to suppress Mary's choice of husband, news slowly leaked out into the kingdom and rumors soon arrived at court of possible revolts, that Mary would be removed from the throne, and Elizabeth and Courtenay would replace her. These rumors only aggravated the already strained relationship between the Queen and Elizabeth. The Queen responded to the rumors by having the two more closely watched and their activities reported to the Queen frequently. Many would not support such an alliance with the Spanish and the Council feared that revolts might in fact break out, as many feared that such an alliance would be an invitation for Spain to invade England; trouble was certainly brewing.

CHAPTER 3. PRELUDE TO REBELLION

Revealed in later court proceedings, the earliest recorded date that a meeting occurred in which the conspirators discussed their plans for a revolt was 26 November 1553. Those present in the meeting, which took place in the Parish of St. Gregory in Castle Baynerde ward London, included Thomas Wyatt the Younger, Peter Carew, William Pickering, George Harper, and several other unnamed gentlemen. They discussed a plan to prevent the marriage of Mary and Philip by any means and would include the Duke of Suffolk who would raise men in the North, Edward Courtenay the Earl of Devonshire and Peter Carew in the West including Devon and Cornwall, and Thomas Wyatt in the East including Kent. The date the rising was to occur was set for 18 March 1554.

It would be safe to speculate that in the last week of November, Wyatt or someone acting on his behalf approached the Duke of Suffolk hoping to secure his support most likely with the intent of placing his daughter back on the throne. A few later historians suggest that Edward Courtenay was the initial leader of the conspiracy, but there are many reasons why Courtenay would not and could not have led such a rebellion as will be described in greater detail later but simply put, he neither had the training or skills required for such an undertaking. Furthermore, during the trial of Nicholas Throckmorton, a Sergeant of the Court revealed that a confession by Crofts indicated that Throckmorton was among the principle instigators and not Courtenay. However, it is often Thomas Wyatt that early history has recorded as the principle leader. However, in all probability, it may not have been just one individual who served as leader, but several acting as a council.

Clearly, the marriage was only one of the reasons that motivated Wyatt and the others and is a little more complex than is sometimes explained. Those that would eventually follow Wyatt may have done so for several reasons, which included the fear of a Spanish takeover of their government and the use of English money to fund Spanish interests without consideration of English needs. Yet others were true and diehard Protestants and the thought of the devout and staunch Catholic Mary allied with another Catholic would be like adding salt to a wound. Religion is often cited as the motivating factor that fueled the revolt, but men of both faiths, Catholic and Protestant, were involved and religion was but one of several reasons. Some may have seen Wyatt as a medium to express their unresolved grievances, while others may have joined because of influence or pressure by friends, family, colleagues, or even landlords.

It was not long before information arrived at Court about some individuals who were conspiring against the marriage, but those who were involved were careful to conceal their plans and had not yet commanded a great deal of attention or concern. Simon Renard, the Emperor's resident Ambassador in England, first mentions these conspirators in a long letter to the Emperor on 17 December:

> "...be that as it may, I must not refrain from repeating to your majesty that a section of the nobility and people is excited about the alliance, and I hear every day that my Lord Thomas Grey and his brother Lord John, brothers of the Duke of Suffolk, the Earl of Worcester, my lord Fealtre, Somerset, the former Admiral, a relative of Courtenay, the late Duke of Northumberland's son-in-law and several others mentioned to me by Pelham, are conspiring to prevent his Highness from landing, though the only argument they have left against the alliance is that the Spanish will wish to govern, for they have heard the articles, which have been proclaimed in general terms by the council. However, as there is unanimity in the Council as to this point, I trust the conspiracy may be checkmated, especially if the Queen surrounds herself with a guard of 3,000 of 4,000 men, as I believe she will do if there is any more talk of disaffection."

Renard continues in his letter to the Emperor with affectation:

> "I am told that the French are fitting out twenty-four warships, four of which are already off the English coast; and spies say that the King of France means to strain every

nerve to hold the Channel against his Highness. Others say that he intends to use the ships to transport his troops to Scotland; but I have from a good source that the Regent of Scotland is doing his utmost to make the Scots hate the French and keep them out of the country, for he fears they may wrest the government from his grasp and rule themselves. [Cal. Letters, Despatches, and State Papers, Mary Vol XII, pg. 40-41]

At the same time as Wyatt and the other confederates designed their plan to prevent the alliance; drafts were composed by the Council of a treaty that would cover all the concerns regarding an English and Spanish alliance. The drafts began in late November and completed in late December and early January of 1554. The treaty in itself spanned twenty-two pages and clearly defined Philip's boundaries. Among the numerous articles outlined was that Philip would enjoy the title of King but the real power over the realm would only belong to Mary. Furthermore, if she were to die without a child and heir, Philip would not have any rights to the throne, but if a son was produced, the son would have the right to claim the throne. Philip would not have any rights to appoint military leaders, alter the laws and customs of the land or remove any jewels, munitions or artillery, or his heir if any were to be, from the country. He was not to allow any Spaniard to act in an unbecoming manner and would only be served by men from the Low Countries and England while in England. Philip's obligation to Spain and his other realms would not change, he would not be allowed to merge Spanish matters into English, and he would be required to obey all English laws and customs.

Though news of the treaty was allowed to leak out before it was completed hoping to appease those that were rumored to be undertaking actions against the marriage, tensions formed as news of the increased unrest arrived at court. In addition to the rumors of a conspiracy forming, worry increased as the relations between England and France continued to break down.

In the last week of November, Renard informed the Emperor that the French Ambassador said in the presence of the full Council that the subjects of his master the King sunk a large number of ships that belonged to the Emperor and the resulting damage totaled a considerable amount of money. The Councilor informed Renard that he had heard of no such sea battle and possibly the French where only boasting again.

Suspicions of any type of French activity had always been carefully reviewed for facts and in the first week of December, the Queen quickly reacted to news that her sister was "lending an ear" to certain French heretics by questioning Elizabeth hoping to learn of her possible involvement and to find out what the French intrigues were. Elizabeth denied any knowledge of, or being involved with, any French activity against England. Antoine de Noailles a French Ambassador in England whose political motives often spurred controversy, wrote to his King that the Lady Elizabeth would gladly wed Edward Courtenay and go with him into the West country (Devon and Cornwall) to lead a rebellion against her sister, but Courtenay had been influenced by some means.

Most likely in a attempt to remove herself from further suspicion and scandal and tired of interrogations, Elizabeth requested leave from the Queen to depart to her childhood home of Ashridge, the home that her father Henry VIII purchased as a nursery for her and her brother Edward VI. Before Elizabeth was allowed to leave, the Earls of Arundel and Paget told the princess that they were suspicious of her activities and wanted to know her intentions. The princess did everything that she was able to do in an attempt to relieve any concerns that they or the Queen had of her and again denied knowledge of any conspiracies against the crown. Unable to gain any useful information, Arundel and Paget allowed her to journey to Ashridge and immediately following her interview, attention switched to Edward Courtenay. Courtenay was questioned in the presence of his mother, an accepted member of the Court for many years. After a long interview and a series of carefully worded questions and equally gauged responses, the Queen was temporarily satisfied with his answers but he and Elizabeth would be watched very closely for any suspicious activity.

By mid-December, Renard had again approached the Queen with the idea of marrying Elizabeth and Courtenay but this time included in his persuasions that he was told by a source that if they were to marry, all the nobility and people of England would support the alliance between her majesty and Philip. Renard revealed that his source may have exaggerated slightly, but he did believe that a marriage between Elizabeth and Courtenay would quiet some. However, there were still those such as Thomas Grey and his brother John both brothers of the Duke of Suffolk and others known to be conspiring to prevent Philip from ever setting foot on English soil.

On 18 December, the Council was informed that the French were preparing warships which would be used to prevent Philip from crossing the channel and four were already positioned somewhere between Calais and Dover. Some also suggested that those ships were to be used to transport French troops to Scotland but the Regent of Scotland was taking steps to make the Scots hate the French and to keep them out of their country. After Mary assured the Emperor that she would do whatever was necessary to ensure the channel would be free of heretics, she was informed that Philip would soon send Ambassadors to England to negotiate the treaty of alliance and to begin preparations for the marriage.

The Queen Dowager of Hungry wrote to the captain of the eight ships that were to sail to Spain and informed him that there were changes in plans. He was to sail to the channel with his ships that were well equipped with artillery, cannon balls and powder, and escort the Ambassadors to England to ensure their journey would not be hindered by the French war ships that were in the channel. The Ambassadors were due to arrive in England during the first week of January.

By 20 December, Renard indicated in a letter to the Emperor that all the articles of the treaty had been revealed and they appeared to address all the concerns that many had regarding the alliance. Renard also informed the Emperor that informants brought him news that the French were no longer able to partisan and the rumors of an uprising from the heretics in England had diminished because of the news of the possible marriage between Elizabeth and Edward Courtenay. Renard assured the Emperor that the Queen had gained the upper hand in those matters and everything that could be done was being done to ensure the safe arrival of the Ambassadors and later the arrival of Philip. Renard also informed the Emperor that views towards the alliance were changing; some had done so out of fear, others out of hope, and some by reason, others out of hypocrisy, and some out of a desire to please.

The Queen requested Renard appear before her on 24 December and inform her of updates on the numerous matters pending in realm. Mary finally gave her answer regarding the marriage of her sister Elizabeth to Edward Courtenay; she was now very against the idea as Paget and other Council members advised her against it and she informed Renard that the nobility no longer desired the union and that the Chancellor had advised Courtenay to seek another wife. Among other issues Mary discussed with Renard was the continuing rumor that certain individuals were secretly trying to persuade Courtenay to seize the Tower of London and remove the Queen from the throne. Unsure of the validity of that information and not willing to take any chances, Renard advised the Queen to increase the guards both in the Tower and around her person. Furthermore, there were rumors that the French were supporting these heretics in their efforts.

Renard informed the Emperor in a letter dated after Christmas that he sent spies into France attempting to discover any information on whether they were in fact plotting, either by themselves or with heretics in England against the crown. He apologized to the Emperor that his spies where unskilled and unable to follow Court activities and the reports they did bring were of no help. Renard concluded that he would do his best to locate intelligent and trustworthy people whom he would send as quickly as he could.

By 1 January 1554, the articles of the treaty of the marriage between Philip of Spain and Queen Mary were finalized at Westminster and preparations for the arrival of the Ambassadors were almost complete. The following day the Emperor's Ambassadors arrived at the Tower of London where many men of distinction greeted them at the entrance to the city. As the Ambassadors dismounted from their horses, all the members of the Council and a large crowd of people who appeared to be happy at their arrival greeted them. The Ambassadors were informed that they would meet with the Queen the following day at two-o'clock after dinner. Several of the men of distinction then escorted the Ambassadors to their chambers where they could relax after a long journey. It is possible that Thomas Wyatt was one of these men who greeted them.

The next day, the same group of men of distinction escorted the Ambassadors to the Queen and displayed respect and warmth as the Emperor would have expected of them. After formally requesting the Queen's agreement in the marriage, which the Queen signified by displaying the ring on her finger, the remainder of the day was spent reviewing the articles of the treaty, then signing it as a sign of their approval as well as addressing other issues relative to the alliance. The remainder of their visit was spent being entertained in Court activities such as playing various games and hunting. They were generally well cared for unaware that several of those who were present with them in the lavish activities were plotting to destroy the very thing they were there to secure.

The Queen, her Council, and the Emperor's Ambassadors were all satisfied with the articles of the treaty, but news of discontent among some who were continuing to seek support against the alliance were constantly arriving at court. Not only were heretics plotting against the marriage of Philip and Mary, but the Queen was also informed that the same heretics were continuing to persuade

Courtenay and Elizabeth to act as their leaders. The names of those heretics had not been discovered, but that was about to change.

News arrived in London that Peter Carew who had once served as the Sheriff of Devon during the thirty-eighth year of the reign of Henry VIII and the first year of Edward VI, was attempting to raise people in the West and attempted to have Courtenay and Elizabeth act as their leaders. The Privy Council Register indicates that as of the result of a meeting held on 2 January a letter was dispatched to Carew ordering him to appear before the Queen and the Council with the intent of confining him in the Tower. They now regarded him as the greatest heretic in England because he was plotting in Courtenay's name and opposing the restoration of religion. It was also reported that the same heretics posted slanderous notices against the Queen by stating that she was going to marry Philip who had all ready promised to marry Maria daughter of Emmanuel I and Eleanor of Austria, sister of the Emperor.

Revealed in later court proceedings, it was now that Peter Carew approached the Duke of Suffolk in an attempt to secure his support as Wyatt had. Realizing that Suffolk was a man of honor, Carew told him that if the Queen would discard the plans of marrying a foreigner, he would continue to serve her and was willing to die for her if it was required. However, if she chose to continue with her plans, he would do everything he could to place either Lady Jane or Elizabeth and Courtenay on the throne and that he was only one of a growing number of men who would seize Mary and throw her into the Tower.

By 7 January, the Council was so worried about the rumors of Carew securing more support as each day passed that they issued another summons to him this time ordering him to appear before them. Nevertheless, he did not giving the excuse that he had no horses with which to travel. The Council sent yet another summons to Carew, his lack of response made it clear to the Council what his intentions were, and they declared him a rebel of the realm. Renard informed the Emperor in a letter that Edward Courtenay and his followers feared that if Carew were captured, he would reveal their secret. The Council issued orders to seize Carew by any means and place him in the Tower.

The following day history has recorded as the day in which Peter Carew decided for reasons that are unknown, to prematurely launch the rebellion instead of waiting until 18 March when conditions were more favorable. Carew, while at Mountsawtrey attempted to "...achieve the death and destruction of the Queen and first declared war against her." Carew dispatched word to Edward Courtenay requesting he should come quickly to Devonshire and promised Courtenay that all the residents of the county would openly support him against the Queen and that horses were placed along his route to expedite his journey from London to Devonshire.

It is unclear what prompted Carew to "jump the gun," but a few theories exist. Nicholas Throckmorton who was close to the activities of the Court probably informed Carew that it was the best time to launch their rebellion. It was later revealed in his court trial that Throckmorton had several conversations with Thomas Wyatt at this point. Other theories include a report released stating that Philip was coming to England before the Feast of the Purification on 2 February: this may have been what Throckmorton communicated to Carew. Another plausible theory suggests that Edward Courtenay confessed during questioning by Stephen Gardiner, before the recorded date of a 21 January interview, of all that he knew of Wyatt, Carew, Throckmorton, and their plans.

Yet, another theory comes from the following letter indicating that Courtenay found out about the uprising suggesting that he did not know it had begun, or more realistically, that it began before the date that he knew it was supposed to have. The Emperor's Ambassadors in England wrote to update the Emperor on the events in England. Included in their letter was a copy of an intercepted letter that the Ambassador de Noailles wrote to the King of France:

> Sire: Since La Marque's departure, I have written twice, on the 21st, and 24th of this month, to inform your Majesty of the state of affairs here, and especially that, as my Lord Courtenay has discovered the enterprise planned in his favour, the authors have been forced to take up arms six weeks or two months earlier than they had intended. I may assure you, sire, that Mr. Thomas Wyatt (Hobiet) has not failed his friends, but has kept his promise and taken the field yesterday with forces that were hourly increasing. The Queen and Council are greatly amazed at this, and mean to send the Duke of Norfolk, the Earl of Hastings (i.e. Huntington) and all the troops they can muster against the insurgents before their numbers swell; but I think the Queen will find it difficult to do this, especially as the very men of whom she now feels sure will soon declare for Wyatt.
>
> The Lady Elizabeth has gone to another house of hers, thirty miles further away, where she is said to have

gathered together a number of people, though the Queen frequently sends letters to her because of her mistrust. I have secured a duplicate of one of her replies to the Queen, which I have had translated into French.

[Cal. Letters, Despatches & State Papers, pg. 65]

Regardless of the reasons, Carew began his campaign earlier than was agreed and he relied heavily on the hope that Courtenay would arrive to take command of the forces. Courtenay would then march to meet the Duke of Suffolk with his forces assembled in the North and Wyatt with his forces from the East where they would all converge and march into London with an impressive show of force to seize Mary and the Tower of London.

Throckmorton and Courtenay did not arrive. Someone close to Courtenay may have influenced him, such as the Chancellor who advised him that it was not a safe crusade and that his participation could result in his return to the Tower, or even his execution. Throckmorton may have realized that there were insufficient supporters to merit the risk, and decided against it.

By now, six to seven nobles and commoners were arrested on suspicion of their involvement in protests against the marriage of Philip and Mary. The Queen responded to the increasing unrest within her realm by issuing an official publication on 15 January announcing her marriage to Philip and had it delivered to all the officers, gentlemen and the servants of her household, requesting their obedience to his Highness. The Queen also issued the same publication to the mayor of London, magistrates, and aldermen of the city of London, all of whom signed, showing their allegiance.

Renard informed the Emperor in a letter of 18 January about situations in England, and among them was an update about Peter Carew:

> "...the council is so penetrated with the danger, that they summoned Peter Carew (Caro), who was plotting in the West Country to induce the people to rise; but Peter Carew did not come, giving as his excuse that he had no horses. They sent again, and he declared himself openly a rebel, thereby plainly showing the evil intentions in his mind. Courtenay and his followers are afraid he may reveal their secret if he comes, but the Council have issued orders to the officers to seize him bodily and take him prisoner to the Tower of London." [Cal. Letters, Despatches, and State Papers, Mary Vol XII, pg. 30-31]

Several of the following accounts of activities in and around Exeter from 18 to 25 January may have come from logbooks kept about that time by guards of the various gates into the city.

It was reported on 18 January that a servant of Carew and another man entered the west gate into the city of Exeter with six horses loaded down with battle harnesses and handguns and that these provisions were brought from Dartmouth. Late in the evening of the same day, a servant of Gawen Carew (Peter's uncle) had entered through the south gate into Exeter to conduct some business and bribed the porter of the watch to allow him to venture out of the locked gates to a ship that was waiting for him. The following evening, a lieutenant of the Queen's guard and several other officers made a thorough search of the city of Exeter for suspicious people before closing the gates for the night. There is no mention if any suspicious individuals were found. At about midnight of the same day, it was reported that a servant of Peter Carew declared at the west gate that Edward Courtenay was seen in the area with two of his servants.

On 22 January, it was reported that Gawen Carew had climbed over the walls of Exeter hoping to avoid detection with the intention of visiting with two individuals on unknown business in the city. His last visit was to replace his boots that he had damaged while en route to Exeter. It was later reported that he departed to Meed with Peter Carew in armor and met with approximately seventy other men who were adherents to the revolt and that Peter Carew posted horses on the route to London and in other areas. It was here that Peter Carew attempted to persuade Walter Raleigh, father to the later famous Sir Walter Raleigh, to join their cause but he declined.

A servant of Carew was instructed to enter Exeter the following day to visit the mistress of Gawen Carew with instructions for her to bring his battle harness hidden in hand baskets to the suburbs of the city where they could meet undetected. All these commotions in and around the city of Exeter began to attract the attention of the Queen's forces stationed there and at about the same time, Sir Thomas Denny received letters from the Queen with orders to apprehend Peter Carew and bring him to London. Orders were also given to seize all battle harnesses, shields, spears, and other weapons and to bring them into Exeter under the control of the Queen's guard.

By some means, Carew received information about the sheriff's orders to apprehend him and dispatched a letter to the sheriff:

Sir Peter Carew and Sir Gawen Carew to Sir Thomas Denys.

Right worshipfull, after our most hertie commendacions. Being this morning enformed that you prepare yourself with power to apprehend and take vs,' ffor what matter we knowe not, we have thought good to send vnto you, and to advertise you that we ar as true and as faithfull subiectes vnto the Quenes highnes as any what so ever they be within the Realme, and entende to observe and folowe her Religion as faithfully as they that most are affected vnto it. Wherefore, knowing our selfes without offence towardes her matie, we can not but wonder for what cause you should prepare, with force, to take vs. And if it be so that you have any such commission from her highnes, or her most honorable counsell, we hertely pray you so to advertise vs, and we shall, without rumor or sterring, immediately repaire vnto you wheres so ever you shall appoint vs. Whereas if you do the contrary, you shall dryve vs to stand to the best of our powers for our libertie vutill such tyme as we may better vnderstand your authoritie. And so fare you most hertely well. ffrom Mouse Awtrey, the xixth of January, 1554.1

Yr loving freende,

P. Carew.

Ga. Carew [Maclean, 144-145]

Though the above letter dated 29 January, the contents seem to indicate that it was perhaps the first letter sent to the sheriff. The following letter is from Gawen Carew and gives some insight about the activities in Exeter during the same period:

Sir Gawen Carew to Sir Thomas Denys.

Mr. Denys, after my harty commendacions. I do not a lytell marvell to hier of suche preparacions as you prepare within the Citie of Exeter, (being, as you are, a wise man) wherof it doth prosede I cannot gesse. Yt should seem by slanderous brutes you have sent and chayned the gates, layed Ordynaunce upon the walles, kepe watche and warde, as it should be beseged by the Quenes highnes enemyes, and not content with this, but also blowen abrode, not only to the vtter ondoyng and clere defasyng of the most parte of gentlemen within this shire toward the Quenes highnes, but also to the discrediting vs among our neighbors, that the gentlemen shoulde practise to take the Quenes highnes' Citie. Yt is more than strange to think what occasion shoulde leade you thus to do. I dare boldely say it was neuer thought by any man to practise so vyle an enterprise agenst the Quenes Matie, that wayes or any other kynde of wayes, whereby her highnes might be offended. I stand owt of all dowtes, from the best to the simplest, there is not one within this shire, but, in defence of her highnes' Citie, or other affayres, lawes, statutes, proclamacions, or prosedinges, but wolde, with the sworde in his hand, defend the same with his bloode to the deth. And farther, yt is bruted that the gentlemen shoulde gather them selves together, and levy a power to stand in the field. I marvell not a lytell to hyer of these Immagenyd lyes. I do assure you, by the faythe I beare to the lyvyng God, there was no such matter of gathering togither of any gentlemen, nor no repayre of any other, but only as heretofore yt hath bene accustomably vsed. And for myne owne parte, I had no more with me than I do accustomably vse to ryde withall, which was but viij persones, and Sir Peter Carew, his housholde servantes. But the very occasion of my repayre to Sr Peter was, that you had gathered a power (as it was shewed vs) to apprehend vs both, and what comission or auctoritie you had so to do we knew not, and vpon that consideracion wrote vnto you our former letter, for if you had sent, declaring that you had suche a comission from the Quenes highnesse, we wolde have comme to you as humble and obedient subjectes, according to our bounden duties. And so I pray you to make reporte none otherwise of vs, for I dowt not but the trouth shall trye vs to be as faythfull and obedient subiectes as any other within the realme, whatsoever they be. And so I byd you most hertely farewell. ffrom Tyverton, the xxiiij of January, 1553.

Your ffreende,

Ga. Carew [Maclean, 146-147]

Thomas Denny wrote to the Council informing them that he had seen Peter Carew during the month of January almost daily. On the day he received the letters from the Council he informed Carew in a letter sent to his house with instructions to meet him at

Exeter at about ten o'clock in the morning but Carew did not come. Instead, Carew sent a letter informing him that he had departed to London to meet with the Council. It was most likely that Peter Carew fled towards France and not London as he alluded to in his correspondence to Denny hoping to gain precious time by deceiving the sheriff thus giving him a head start:

> Sir Peter Carew to Sir Thomas Denys (Sheriff of Devon.)
>
> Whereas I promysed by your messenger to repayer this daye to Exeter vnto you, and thinking you have some cause to allege vnto me for that I have byn sent for to the courte & have not made suche speede thyther as the counsell ha-the lookyd for, and to avoyde alle rumors that may ensue for my supposed disobediens, I haue, sithen the departure of your said messenger, thought good to advertise you that I am this daye departed from hens toward London, with as moche speade as I possiblye can, not doubting but I shall be abull so to answer the cause as myne honestye shal be nothing impayred, whatsoever myne enemyes shall allege agenst me; most hartelye praying you so to vse your authoritye, whatsoever it be, as you may receave no evyll opynyon at the Quenes highnes handes, nether to use th'extremyte thereof (so as the same may be to my vtter defacing), whereof I have no mistrust of you for that you know my demeans hath not geaven the occasion hereof. And knowing this shall suffice to such an assured friynde as you are, I bid you ffarewell. ffrom Mohouns Ottery, this tewsdaye the xxiij of January, 1554.
>
> Yr assured ffrynde,
> P. Carew [Maclean, 145-146]

It is quite probable that Thomas Wyatt received information about Peter Carew at this point, or perhaps a week before, causing Wyatt to launch his campaign prematurely.

Late in the day or evening of 24 January, with plans to enter Maidstone the following day to issue a proclamation, Wyatt wrote a letter to Sir Robert Southwell, the Sheriff of Kent, hoping to secure his support. A gentleman by the name of Thomas Monde delivered the letter:

After heartie commendations, there hath been betwene you and me many quarelles' and grudges, and I euer the sufferer, and yet haue you sought the ende whiche is nowe frendlye offered vnto you, if you bee willing to receiue it. But whatsoeuer priuate quarell you haue to me, I doubte not but youre' wysdome is to muche, seying so manye perilles' at hand to vs both (this pretensed marriage taking effect) to dissent from vs in so necessarie a purpose, as wherin we nowe determine to entre for the common wealthe of the whole realme. And that you may the better vnderstand our pretence, I send you the copy of our proclamation compre- hending the somme and effect of our meaning whervnto if the commen wealth shal fynde you an enemie, saye not hereafter but that you were fre-dly warned we forbeare to write to the lorde Aburgaueny, for what you may do with him, if you list, we know. [Proctor, 8]

The following is a copy of the proclamation agreed to by Thom- as Wyatt, George Harper, Anthony and William Knevet and sent to Sir Robert Southwell:

Forasmuche as it is now spred abrode, & certainly pronounced by the lorde Chauncelour and other of the counsell, of the Qnenes determinate pleasure to marry wt a strauger: &ce. we therefore write vnto you, because you bee oure neighbours, because you be our frendes, and because you be Englishemen, that you wyll ioyne with vs, as we wil with you vnto death in this behalfe, protestyng vnto you before God, that no other yearthly cause could moue vs vnto this enterprise, but this alone, wherein we seke no harme to the quene, but better counsel & cousel- ours, which also we would haue forborne in all other thinges saue onely in this. For herein lieth the helth & welth of vs al. For trial herof & manyfest profe of this in- tended purpose: lo now euen at hand, Spaniardes be nowe already ariued at Douer, at one passage to the nombre of an hundreth passing vpwarde to London, in companies of ten, foure and vi. with harnes, harquebusses and morrians with match light, the formest company wherof be already at Rochester. We shall require you therfore to repaire to such places as the bearers hereof shal pronouce vnto you, there to assemble & determine what may be best for ye ad- uauncement of libertie and commen wealth in this behalfe,

& to bryng with you suche ayde as you may. [Proctor, 8-9]

Thomas Monde remained with the sheriff until he had finished writing his answer then delivered the following to Wyatt shortly thereafter:

Neyghbour Monde, rather to satisfie your importunitie, the to answer Wyates' letter, whom in this case I disdaine to answere, or to speake with you apart coming from a traytour, you may say vnto him that as in dede I haue been desierous of his frendship for neighbourhoodes sake, so haue I muche more desired his reformation in diuers pointes of great disordre, wherby he certainly knew as well by my spech to him selfe, as other meanes coming to his knowledge, that I haue sithens the beginning of the Quenes' reigne holden him and some of his coleges in this cospiracie vehemently suspected for like matters as nowe they haue attempted.

Wherein seyng he hath not deceiued me, but by opening him self hath manifestly verified myne opinion conceiued of him, I purpose not to purchase his frendship so deare, as for the gaine of him to lose my self & my posteritie in perperual infamye. And if suche thinges whiche his fonde headded hath wayed for perilles', to the condempnation of the whole wisedome of the realme (thei allowing the same for good) had been in dede as perillous, as he with others, for want of due consideration, demeth them, his duetie had been to haue opened his opinion therein as an humble & reuerent peticioner to the Quenes' highness, or to some of her graces counsell. But to presse his soueraigne in any suite or vpon any occasion with weapon & armour by sturring her subiectes to rebellion, that is and alwaies hath been accompted the parte of most arrogant and presumptuous traytours, and so do I note him and his mates as you may tell them, & shall God willing prouide for them accordingly. Nowe goodman Monde it shal be in your choyse whether you will carie this message or no. But as your frende I shall aduise you to seeke out better company. [Proctor, 10,11]

On 25 January 1554, Thomas Wyatt accompanied by his cousin Thomas Isley and several others entered Maidstone to issue a proclamation against the English/Spanish alliance. It was a perfect day for Wyatt to present his proclamation because it was market day in Maidstone, and more people would be present and so he might rally all his neighbors, friends, and Englishmen to join with him and his confederates to defend their realm from the Spanish. It has been suggested that in addition to the proclamation that Wyatt issued to the crowd, he mentioned that certain nobles and other gentle-men had joined his cause, hoping to alleviate concerns that he was without support and acting on his own in this traitorous activity by telling them:

> "That all the Nobility of the realm and the whole [Privy] Council (one or two only except) were agreeable to his pretensed treason, and would with all their power and strength further the same; (which he found most untrue, to his subversion): and That the Lord ABERGAVENNY, [Sir Thomas Cheyney,] the Lord Warden [of the Cinque Ports], Sir Robert Southwell, High Sheriff, with all other Gentlemen would join with him in this enterprise, and set their foot by his, to repel the Strangers." [Pollard, 209].

Though Wyatt's claims were untrue, the crowd did not know that and several began to question what Thomas Wyatt was telling them.

> "Sir, is your quarrel only to defend us from overrunning by Strangers and to advance Liberty; and not against the Queen?"

> "No," quod wyat. "we mind nothing less than any wise to touch her Grace; but to serve her and honour her, ac-cording to our duties."

> "Well," quod they, "give us then your hand. We will stick to you to death in this quarrel!"

> That done, there came to him one other, of good wealth, saying, "Sir," quod he, "they say I love potage well. I will sell all my spoons, and all the plate in my house rather than your purpose shall quail; and sup my potage with my mouth. I trust," quod he, "you will restore the right religion again."

> "Whist!" quod Wyat, "you may not so much as name religion, for that will withdraw from us the hearts of many. You must only make your quarrel for overrunning by Strangers. And yet to thee, be it said in counsel, as unto my friend, we mind only the restitution of GOD's Word.

But no words!" [Pollard 210]

Having finished at Maidstone, Wyatt accompanied by a small force of well-armed men possessing various types of weapons, departed for Rochester. As Wyatt and Isley were attempting to gain additional support, other confederates were doing the same in Milton and Ashford and other towns in Kent and so far without encountering any resistance.

Christopher Roper a well-respected man of Milton challenged the proclamation then was taken prisoner by Wyatt's men. Master Tucke and Master Dorrel of Calehill both gentlemen and also well respected were taken from their houses as prisoners. Roper, Tucke, and Dorrel were taken to Rochester under guard and Wyatt would later determine their fates. John Twine the Mayor of Canterbury stated that regardless of the zealous attempts by the heretics to raise the people, not one person had outwardly joined Wyatt or any other of his confederates. At the very least, there must have been some in the various towns who had questioned the validity of Wyatt's proclamations. Nevertheless, history has recorded that Wyatt's numbers were increasing, so there must have been some who joined the cause. The reputation of the Wyatt family would have also played a part in securing loyalty.

Wyatt, Harper and the others arrived in Rochester late on the same day and issued their proclamation, seized the bridge and fortified the East part of Rochester. Wyatt stationed men on the bridge who threatened anyone that would attempt to cross by telling them they should be silent about their presence and took their weapons from them if they had any before allowing them to continue on to wherever they were headed. Try as they may to prevent it, it did not take long for word to reach London.

Mary reacted quickly to the rebellion in Kent as the news arrived perhaps late that same night or early the following day. Among the steps she took in an attempt to maintain control was writing to Elizabeth offering her a choice; either come on her own or be brought to her.

> Right dear and entirely beloved sister, We greet you well: And whereas certain evil disposed persons, minding more the satisfaction of their own malicious and seditious minds than their duty of allegiance towards us, have of late foully spread divers lewd and untrue rumours; and by that means and other devilish practises do travail to induce our good and loving subjects to an unnatural rebellion against God, us, and the tranquillity of our realm; We, tendering

the surety of your person, which might chance to be in some peril if any sudden tumult should arise where you now be, or about Donnington, whither, as we understand, you are minded shortly to remove, do therefore think expedient you should put yourself in good readiness, with all convenient speed, to make your repair hither to us. Which we pray you fail not to do: Assuring you, that as you may most safely remain here, so shall you be most heartily welcome to us. And of your mind herein we pray you to return answer by this messenger.

Given under our signet at our manor of St. James's the 26th of January in the 1st year of our reign. "Your loving sister

Mary, the queen. [Aikin, pg. 137]

When the letter arrived Elizabeth's officers replied to the Queen that she was sick and confined to bed. They advised Elizabeth that by not addressing the Queen's request soon, her action might give the wrong impression. The French Ambassador de Noailles said that Elizabeth's illness was "a favorable illness" as to avoid any punishment from her sister and there were rumors that Elizabeth was pregnant with Courtenay's child.

With events beginning to unfold in London and nearby Kent, the Duke of Suffolk summoned a servant of his to meet him at Sheen with orders to proceed to London and retrieve a sum of money then inform the Duke's brothers Thomas and John to leave London that evening then the servant was to meet the Duke at Leicester. The servant completed his task in London and accompanied the Duke's brothers when they left the same evening by the way of Enfield Chase. Later that evening they called on a Mr. Wroth who was at Cheshunt. Wroth greeted the men with another man John Harrington as the Duke's brothers attempted to convince Wroth and Harrington to join their cause but the two decided against it on such short notice. They continued on their way through St. Alban's not stopping to rest until they arrived at Towcester where they expected to meet up with Suffolk. They eventually met with the Duke at a tenant's house in Lutterworth and departed for Bradgate the following day.

On 27 January, the Queen issued a type of circular letter most likely addressed to the sheriff and other officials desiring them to exert themselves in the suppression of the rebellion:

By the Quene. Mary the quene.

Trusty and right welbiloved, we grete you well. And where the duke of Suffolke and his brethern, with dyverse other personnes', forgettyng their trewth and dyutye of allegiaunce which they owe to God and us, and also the greate mercye which the sayd duke hath lately receyved of us, be as we are surely enformed revolted and malytyously conspyred togethers to styrr our people and subjectes moost unnaturally to rebell agaynst us, and the lawes lately made by aucthoritie of parlyament for the restitution of the true catholique chrestian Religion, making theyr only pretence nevertheles (though falsely) to let the cumming in of the Prynce of Spayne and his trayne, spredding most false rumours that the sayd Prynce and the Spanyardes entende to conquer this our Realme Wheras his sayd cumming is for the greate honour and suretye of us and our sayd Realme, as we doubt not God' wyll in the end make a most playne demonstration to the comforthe of all our good subjectes. Therfore trusteng in your fidelitie, valyantnes, and good courage to serve us and our sayd Realme agaynst the sayd traytours and rebelles' We requyre you immediatly upon the sight hereof to put yourself in order to represse the same with all the power, puissance, and force ye can possibly make of horsmen and footmen, as well of your own ffrendes, tenauntes, and servauntes, as others under your rule. To the levyeng, rayseng, and leading of which force we gyve you full power and aucthoritie by thies presentes. Willeng you further to have a vigilant eye to all suche as spredde those false rumours, and them t'apprehende and commyt to warde to be ordred as the lawe requyreth. And to th'intent our good subjectes' shall fully understande uppon howo false a grounde the sayde traytours buylde, and howe honorably we have concluded to marye with the sayd Prynce, we sende unto you th'articles of the sayd conclusion for Mariage. Wherfore, right trusty and right welbiloved, as ye be a man of courage, and beare good harte to us your liege Lady and countreyc, nowe acquyte yourself according to your bounden dieutye which ye owe to God and us, and we shall considre the same God willing as shalbe to the good eomfortes of you and yours. Yeven undre our Signet at our Manour of St. James the [27th] of January the first yere of our reigne. [Nichols, 186]

On the same day, being market day at Malling, the Sheriff Sir
Robert Southwell took advantage of the large crowds, who gathered to listen to an exhortation he had written the night before,
hoping to persuade them not to follow Wyatt:

> Louinge neighbours & frendes, where of late there ha-
> the been most pestilent & trayterous proclamations, as ye
> haue hearde set furth by Thomas Wyat, George Harper,
> Henry lsley, & others, as most arrant traitors to the quene
> & the realme, some of the quenes ancient enemies afore
> time, & double traitors, yet notwithstanding, accompany-
> ing themselues to be the best of the shire in their proc-
> lamations, & in the same puting & pronouncing other
> as traitors, who ye all can witnes to haue been from time
> to time, true & faithful subiects to the quene & this our
> common weale: as the lord Aburgauenye here present,
> myself & other gentlemen now prest & readie with you,
> according to our duetie, to serue our noble quene: I shal
> need to spend the lesse tyme to declare vnto you, howe
> euil thei be, or howe euil their enterprise is, that thei haue
> take- in hand: for asmuch as this their arrogant presump-
> tion & presumptuous pride in advancing themselves so
> far from all trueth, & in deprauing of other so malliciously
> for executing their bounden duetie, ought abundantly to
> persuade what they be to all of consideration without
> further circumstance. But for as much as in their procla-
> mations, thei [document damaged] quenes's liege people
> with grosse & manifest lies to styrre them against her
> grace, in the utterance wherof thei vse this demonstra-
> tion, lo, signifiyng some notable thing neare at hand for
> credit worthie impression in their memorie, as lo, a great
> number of strangers be now arriued at Douer in harnes,
> with harquebusses, [unclear] match light I say vnto you
> neighbors and frendes vpon paine to be torne in peces with
> your hands, that it is vntrue & a manifest lie, invented by
> them to prouoke & irritate the quenes' simple people to
> ioine with them in their traiterous enterprise. And ther-
> fore I have perfect hope, that you being afore time abused
> with their craftie & deceitful treasons, wil not now ones
> againe hauing experience of their farmer euil be trapped
> for any persuasions in so heinous a snare as this most vile
> and horrible crime of treasons. Do you not see & note [?]

as in the beginninge of the quenes' most gracious raigne, some of them sought to depriue her grace of her princely estate & rightful dignitie, minding to advance thervnto the ladye Jane doughter to the duke of Suffolk. So are thei & others newly concedered ... the duke & his brethren, being armed at this present for ye same purpose, & daili looking for aid of these traitors & other of their co-spiracie as by the quenes' most gracious letters signed with her owne hand and redie to be read here, may plainly apeare vnto you? And wil you now neueritheles ayde them any waies, or sit stil while they go about thus wrongfully & traitorously to depose their & our most gracious soueraigne lady & quene, the comfort of vs all, the staye of vs al, thonly sauegard of vs al, to whom can no displeasure or daunger chance, but the same must double redoubt to all & euery of vs? Ah frendes & neighbours, I trust neuer to liue to se you so far abused. Thei go aboute to bleare you what matters of strangers, as though thei shuld come to ouerun you & vs also. He semeth very blinde and willynglye blinded that will haue his sight dimmed with such a fond mist. For if they ment to resist strangers, as thei mind nothing lesse: thei [?] them prepare to go to the sea coastes, & not to the queen's most roial person with such a company in armes & weapon. Ye can consider I trust, this noble gentleman the lord Aburgaueny here present being of an ancient and great parentage, born among you, & such other gentlemen as you see here, which be no strangers vnto you my self also (although a pore gentleman, who I trust at no time hath abused you) hath so-what to lose as well as thei, & wald be as loth to be ouer run with strangers as thei, if any such thing were ment. But for that we know most certainly that ther is meant no maner of euil to vs by those strangers, but rather aide, profit & comfort against other strangers our ancient enemies, with whom they as most arrogant and degenerate traitors do in deed vnkindly & vnnaturally [unclear]: we in her graces defense wil spede both life & what we haue beside to the vtter most peny against them. Wel, 1 can na more now sai vnto you, but vnderstanding ye quenes' highnes as a most merciful princesse to be ones again determined to pardon as many as by their traiterous & deceitfull proclajmations, & other illusions wer allured to this last treason, so they repaire to their habitations within xxiiii houres after her graces prociamation read, & become true subiectes to her grae, to aduise such as hath taken part with those traitours, or haue withdrawe themselues contrary to their ailegiance, from the aiding & seruing of their soueraigne, according to their duties against her enemies, thankfullye to accept & imbrace her most gracious pardon & vse meanes of themselves to ap' prehend those arrogant and principall traitaurs, & make a present of them to the quenes' highnes, or leaue them to themselves as most detestable traitors: who being once so graciously & mercifully forgeuecould not but cary the demcie of the same in their hartes to the furtherance of all obedience whiles thei liued, if ther had been any spark of grace in them. And further I haue to say vnto you, that as these traitors by their proclamations without authoritie haue moued you to styr against the quene your soueraigne, & apointed you [unclear]; wher to mete & consult for the furtherance of their traiterous purpose, & to bring with you such aid as you can, so shall I require you, & in her graces name charge you that be here present, not to come there, but that you & such as be absent taking knowledge herby, repair to such places as I the quenes' shireffe & of' ficer shal appoint you, with such ayde as you can bring for the better seruice of the quene & the shyre, where you shalbe assured to receyue comforte, thankes, and honestie to the ende of your liues and your posteritie. And th other waye but endless shame and vtter vndoinge to you and yours, whiche shall be worste to your selues, and yet a gre' ate griefe to vs your neyghbours, whose aduise in al other your private causes you haue been content to folowe, & nowe in this waightiest that hathe or maye happen to you, wyll refuse vs and folow them that hathe euer abused you to your and their vtter confusion.

At Mallynge the seuen and twenteth daye of Ianuarye. Anno Mariae primo.

God saue Queene Marye and all her weil wyllers.
[Proctor, 18-25]

At the same time the sheriff was busy in Malling, Sir Henry Is' ley, Anthony and William Knevet, accompanied by others, issued a proclamation at Tonbridge informing anyone that would listen that Southwell, Clarke, and Abergavenny were traitors to God, the crown and the commonwealth by raising the people to defend the evil and wicked intensions of the Council.

The following is a copy of the proclamation that Henry Isley issued in Tonbridge:

> "You shal vnderstand that Henry Lord Aburgauenye, Robert Southwell knight, George Clerke gentleman, haue most traitrouslye to the disturbance of the common wealth, styrred and raysed vp the Queenes' most louing subiectes of this realme, to defend the most wicked & deuilishe enterprise, of certen of ye wicked and peruerse couselours, to the vtter confusion of this her graces realme, and the perpetuall seruitude of all the Queen's most louynge subiectes. In consideration wherof, we syr Thomas Wyat knight, syr George Harper knight, syr Henry Isleye knight, Anthony Kneuet Esquer, with all the faithful Gentlemen of Kent, and trusty commons of the same, do pronounce the sayde Henry Lorde Aburgaueny, Robert Southwell, and George Clerke gentleman, to be traytours to god, the crowne, and the common wealthe. [Proctor, 13]

When they were finished at Tonbridge, they departed for Sevenoaks to issue a proclamation there before going on to Rochester to meet up with Wyatt.

Meanwhile at Rochester, a trumpeter and a herald wearing a coat of armor with the Arms of England on his back sent by the Queen summoned Wyatt, who met them at the foot of the bridge leading into town, but they were not allowed over the bridge. Wyatt and only a couple of his men listened as the herald recited his message informing them that the Queen promised a pardon to anyone who would return to their homes within twenty-four hours and remain a quiet citizen. Wyatt would not allow anyone else to hear the herald's message.

The following is a copy of a pardon issued by the Queen to "...all such as would desist from their purpose,"

> Mary, the quene:
>
> The Quenes' highenes most excellent Ma'tie understanding how Thomas Wyat, confederal with other lewde and evill disposed personnes', have, under the pretense of the benefite of the commenwelthe of the Realme to withstande straungers, sette furthe a Proclamation, therby to assemble her highenes good, true, and lovinge subjectes', to

the disturbaunce of the realme, the confusion of this com-
monwelth, and the destruction of her most noble personne
and astate (which God forbidde), her saide highnes being
mercifully moved towardes the conservation of her subjectes' from all pcrill and daunger, and glad to relievesuche
as shulde be by sinistre motions abused and seduced: hathe thought goode to signifie to her saide subjectes' that
whosoever upon any proclamation made and sette forthe
by the said Thomas or any other private man, to the purpose aforesayde, shall happen to assemble accordinge to
the same, and upon knowlege herof shall, within xxiiij
houres after, returne to their houses and live there quietly
and obediently: her highenes is contented to pardonne
that their doinge in the saide assemblie, and to defende
and manteyne them as her highenes good subjectes', to the
benefite and comforte of them and their posteritie. [Nich-
ols, 186-187]

At about the same time, Sir Thomas Cheyney, the Lord Warden, acting as a true and faithful subject of the Queen, sent Wyatt
a letter which described his feelings of contempt and defiance, his
disapproval of Wyatt's intentions, and furthermore stating that he
would take any advantage necessary to repress Wyatt's action with
force if required in that shire.

That evening, Lord Abergavenny, the Sheriff Warran Sentleger
and other gentlemen assembled about four miles from Rochester, at
Malling. They led a small force of five hundred white coats (a term
given to men trained in London who wore a type of uniform taken
from the English national flag with a red cross of St. George) and a
number of the royal guard. They received information that Henry
Isley and the Knevet brothers were leading a force of five hundred
men at Sevenoaks and would march towards Rochester early the
following morning to meet Wyatt and lend assistance in Wyatt's
confrontation with the Duke of Norfolk's forces that were en route
to Gravesend with an additional five hundred white coats.

Early the following morning 28 January, Lord Abergavenny,
Warran Sentleger and other gentlemen with a force of between five
hundred to six hundred foot soldiers, departed Malling marching in
perfect order. Abergavenny arrived at Wrotham Heath and waited
until they heard the advancing drums of Isley's forces. As soon as
the drums could be heard in the near distance, his forces quickly
took out after the rebels and pursued them to Barrow Green where

Abergavenny's forces planned to intercept Isley's forces that had departed from Sevenoaks and were en route to destroy and burn the house of George Clerk before continuing on to Rochester.

Lord Abergavenny was confident of his securing Barrow Green and sent out a few men to locate Isley's forces and the men quickly returned informing Abergavenny that the rebels were marching towards them in a quick pace and where very close. Abergavenny reacted quickly by placing his men in strategic locations to prevent Isley's forces from advancing by either overtaking them or over-throwing them. It would appear that Henry Isley had somehow received information of Abergavenny's intent and for some reason, possibly because Isley disliked the match of forces or the possible less than favorable location for a match to take place, dispersed and secretly hid in a by-way as Abergavenny's men were positioning themselves. By the time Abergavenny received word that Isley escaped interception, it was too late because the rebels had slipped by. Abergavenny had taken out after them with such haste leaving behind a large number of his footmen.

Abergavenny first regained sight of his quarry as they ascended Wrotham Hill near Master Peckham's house where Isley's forces had confidently displayed their ensigns believing they had taken the hill. Their confidence would not last long as Lord Abergavenny, the Sheriff, and their remaining forces began the arduous task of ascending the hill attempting to hold Isley's advancement with the use of horsemen and eventually overtook the rebel forces at Black-soll Field in the parish of Wrotham about a mile from the top of Wrotham Hill.

Both sides met then exchanged shots and arrows wounding men on both sides during the skirmish but history has not recorded any deaths. Isley's forces fled the fight and chased for about four miles to Hartley Wood where several were taken prisoner. It was reported that Henry Isley hid in the woods all night, evading capture, then fled to Hampshire the following day. The Knevet brothers escaped on horseback and pursued so hard that they had to abandon their horses and fled into the woods where they discarded their boots and managed to evade capture as darkness settled in. That evening, Anthony Knevet made his way to Wyatt in Rochester and informed Wyatt of the events of the day.

During the night, George Harper slipped away from Wyatt's camp to turn himself over to the Duke of Norfolk, who arrived at Gravesend at about four o'clock that day. It is suggested in the following letter that a few other rebels may have gone with Harper. As soon as Norfolk arrived in Gravesend, he dispatched a letter to the Council in London with an update on the rebellion:

My very good lordes,

Theis shal be t'aduertise ye on this daye aboute foure of the clock I arryved here at this towne, fyndeng here my L. Cobham, Mr. Vice chamberlaine and Sr Ihon Fogge, without any cumpany savynge suche as the same Vice-chamberlaine and Fogge brought with them, not passinge CCC. And whereas Sr George Harper did sende before to Mr. Vice-chamberlaine to have his pardon, as I dowte not ye knowe by the purporte of the said Mr. Vice-chamberlaines l're. This night at v of the clock, the said Sr George Harper arryved here, and is stollen frome the rebells, and hath given in commaundement to all men being in nomber as he saieth above CC. to steale away from Rochester before day, sayeng farther y» he dowteth not, that there shalbe to morowe by none, right fewe of the rest lefte in Rochester with the rebells. And to morowe by none with gods grace I will not faile to be at Rochester, I here no worde of my L. Warden, nor what power he hathe, I have y» present houre wrytten to hym aduertiseng hym to be vigilant yt Wyot nor Isley escape not out of the realme by water. And to cum with his power towardes Rochester. I here no worde of my brother Wm his cummynge but I have put order of his intended purpose, in prepairenge of botes to beate the brydge at Rochester. And as for my L. Abergevenny, I here say he is gone to Senock to saue a gentlemanes' house yt Henry Isley is mynded to destroye and robbe there.

My very good lordes. [Cruden, 175]

As the rebellion continued to gain momentum in the Southeast, the Duke of Suffolk ordered a servant of his to write Robert Palmer of Kegworth and request his support. As the servant drafted the letter, another gentleman and Suffolk were in his chamber drafting a letter to be sent to the Queen. A form of proclamation was also drafted then sent to his brothers Thomas and John for publication and distribution.

On the same day at about noon, the Duke of Norfolk departed Gravesend and marched in the cold and rainy weather towards Rochester to confront Wyatt. George Harper and Sir Henry Jerningham accompanied Norfolk with a force of about three hundred men and Captains Bret and Bryan Fitzwilliam with about six hundred men and six pieces of ordnance of the Queen's army.

Before Norfolk departed Gravesend, he dispatched the following letter to the Council:

> My veray good L. theis shalbe t'aduertise you that I haue bene here redy for the departyng out of this towne since sonne rose, but for asmoche as I haue none other here with me, but Mr. Vicechamberlaine and his cumpanye and Mr. Fogge. And that dyvers others were cummyne to me from Dartford, I wolde not go hence till they were cum. And now being furnisshed with vii or viiic men, woll departe out of ye towne towardes Rochester within little more than an houre. And my L. Cobham shall mete me on the waye with at the leaste cc of his cumpany. I here no worde from my L. Warden, nor from my L. Aburgeynye, they have fortefied the bridge at Rochester, so that I think it wilbe harde passinge there, howebeit we shall do the best we can. This present houre I have receiued a letter from my L. Cobham, which you shall receiue herewith. And by the same you may perceive of Wyotf' s braggs, and wherein I byleve he will breke promes, and not to feight it out. And where his trust is, ye the garde and pentyoners with the Londoners woll take his parte. I pray God contynewe his purpose in yt behalfe. I shall with God's grace be within theis iiij houres at Strowde, where if he will haue free passage with his hole companye I shall give hym and them leave to come over the bridge to trye ye matter, and if he will not, I shall make hym ill rest in ye towne with sending messages of such sorte as I have here with me. If my L. Aburgeyny, M. Southwell, and other gentlemen with them woll go over the water, and cum in ouer the back side of them, and so joyne with my L. Wardeyn, of whome as yet I here no newes, I dowte not ye shall shortely here of their repulse out of the said towne of Rochester. Desirynge yor good L. to conceyve no ill opinion of such lordes and gentlemen as were appoynted to cum hither vnto me, for I thinke they have an honest excuse, the wether being so terryble y' no man can stire by water or yet well by lande. And thus most hartely fare you well from Gravysende this xxix of Januarye.

> Yo lordeships asseweredly, T. Norfolk.

"To my veray good lordes the lordes of ye quenys' Mat-
ies most honourable pryvie Counsaile in hast post.
From gravesende at xi of the clock. [Cruden, 176, 177]

The Duke of Norfolk arrived at Strood at about four o'clock
with his forces and Captain Bret and five other of Norfolk's captains with about five hundred men had remained behind at Spittle
Hill while Norfolk continued into town to ensure that the ordnance
was set up properly. In the meantime, Wyatt continued to maintain
his position on the bridge into Rochester with their flags displayed
on the bridge wall.

With his ordnance charged, Norfolk ordered a shot to be fired
into Rochester. As the gunner fired his shot, the son of Sir Edward
Bray came to the Duke and informed him that the Londoners would
betray him. The Duke of Norfolk turned around to find just that:
Bret and the five Captains with their forces behind them shouting,
"We are all Englishmen, we are all Englishmen," as they moved to
form an arch in front of the surprised Duke with their weapons all
pointing in his direction, ready if he gave any resistance. Norfolk
ordered the ordnance pointed at Rochester to be turned upon his
new enemy, but reconsidered firing a shot, as he saw that it would
be in vain, then commanded his remaining forces to step aside as
he had new adversaries in front and behind him, leaving behind six
pieces of ordnance.

Wyatt and a couple of his close associates came forward to meet
the six captains who accompanied George Harper. One story has
them at first saluting each other, then embracing and shaking hands.
Wyatt was so pleased with the occurrence that he dispatched a letter to the Duke of Suffolk but the letter was intercepted at the ferry
at Gravesend.

On the same day, Cobham wrote a letter to the Duke of Norfolk
requesting orders and mentioned that he had concerns about de-
fections. It could be possible that Norfolk received the letter after
the defection of his captains or felt that Cobham's message was not
worthy of attention. It would appear rather unfortunate for Norfolk because he had not requested Cobham's forces to assist him at
Rochester.

Lord Cobham to the Duke of Norfolk

Pleasith yt youre grace to be aduertisyd at my comyng
home from you, Wiat percyuyng of my departure [did]
sende an espiall vnto my house and made an errande to

speake with on [one] of my house, when he kam ther, my stewarde percyving that he talkyd and whisperyd cmong-ste my Tenaunts, toke hym aparte into his chamber, and examyned hym and serched hym and founde a letter upon hym wherein is declaryd that bothe pentioners, Garde and Londoners wolde tak suche parte as he dyd. And also trust-ing that his cosyns wolde not se his blod shulde perishe. It may please your grace, if he be not gone this mornyng, he intendeth to fight yt out, for he maketh rekenyng of the saide pentioners, garde, and Londoners with diverse other of your company: therfor my opynion is that youre grace be not to forwarde vnto such tyme your company come together. And that Harpar do not practise to [too] moche with some other, beseching your grace to sende me worde, whether ye will remove this day or noo, and whether ye will, I bring my men vnto your grace to Gravesende: for I haue no weapons for them, but a fewe blacke bills. I have written to my lorde Warden according to your commaun-dement. thus the lorde preserve your grace with moche honor. From my house at Cooling the xxix of January. Your graces to commande,

G. Cobham.

The carrier of this letter unto the Dukes grace is Downyn of Gravysende. [Cruden, 178]

News arrived quickly to Lord Abergavenny, who was in Malling, and to the Sheriff in Maidston who immediately departed to Malling after receiving the information. Upon his arrival there, he was advised to seek the advice of the Council in London as to what he should do next.

Lord Cobham wrote to the queen informing her of events that occurred after his departure:

Lord Cobham to the Queen.

It may please yor most excellent Malie to be aduer-tysed that yesterday the xxviii'h of this moneth, beyng at Gravescnd with Mr. Vicechamberlayne conferyng with hym for our settyng forth towardes the rebelles', we then thought good to deferre our purpose vntill the commyng of my Lord of Norfolk with his force; vppon whose repayre thither we then consulted with hym what was ferther to be don, who uppon consultacion determyned to do noth-

yng vntill my Lord Admyralles' comyng thither with his
assembly, whereuppon the next mornyng early I repayred
to my Castell, puttyng my self in a redynes with my men,
and at my commyng thither 1 did vnderstand that ther
had byn in myne absence [a spyall] sent from wyat to my
sonnes who were with me at Grauesend. I then forthwith
did wryte vnto my Lord of Norff. the copy wherof I send
vnto your highnes herin inclosed aduertysyng hym aswell
of the sayinges of the spyall which your malle may perceyve by the seid copy, as also admonyshyng hym that in no
wyse he should not be to (too) foreward to make ageynst
the rebelles' vntill my seid Lord Admyralles' assembly
came, desyring his grace by the same L're that I might
be aduertysed with spede of the tyme of his remove from
Grauesend towardes the rebelles', to th'end I might either
mete with him with my force by the way, or elles come
vnto him to Grauesend, and so to joyne forwardes together. So resting vppon his ferther aduertysement therin, he,
contrary to his former determynacion with me, marched
with his small power towardes Rochester immedyatly after my departure from hym, not sendyng me eny knowlege
therof vntill he was almost at Rochester. And I beying then
in a redynes when the messynger came, I forthwith, with
all spede, made to hym, but before I was half wey I was
aduertysed that his men had forsaken hym and were fledd
to the rebelles'; so that his power beying gon, he was compelled to retyre, and I heryng thereof retyred also to my
castell ageyne. Also your highnes shall resceyve a L're sent
to me by wyat yesternight herin inclosed, wherby your
grace may perceyve his meanying, cntendyng to marche
towardes London shortly; wherfore it may please your
highnes that I may vnderstand your graces pleasure what I
shall do herin, which accordyng to my allegeaunce which
I shall contynually beare vnto yr highnes I will accomplys-
she effectually to the vttermost of my power. Thus prayeng
to God for the preservacion of your matle with the victory
ouer your enemyes I most humbly take my leave of your
grace.

From Cowlyngcastell the xxixth of Janurij 1553.
[1554.] Your most humble and true Subject & servaunte.
G. Cobham.

To the Queenes' most excellent matie. [Cruden, 178-179]

The following letter, written by Thomas Wyatt, was enclosed with Lord Cobham's letter:

My Lorde you vnderstande in what state we now are, thanks be given to God, I am right sorye that you are so far behinde hande, yet I will not forsake you in this my ioy, but wolde wishe you to be parteners of the same. I pray you to be her to morowe for we will march then to london. far your Lordship well, from Rochester the xxix of Januarie 1553. [1554.]

Youre frend and cosyn,

thomas Wiat.

I pray you take some order for the taking of the Duke whereso that he be between this and london, wherein you shall gratifye the state of the realme. [Cruden, 179]

The Duke of Norfolk and the Lord Abergavenny withdrew to contemplate their defeat and Abergavenny's emotions are clear in the following letter he dispatched to the Privy Council:

Lord Abergavenny to the Privy Council.

After my verye hartie commendacions unto your good and honorable Lordships. Theis maye lieke the same to understand that receyving your letters datyd the 30th of this present, willing me therbye to followe Wyat and others the Quene's' Matie' ennemys on the backe, and for the better service thereof to call apon the L. Warden for his ayde: from whome in all this trobelousome tyme I have not herde, nor yet from the L. Cobham. I notwithstanding, with the companye that I hadd made, to the nombre of ijm at the leaste, lying yesternight at Maydeston, to have marched towards Rochester, receyved knowledge about mydnight that the Duke of Norff: whole bande hadd forsakyn hym, with the whiche brute [bruit or report] my souldiors some repayred to Wyat, some to their habitacions, and the resydue being not many besydes my household servauntes, accompanyd me to my cosyn Southwells' howse, where I looke hourely they will assault me, as I am informyd. Yet sorye I am that the Duke of Norff. dyd this enterprise without making me and other gentlemen in the partes where I am pryvie, that wer redye to have assisted hym yf wee hadd heard from hym in tyme. Howebeyt by reason my souldiours ar dissperst as aforsaid, leving me in mannr withowt armour, artillerye, and money, am hable to do nothing sodenlye, wherof I am right sorye that I cannot do my dutye accordingly. And thus I take my leave of your good and honorable Lordships for this tyme. From Mere-worth the last of January [1554.]

Your L. assuryd to his poore (power), Henry Aurgavennye.

[Cruden, 180]

Because of the disaster at Rochester, the Duke of Norfolk had no further involvement in the suppression of the rebels, whereas Wyatt, now confident with the victory and the increase in the size of his forces, set his sights on London with renewed vigor.

CHAPTER 4. LONDON BRIDGE HAS FALLEN DOWN

The Queen reacted quickly to the news that uprisings were occurring within her realm by issuing and sending proclamations to several locations carried by riders with great haste. The following is an example of one such proclamation:

> Mary the quene,
>
> The quene our Soveraign Lady geveth knowledge to all and singular her true and loving subjects, That Henry duke of Suffolk, with the Carews, Wyat and others, conspyring with hym, have by sowing of false and sedicious rumours raised certain evill disposed personnes' in Kent unnaturallie to rise and rebell against Mr heighnes. Mynding her graces destruction and to advaunce the lady Jane bis daughter, and Guilforde Dudley hir husbande, the duke of Northumberlandes' sonne, her graces traytours attaynted unto hir Majesties Crowne. And therefore hir Majestiewilleth all Maiors, Shirieffs, Bailieffs, Constables, and alle other hir officers, ministres, and good subjects to whom it apperteyneth in this parte, To proclayme unto all hir graces loving subjectes' within their severall offices The said Duke of Suffolk, his brethcrne, and Thomas Wiatt of Kent, and all other thiere confederates, to be false traytours unto hir heighnes and hir crowne, and dignitie roiall

And that hir Majestie hath sett fourthe her puissaunce to subdue the said traitours Trusting by the healpe and grace of God and the aide of hir said loving subjects utterly to confounde the said traitours. Wherfore hir Majestie exhorteth all her true subjectes' bearing true heartes to God and hir and hir crowne, and the realme of Englande, to put them selfes in order and redynes to resist the said duke and all his adherents and commaundementes, which service of hir Majesties loving subjectes' hir grace shal consider to all their comfortes, besides that God will undoubtedly rewarde thier service. [Nichols, 185]

The Duke of Suffolk who was at first reluctant to join Wyatt's cause, perhaps received news of the white coats joining Wyatt at Rochester despite the intercepted letter sent by Wyatt and he and his brothers departed from Sheen and rode to the town of Leicester to issue the same type of proclamation that Wyatt had elsewhere. Suffolk found the support he was promised was not there and no one was willing to listen to his proclamation much less join him. Before arriving, the Duke was told that Thomas Dannett had assembled four hundred armed men for him at Leicester, but this was not true.

On 30 January, the Duke of Suffolk rode towards Coventry with his party. When they arrived within a quarter of a mile from the town, Suffolk sent a man ahead to the gates that led into the city and the man soon returned with news that the gates were shut against him and that no man would support his traitorous cause. They were unaware that the Earl of Huntington already warned the town of their arrival and prepared the townsfolk by supplying armor and arms to help them prevent Suffolk from entering. Now they were beginning to understand why Leicester was not open to them.

Discouraged by the lack of promised support and afraid to proceed, they departed to the Duke's home in Astley, about five miles from Coventry. Once there, every man removed their battle harnesses and Suffolk's brothers Thomas and John changed into the coats of their servants to serve as a disguise. A servant of Suffolk returned after attending to the horses to witness money being divided between the men that gave him a sinking feeling. The servant was later quoted as saying in his deposition, "Then I wished I had never known service to see that change, so havie a companie as theare was!" As Suffolk's brothers were departing, the servant of Suffolk was attempting to do the same when the Duke summoned him to give him his coat as well, to serve as a disguise, and the servant said that he was sorry that it had arrived at that and gave the Duke his coat, then they departed on their separate ways.

The Earl of Huntington picked up their trail and pursued them to Coventry, where, with a dog, he eventually located the Duke of Suffolk hiding in a hollowed out tree and found his brother John hiding in a stack of hay. The Duke of Suffolk's other brother Thomas had fled to Wales but was eventually captured when he returned to the inn where he had spent the night, to claim his money and cap that he forgot. The Earl of Huntington took all the prisoners to London.

Yet unaware of Suffolk's failure in the North, Wyatt and his increased size of forces left Rochester the same day on a crossroad leading to Cooling (Cowling) Castle with his newly acquired ordnance and traveled about four miles to the castle which was held by Lord Cobham. The Emperor's Ambassadors in England informed the Emperor in a letter of the events of the rebellion and that Wyatt removed several pieces of artillery from the Queens ships anchored on the Thames River possibly in or near Rochester. Regardless of how, Wyatt now had a greater number of artillery pieces and upon their arrival at the castle, Wyatt had his gunners place the cannons facing the gate into the castle then fired several shots before setting the wooden gate on fire. After several more shots were fired at the gate, it was finally destroyed and the castle received a great deal of additional damage. Wyatt requested that Lord Cobham surrender, but having only a small force with him, Cobham defended the castle as best as he could with the limited supply of munitions that were available. Cobham fired his pistol at those who entered through the destroyed gate but history has not recorded whether his shots were effective in either wounding or killing any of Wyatt's men though Cobham did lose four or five of his men during the skirmish before surrendering the castle to the superior forces of Thomas Wyatt. Though the castle was of no military value, the defeat appears to be more of a personal significance to Wyatt, perhaps even a resolution to a past vendetta.

That evening Lord Cobham dispatched a letter to the Queen describing the events of the day:

> Lord Cobham to the Queen.
>
> It may please your most excellent matie to be aduertysed that this day at xi of the ciok, wyat with his hole force of ijm men and above, removed from Rochester and approched to my castell, assalting the same in most forcy-

ble manner they could: but I declaryng my true subiection towards your highnes and callyng them traytours, made to them defyaunce, resystyng their force, and defendyng my castell with such power as I had vntill v of the clok at after none, havying no other munycions or wepons but iiij or v hand gones, pykes, and the rest blakbylls, the fault whereof I may well ascrybe vnto your graces offycers of the bulwerkes and ships, makyng ernest request as well to my lord of Norfolk as to theym for the same, howbeit I could never get none.

The rebells perceyving that I was bent to resystt theym, havyng ij great peces of ordynnaunce that the Duke of Norfolk left amongs theym at his retyre, layd battery to the gate of the castell, and also did fyre the same and leyd foure other peces to another syde of the castell, which did so sore batre the castell and the gates, that without that they could neuer have prevayled, at which assault iiij or v of my men were slayne and diuers hurt, which did so discorage the comons that I had thyre assembled for the servyce of your highnes, that they begonne to mutney and whisper one to another, and I their standyng in defence at the gates, with my sonnes ageynst theym in a doubtful as-salt, vntill my gates with the drawe-bryges were so hatred and fyred downe that they were redy to invade me, I perc-eyving behynde me both my men to shrynke from, and my shote to be wasted, was then compelled to yeld, whereof if power had seruyd to my true hart and servyce towards your highnes, I wold have dyd in your graces quarrell. If your grace therefore, will assemble such force in conveny-ent tyme as were able to encounter with so fewe in nom-bre beyng not above ij, and yet not vc of theym able and good armed men, but rascalls and rakehells as lyve be (by) spoyle; I doubt not but your grace shall have the vyctory of theym, so that they be guyded and man handled by such an approved Captayne as can discretely lede theym. They en-forced me to promyse them vppon myne honor, to be with them to morowe at Gravesend, yet notwithstandyng I will remayne faithful in hart towards your highnes, aduerty-syng your grace from tyme to tyme of their proceedyngs. And for the better tryall of my good servyce towards your highnes to be don unfaynedly, yea and more effectually then I have wryten. It may please your grace to send some one whom your grace shall appoynt, to viewe my house, wherby your grace shall vnderstand that I have, as well in this as in all other your graces former commaundements, showed myself a true and redy servyteur towards your highnes, although I understand I have byn otherwise reported to your highnes, wherin my doyngs and the contrey shall vtter and witness the truth, as my conscynce hath inwardly merit good fayth towards your grace, which I shall so contynually beare whiles lyfe doth last. Thus makyng my contynual prayer for the preservacion of your highnes with strength and fortune to subdue your enemyes, I most humbly take my leave of your grace from Cowling Castell, in hast the xxxth of January, 1553. [1554.]

Your graces most humble and true subiect and seruante to th'end,

G. COBHAM.

To the Queenes' most excellent matie. [Cruden, 180-181]

Having successfully taken the castle from Lord Cobham, Wyatt moved his forces to Gravesend where they camped and rested for the night. History has not recorded the disposition of the castle after Wyatt left, but most likely Cobham would have regained control even damaged as it was.

On 31 January, Wyatt and his forces marched out of Gravesend to Dartford, which was about a seven-mile journey. Upon their arrival, Sir Edward Hastings and Sir Thomas Cornwallis both members of the Privy Council and sent by the Queen, arrived at Wyatt's camp to meet with Wyatt who had just returned from the West side of town. Wyatt had ensured that all of his artillery were in place and greeted the two men with a halberd (a weapon with a long handle with a combined spearhead and battleaxe) in his hand.

Sir Edward Hastings was the first to address Wyatt:

"The queens majesty requireth to understand the very cause wherefore you have thus gathered together in arms her liege people, which is the part of a traitor; and yet, in your proclamations and persuasions, you call yourself a true subject: which cannot stand together."

Wyatt replied, "I am no traitor and the cause whereof I have gathered the people is to defend the realme from our overrunning by strangers; which follows, this marriage taking place."

The Council members continued their questioning, "Why, there be no strangers yet come whome either for power or number ye need to suspect. But if this be your only quarrel, because, ye mislike the marriage; will ye come to communication touching that case? And the queen of her gracious goodness, is content ye shall be heard?"

Wyatt responded, "I yield therto, but for my surety I will rather be trusted than trust. And therefore I demand the custody of the Tower and her grace in the Tower; the displacing of certain councilors, and placing others in their room as to me shall seem best."

The conference continued between them for a while longer with Sir Edward Hastings ending their conference by replying sternly, "Wyat, before thou shalt have that thy traitourous demand granted, thou shalt die and twenty thousand with thee." [Holinshed, 1095-1096]

Having obtained as much information as they could, the Privy Councilors departed Wyatt's camp for London to inform the Queen of Wyatt's intentions. After the Councilor's departure, some of Wyatt's men discussed how he addressed the first of the Queen's heralds at Rochester in a rather private conversation and how Wyatt would not allow the herald to read the Queen's proclamation. Now his handling of the two Privy Councilors at Deptford had many of his men questioning their loyalties to Wyatt and wondered if he was being truthful with them.

On 1 February, a proclamation was made in London delivered by a herald of the Queen informing the people that the Duke of Suffolk's forces, including Gawen Carew and William Gibs, were scattered and that he and his brothers fled to avoid capture and Peter Carew fled to France. Regardless of the news of the captures, news of Wyatt's march to London began to alarm many in the city, including several of the foreign Ambassadors who quickly fled by the Thames River in the opposite direction as soon as they could to avoid any danger.

The Queen was advised to leave Westminster by members of her Council and seek the safety of the Tower, but they were unable to persuade her to do so as she had other plans. Several Council members then escorted the Queen, members of the guard and other gentlemen to Guildhall where as soon as the Mayor had quieted the increasing crowd, the Queen gave a speech.

[**Editor's note**: We found this document particularly difficult to transcribe as the original is reproduced from a 1586 edition; we have attempted to present as accurate a copy as possible.]

I am (quoth shee) come unto you in mine owne person, to tell you that which already you doo see and know, that is how traitorouslie & seditionslie a number of Kentish rebels have assembled themselves togither against both us and you. Their pretense (as they said at the first) was onelie to resist a mariage determined betweene us and the prince of Spaine. To which pretended quarrell, and to all the rest of their evill contriued articles ye haue beene made priuie. Since which time, we haue caused diuerse of our priuue councell to resort [unclear] to the said rebels, and to demand of them the cause of their contunuance in their seditious enterprise. By whose answers made againe to our said councell, it appeared that the marriage is found to be the least of their quarrel. For they now swaruing from their former articles, haue betraied the inward treason of their hearts, as most arrogantlie demanding the possession of our person, the keeping of our tower, and not onelie the placing and displacing of our councellors; but also to use them and us at their pleasures.

Now loving subiects, what I am, you right well know. I am your queene, to whome at my coronation when I was wedded to the realme, and to the laws of the same (the spousall ring wereof I haue on my finger, which neuer hither to was, nor hereafter shall be left off) ye promised your allegiance and obedience unto me. And that I am the right and true inheritor to the crowne of this realme of England; I not onelie take all christendoome to witness, but also your acts of parlement confirming the same. My father (as ye all know) possessed the regall estate by right of inheritance, which now by the same right descended unto me. And to him always ye shewed your selves most faithfull and louing subjects, and him obeid and serued as your liege lord and king: and there fore I doubt not but you will shew your selues likewise to me his daughter. Which if you doo, then maie you not suffer anie rebel to usurpe the gouernance of our person, or to occupie our estate, especiallie being so presumptuous a traitor as this Wiat hath shewed himselfe to be; who must certeinlie, as he hath abused my ignorant subiects to be adherents to his traitorous quarrel; so dooth he intend by colour of the lawe, to subdue the lawes to his evill, and to give scope to the rascall and forlorne persons, to make generall hauocke and spoile of your goods. And this further I say unto you in the word of a prince, I cannot tell how naturallie a mother loueth her children, for I was neuer the mother of anie, but certenilie a prince and gouernor may as naturallie and as earnestlie loue subjects, as the mother dooth her child. Then assure yourselves, that I being souereigne ladie and queene, doo as earnestlie and as tenderlie loue and fauour you. And I thus louing you, cannot but thinke that ye as hartilie and faithfullie loue me againe: and so louing together in this know of loue and concord, I doubt not, but we together shall be able to giue these rebels a short and speedie ouerthrow.

And as concerning the case of my intended marriage, against which they pretend their quarrel, ye shall understand that I entered not into the treatie thereof without advise of all our priuie councell; yea, and by assent of those to whome the king my father committed his trust, who so considered and weighted the great commodities that might inuse thereof, that they not onlie thought it very honorable, but expedient, both for the wealth of our realme, and also of all our louing subiects. And as touching my selfe (I assure you) I am not so desirous of wedding, neither so presise or wedded to my will, that either for mine owne pleasure I will choose where I lust; or rise so amorous as needs I must haue one. For God I thanke him (to whome be the praise thereof) I have hitherto liued a virgine, and doubting nothing but with Gods grace shall as well be able so to liue still.

But if as my progenitors haue done before, it might please God that I might leaue some fruit of my bodie behind me to be your gouernour, I trust you would not onelie reioise ther at, but also I know it would be to your great comfort. And certeinlie if I either did know or thinke, that this marriage should either turne to the danger or losse of anie of you my louing subiects, or to the detriment of impairing of anie part or parcel of the roiall estate of this realme of England, I would neuer consent there unto, neither would I euer marrie while I liued. And in the word of a queene I promise and asure you, that if it shall not probablie appeere before the nobililitie and commons in the high court of parlemient, that this marriage shall be for the singular benefit and commoditie of all the whole realme; that then I will absteine, not onelie from this marriage, but also from anie other, whereof peril maie insue to this most noble realme.

Wherefore now as good and faithfull subiects plucke up your harts, and like true men stand fast with your lawfull prince against these rebels, both our enemies and yours, and feare them not: for assure you that I feare them nothing at all, and I will leaue with you my lord howard and my lord treasuror to be your assistants, with my lord maior, for the defense and safegard of this citie from spoile and saccage, which is onelie the scope of this rebellious companie. [Holinshed, 1095-1096]

History has recorded that the Queen's speech had a positive effect on those who listened as she comforted some and answered the many questions that most had because all they had heard prior to her speech were rumors. Her speech motivated many to make preparations for the defense of their city, not against the Spaniards, but against Wyatt. Following the speech, Mary and her Council returned to Whitehall to discuss with Sir Thomas White and William Howard their plans for the defense of London and also prepared an army to be led by William Herbert the Earl of Pembroke and to leave London immediately with only one task: stop Wyatt.

Aware of the occurrences in the realm and wishing to join the search for Wyatt, Sir Thomas Cheney was eagerly awaiting a response to the letter he sent to the Council several days before:

Sir Thomas Cheney to the Privy Council,

Forasmuch as I have sent letters to the Queries Matie and also to your Lordeshippes' as well by Mr. Everhed, Gentleman Huisher, as by thre or foure of my servaunts at sundrye tymes, and as yet have receyved no woord of aunswere agayne, whereof I do not a litle marvaile, being therfor in great doubte they be staied or apprehended by the waye, which hath byne my onely staye, and for that I am not sure of ten of my nowne men that will take my parte in this quarell: all this notwithstanding vpon her Highnes pleasour or commaundement signified unto me, I will give thadventure against these rebelles', althoughe I shuld not have one man to take my parte but myself, let God doo with me what shal be his will: for I had lyver dye if I had a thousand liefs, in this quarell against theis traitours, then lyve otherwise. Yt is a great dele more then straunge to see the beastlyness of the people to see how earnestlye they be bent in this theyr most develishe enterprise and will by no meanes be persuaded to the contrary but that it is for the common welthe of all the Realme, and they say and protest before god they meane to her grace no hurt, but for all that I pray god kepe her out of their daungier, as my verey trust is He will: most humbly desireng to here from your lorde-shippes' by this bearer my servaunte whom I trust verey well, and that he will not deceyve me. The abhominable treason of those which came with my Lorde of Norffolke hath wonderfully discoraged almost all serving men and others, that I wold to god my said Lord had forborne but that clay and then I am out of doubte they had all ryn away the same night, for I had suche woord the next morneing from thence. Thus I beseeche almightye god to preserve the Quenes' matie and your lordshippes' and to send us a more quiet worlde, and that shortely. From Sherlond this first of February aboute 3 of the clock in the afternoone.

At your Lordshippes' commaundement to th'uttermost of my lief and powre, T. Chetne.

Postscript. Being enformed that my Lord Penbroke is comeng against them with a great nombre, which I think shall abasshe them wonderfully, I wold wisshe he shuld not be to hastye, for the longer he taryeth the more will theyr company waiste. If my men forsake me not, I will not be farre from theyr backs with as many as I am hable to make. Yt shall not be best to go to rasshley to woorke, for there is an old sayeing, that haste oftentymes maketh waiste. I have no waye to conveye my l'rs but onely by wa-ter. [Cruden, 183-184]

Meanwhile Wyatt, now displaying fourteen ensigns and with an estimate of four thousand men, marched to Deptford Strand, just eight miles from Dartford and only four miles from London. Wyatt's spies returned with information that the Queen was at Whitehall and that her speech had motivated the people of London against them. Wyatt decided to camp at his location for the night and the entire following day, perhaps hoping that the city would cool down, but several of Wyatt's closest advisors were not happy with the delay. They recommended that they continue to London because any delay would give the Queen's forces more time to increase their strength, but Wyatt remained. This decision may have been his first real tactical error. Sometime during the first night, three prisoners escaped even though they had promised Wyatt they would not do so.

As news of the revolt spread, officials were notified to watch for similar activities elsewhere. One result of this was that a servant of the Duke of Suffolk was caught in possession of a notice issued by the Duke before his capture. The notice was to be posted in as many locations as could be, announcing that twelve thousand Spaniards were at Calais and even more were ready in invade England at any time, and that the English people should take up arms immediately to defend their home. This notice could very well have induced panic in many areas, as it was intended to do, if his plans had not been discovered in time. The man was later hanged for his crimes.

On 3 February, Wyatt and his forces left Deptford Strand and marched to Southwark. When he arrived at the foot of the London Bridge, he called for the gates to be opened to him, but the attendants would not comply with his request. Wyatt had not anticipated this development and expected a more encouraging reception: the gates open and additional support ready to escort him into London. Several of his advisors said his delay at Deptford Strand had allowed the Queen's speech to work against them. Wyatt remained optimistic and, drawing upon his past military training and discipline, he had a deep trench dug between the bridge foot and his encampment, then positioned his men and two pieces of artillery at the foot of the bridge.

Word quickly spread in London of Wyatt's arrival, causing alarm and in some cases, panic. There exists an account of these events that Edward Underhill recorded in *Underhyll's Anecdotes of Wyatt's Rebellion:*

> Sir Homffrey Rattclyffe was the levetenauntt off the pencyonars, and alwayes favored the Gospelle, by whose merinos I hadd my wagis stylle payde me. When Wyatt was cume into Southwarke, the pencyonars weare commaunded to wache in armoure thatt nyght at the courte, whiche I hearynge off, thought it best in lyke suerte to be there, least by my absens I myght have sume quarell piken unto me, or att the least be strekon off the boke for reseavynge any more wagis. After supper I putt one

my armoure as the rest dide, for we weare apoynted to wache alle the nyght. So beyng alle armed, wee came uppe into the chamber of presens with ower pollaxes in ower handes, wherewith the ladies weare very fearefulle; sume lamentynge, cryinge, and wryngynge ther handes, seyde:

"Alas, there is sume greate mischeffe towarde; we shalle alle be distroyde this nyght. Whatt a syght is this, to se the quenes' chamber full of armed men; the lyke was never sene nor harde off."

Then Mr. Norres, who was a jentyllman ussher of the utter chamber in kynge Henry the viij tyme, and all kyng Edwardes tyme, always a ranke papist, and therfore was now the cheffe ussher off quene Maryes' privy chamber, he was apoynted to calle the wache, to se yff any weare lackynge; unto whome Moore, the clarke of ower cheke, delyvered the hole of ower names, wiche he parused before he wolde calle them att the curbarde, and when he came to my name, "Whatt (sayd he) whatt dothe he here?"

"Syr (sayde the clarke) he is here redy to sarve as the rest be."

"Naye, by God's body! (sayde he) that herytyke shall not wache heare; gyve me a pene." So he stroke my name owt off the boke. The clarke of the cheke sought me owte, and sayde unto me:

"Mr. Underhyll, yow nede nott to wache, yow maye departe to your logynge."

"Maye I? (sayde I) I wolde be glade off thatt," thynkynge I hadde byn favored, because I was nott recovered off my sykenes: butt I dyde not welle truste hym because he was also a papist. "May I depart in dede (sayd I), wylle yow be my discharge?"

"I tell yow trew (sayde he), Mr. Norres hathe strekon you owt off the boke, sayng these wordes ' That herytyke shall nott wache here; I tell you trwe what he sayde."

"Marye [exclamation], I thanke hym (sayde I), and yow also; yow could nott do me a greater plesure."

"Naye, burden nott me withall (sayde he), it is nott my doynge." So departed I into the halle where ower men weare apoynted to wache. I toke my men with me, and a lynke, and wentt my wayes. When I came to the courte gate, ther I mett with Mr. Clement Througemartone, and George Feris, tindynge ther lynges to go to London. Mr. Througemarton was cume post frome Coventry, and hadde byne with the quene to declare unto her the takyngc of the duke of Suffoke. Mr. Feris was sentt from the councell unto the lorde William Hawwarde, who hadde the charge of the whache att London bryge. As we wentt, for thatt they weare bothe my frendes, and protestanes, I tolde them my goode happe, and maner of my discharge off the whache att the cowrtt. When we came to Ludegate it was past aleavene of the cloke, the gate was fast loked, and a greate wache within the gate off Londonars, but noone withowte, whereoff Henry Peckham hadde the charge under his father, who belyke was goone to his father, or to loke to the water syde. Mr. Througemartone knoked harde, and called unto them, saynge, "Here is iij or iiij jentyllmen cum from the courte thatt must come in, and therfore opon the gate."

"Who?" cothe one, "Whatt?" cothe another, and moche laughynge they made.

"Cane ye tell what ye doo, syrs?" sayd Mr. Througmartone, declarynge his name, and that he hadd byne with the quene to showe her grace off the takynge oft the duke off Suffoke, "and my logynge is within, as I am sure sume off you do know."

"And," sayde Ferris, "I am Ferris, that was lorde off misrule with kynge Edwarde, and am sentt from the councell unto my lorde William, who hathe the charge of the brige, as yow knowe, uppon weyghtie affayres, and therfore lett us in, or eles ye be nott the quenes fryndes."

Stylle there was mouche laughynge amoungst them. Then sayd too or three off them, "We have nott the keyes, we are nott trusted with them; the keyes be carryed awaye for this nyghte."

"Whatt shall I do?" sayde Mr. Througemartone, "I am wery and faynte, and I waxe nowe colde. I am nott aquaynted here abowte, nor no mane dare opone his doores in this daungerous tyme, nor I am nott able to goo bake agayne to the courte; I shall perishe this nyght."

"Welle (sayde I) lett us goo to Newgate, I thynke I shalle gett in ther."

"Tushe (sayde he), it is butt in vayne, we shalbe aunswered ther as we are here."

"Welle (sayde I) and the worst of all, I can loge ye in Newgate; yow know whatt acquayntaunce I have ther, and the keper's' doore is withowte the gate."

"That weare a bade shifte (sayde he), I shoulde almost as lyffe dye in the stretts; yett I wyll rather wander agayne to the court."

"Welle, (sayde I) lett us goo prove. I beleve the keper wyll healpe us in att the gate, or eles lett us in thorow his wardes, for he hatthe a doore on the insyde also; yff all this fayle I have a frend att the gate, Newmane the ierin-mounger, in whose howse I have byne logede, where I dare waraunt yow we shall have logynge, or att the lest howse-rome and fyer."

"Marye, this is wel sayde," (sayethe Ferris;) so to New-gate we wentt, where was a greate wache withowte the gate, wiche my frende Newmane hadde the charge off, for that he was the cunnestable. They marveled to se those torches cumynge thatt tyme off the nyght.

When we came to them, "Mr. Underhyll (sayde New-mane), whatt newes, thatt you walke so late?"

"None butt goode (sayd I); we cum from the cowrte, and wolde have goone in att Ludgate, and cannott be lett in, wherfore I pray yow yff yow cannott helpe us in here, lett [us] have logynge with yow."

"Marye, that ye shall (sayde he), or go in att the gate, whether ye wille."

"Godamercy, gentyll frende (sayde Mr. Througemar-tone); I praye you lett us goo in yff it maye be." He called to the cunestable within the gate, who opened the gate forth-with. "Now happye was I (sayde Mr. Througemartone) that I mett with you, I hadd byne lost eles." [Nichols, John Gough, 128-130]

As Wyatt and his men were considering an assault on the gates of the London Bridge, several of Wyatt's men wandered away and pilfered the house of the Bishop of Winchester. When Wyatt received the news, he threatened to hang the men for their acts. Wyatt felt that if he allowed that type of behavior to continue it would give the impression that they were all just common criminals and history records that Wyatt was clearly offended by their actions.

There exists an account of what Wyatt's men had done, though it seems rather exaggerated:

> Notwithstanding, forthwith divers of his company, be-
> ing gentlemen (as they sayed) went to Winchester place,
> made havocke of the bishop's goods, (hee being lord chan-
> cellor), not onely of his victuals, whereof there was plenty,
> but whatsoever els, not leaving so much as one locke of
> a fore but the same was taken off and carried away, nor
> a book in his gallery of library uncut, or rent into pieces,
> so that men might have gone up to the knees in leaves of
> booke, cut out and throwne under feete. [Stowe]

John Nichols, in his *Chronicle of Queen Jane*, indicates, "Proctor, who was much prejudiced against Wyat, admits that he (Proc-tor) immediately checked the spoil of Winchester house, and so sharply threatened a certain young gentleman, who was the most active partly therein, that he made divers believe that he would have hanged him on the wharf." John Proctor's record of the Wyatt rebellion was published shortly thereafter and though Proctor may have visited the Winchester house after Wyatt left, there are no in-dications or mentions in his account that he himself was to or had disciplined anyone for their actions.

Nevertheless, history has recorded that prior to the ransacking of the Winchester house, Wyatt had a conversation on 22 January with several of his men regarding the very same issue before the revolt began hoping to prevent something similar to that from hap-pening. These men hoped to justify the act of pilfering by debat-ing with Wyatt that the money was needed to keep their campaign going. In the preliminary planning stages, Wyatt had foreseen the problem of finances and told the men that many who had joined their ranks brought enough money to sustain themselves for nine days and could assist with others if so required. This did not ap-pease the men who continued to debate that they could apprehend several important individuals such as Lord Abergavenny or Sir Rob-ert Southwell who could be worth money. They also pointed out to Wyatt that many of the citizens in London had money that they could use to further the uprising. History has recorded that Wyatt stood firm on his moral beliefs and indicated that pilfering from the citizens would not be tolerated and that once the Tower had been secured, they would have enough money to sustain them for quite some time. Wyatt concluded by explaining that they should show that their only dispute was against strangers in England.

Wyatt and his men maintained their position for the remainder of the day at Southwark as Lord William Howard and the mayor of London stood watch over the London Bridge with three hundred men. Wyatt maintained a close watch of the activities on the other side for the remainder of the day and noticed that as additional safeguards, the drawbridge had been removed and thrown into the Thames River to prevent Wyatt from crossing and they fortified their side with armed soldiers and artillery. During his time at Southwark, Wyatt composed a letter then dispatched it to the Duke of Suffolk requesting him to meet at Kingston Bridge then accompany him to London as Wyatt really could have used the additional support at that point in time.

Wyatt returned to the London Bridge later that evening at about eleven o'clock after most of the commotion had settled down on the London side. He realized that it was safer to execute a plan now and had his men remove a wall from a house near the foot of the bridge that could be used to connect the gap where the drawbridge had once been. By the light of flickering torches, Wyatt advanced across the bridge as quietly as possible. He found the porter in a state of slumber and his wife accompanied by a few others awake and warming themselves around a small pile of coals. They were startled and surprised to see Wyatt who quickly responded to their surprise, "As you love your lives, sit you still, you shall have no hurt". They were so glad of the assurance that they did just as they were told and remained quiet as Wyatt and his men proceeded as far as the drawbridge. Wyatt sat and listened for quite some time viewing the artillery and a flurry of activity then returned back to his men undetected and informed them, "This place is too hot for us" and abandoned the plan of attempting to cross over into London at that point.

Wyatt and his men stood around the light of a small torch and discussed their options. Some advised that it would be best to return to Greenwich where they could pass across the river into Essex and secure additional support then enter London by Aldgate. Others felt that it would be best to go to Kingston-upon-Thames, and some even farther westward. Some, including Wyatt, felt that by returning to Kent to meet with the Lord Abergavenny, the sheriff, and others who had left Rochester and were enroute to London, could find more support and increase their numbers as when Captain Bret had joined their campaign. A few felt that Wyatt's main motivation with that plan was to flee from what was believed to be a failed attempt and possibly leave for France. Wyatt chose to remain at the foot of the bridge.

As Wyatt sat at the well fortified London Bridge, Sir Thomas

Cheyney arrived in Rochester acting upon orders given earlier with a large garrison of men and horses and sought to take out after the rebels with great haste. Several of his advisors met with him to discuss their options and Cheyney decided to refrain from his overenthusiastic ambition until he had received directions from the Queen and sent a message to London. The following day he sent word to the Privy Council and soon after left Rochester with his garrison to pursue Wyatt.

Sir Thomas Cheney to the Privy Council.

It may please yours honors that, I have receyved the Quenes' Ma'tie proclamacion and your lordeshippes' l'res of the third, and have sent copies of the proclamacion to Canterbury, Dovor, and to diverse other townes along the coste: assuring, your said l'res hathe somewhat revived me trusting my slacknes shall well appeare yt was not for wante of goodwyll, for lack of stomake, or for the savyng of that litle I haue of my nowne; but onely for lack of trew and trusty men to take my parte, as, by any thing I could perceyve, I had verey few, and then if I shuld have set furthe and have byn takyn or slayne, I think it shuld have byn but a small furtherance for the pacefieng of theys abhominable traytors and the rankest rebells that ever was. I wold be full sory for my parte that any one of them shuld escape, and in especiall any one that beareth the countennaunce of a gentleman or substanciall yeoman that, is woorthe any maner way C. I was yesterday at my comyng out of th'yle (Isle of Sheppey) fayne to leave the most parte of my best horse and geldyngs standing at the watersyde, where as I think they are yet, and whether they have a good standeng there or no, in suche a night as this hath byn, my lord Privie Seale and others that doth knowe the place can tell. Thus I betake your lordeshippes to god. Frome Sittingbome, this 4th of February, as I was settyng my foote in my stirrop to Rochester ward, from whence I hope to asserteyne your lordeshippes' of suche nombre of horsemen and footemen as shall be of our company. Your lordeshippes' alwayes at commaundement,

T. Cheyne. [Cruden, 184]

Still unable to proceed across the bridge and with no signs of additional support, Wyatt spent his time studying his adversary, hoping to spot a weakness that he could exploit. He noticed that the Lord Admiral was maintaining a stronghold on the bridge with an estimate of three hundred men who would stand watch until eight o'clock at night, and their relief would consist of another three hundred men, all well armed and wearing armor, so the London Bridge was guarded both day and night. Wyatt was surprised and troubled by the lack of support from the Londoners and so far, how strongly they were standing against him. Perhaps as a result, Wyatt's advance stalled for a short while. Captain Bret voiced his concerns as an experienced military leader and freely gave his advice to Wyatt, pointing out that Wyatt and all his men were in a town and boxed in, which made getting away in a hurry more difficult, if not impossible. Furthermore, if Wyatt did in fact leave for Kent, as many of his men thought he might do, it would be a severe blow to the morale of the men who had come so far with him.

Bret continued by pointing out that if Wyatt did not advance soon, many of his men would abandon him only weakening his forces giving the enemy the advantage. Captain Bret pulled Wyatt aside from the ears of the others to talk with him alone as he received word that Wyatt now had a bounty on him of one hundred pounds to anyone who would bring him to the Queen. He continued to express his concern that should his men hear of the bounty coupled with the issues he had already discussed, many of his men's thoughts would most certainly change.

After Bret turned and walked away, Wyatt turned to his cousin and long time friend Henry Isley:

> "Ah, cousin Isley, in what extreme misery are we? The revolt of these Captains with the White Coats seemed a benefit in the beginning; and as a thing sent by GOD for our good, and to comfort us forward in our enterprise: which I now feel to our confusion. Ah, cousin, this it is to enter such a quarrel, which notwithstanding we now see must have a ruthful end; yet of necessity we must prosecute the same."
>
> [Pollard, 247]

Now, among Wyatt's many worries, he was concerned about the traitorous captains once again becoming traitors, but to him this time.

On 6 February, called Shrove Tuesday, Wyatt left Southwark at six o'clock in the morning and marched to Kingston-upon-Thames, about a ten-mile march. They arrived at four o'clock that afternoon to find about thirty feet of the bridge missing with only the posts remaining. Wyatt found a couple of able-bodied men to swim over to the other side of the river and retrieve a barge moored at the banks and return with it. Wyatt and several of the gentlemen with him then crossed over the Thames on the barge while the others stole beams and planks from anywhere they could and fabricated a bridge by tying them together with ropes. By ten o'clock, they were ready to transfer from one side to the other and by eleven o'clock all of Wyatt's forces and ordnance had crossed over their makeshift bridge safely without opposition and with renewed spirits after finally overcoming one of their largest hurdles, the Thames River, headed towards London.

Though their spirits may have been high after finally crossing the Thames, they deteriorated during the long march in the cold January morning. The cold and weary men finally arrived at about nine o'clock, Ash Wednesday, at Hyde Park. The exact path Wyatt followed is not certain but it is possible that Wyatt came in on the west side of Saint James and as soon as they approached the field near Saint James Park, his advance scouts informed him there were soldiers of the Queen's army on both sides of the path. These were the forces of the Earl of Pembroke, who received information from his spies about what path Wyatt would most likely take, and placed his men of arms and demi-lances in a field on the west side of Saint James. The remainder of his forces, which consisted of light horsemen where placed in the lane next to the park. Pembroke placed his artillery on the highest location possible, which happened to be next to Saint James and placed additional pieces of artillery on each flank. Because a conflict was now imminent, both groups of Pembroke's forces were now under the charge of Lord Clinton, marshal of the field. Wyatt quickly realized that his delays had given Pembroke time to set up his forces, but it was too late to change plans now.

Wyatt and Pembroke's forces met, then charged each other as the artillery thundered to life from both sides, though not yet effective, as the gunners had to dial the guns in on their targets. As Wyatt arrived at the corner of Saint James Park, he realized that it would be disastrous if he continued in the same direction and veered off towards Saint James. Pembroke's forces quickly reacted to Wyatt's change in direction, then charged, causing Wyatt's forces to split their ensigns into different directions with some, including Wyatt, fleeing in the direction from which they had come.

It has been suggested that the others were led by one of the Knevet brothers and escaped by slipping along the west side of Saint James towards Westminster, then towards the Tower, perhaps along King's Street or Parliament Street, but found the gates closed to them. Hoping to avoid further conflict with the Queen's forces by hiding, Knevet and his small group remained where they were for a while, shooting arrows into any window that was available (perhaps in and around the area of the Palace of Whitehall). Furthermore, they shot arrows over a garden (very likely the Privy Garden); history has not recorded whether these shots had any effect or not. Knevet realized that their numbers were too few to make a difference and gathered his men, then departed to rejoin with Wyatt, who was heading towards London. As they arrived at Charing Cross, they encountered members of Pembroke's forces led by Sir Henry Jeringham, captain of the Queen's guard, and Sir Edward Bray, master of the ordnance, with a band of archers and small cannons. The Queen's forces opened fire on the rebels with cannons, then charged with pike poles into Knevet's ranks that were not well armed, and only half armored, causing them to split up. Some fled down the lane back towards Saint James and the remainder went towards the Thames River. Twenty of Knevet's men were killed in the skirmish but it is unclear whether any of the Queen's forces were killed or wounded.

Meanwhile, Wyatt and his remaining forces marched along the wall of Saint James, trying to avoid Pembroke's forces, and arrived at an inn called the Bell Savage near Ludgate hoping to find much needed support, but found the gate closed to them and strongly guarded by members of the Queen's guard and citizens of London. Wyatt had anticipated, or hoped for support when they arrived at that point, but not having received it, they turned around to return to Temple Bar, hoping to regroup their forces, then proceed into London. Wyatt had suffered several defeats at this point, but even with his forces split by the attacking forces of the Queen and numerous desertions by men who fled hoping to live another day, he continued to remain optimistic that support would arrive at any time.

Instead of meeting additional support, Wyatt was met by a herald sent by Pembroke ordering him and his men to desist from his rebellious enterprise; but Wyatt ignored what the herald said and continued toward Temple Bar.

Edward Underhill's account of the rebellion continues at this point:

> When Wyatt was cum abowte, notwithstandynge
> my discharge of the wache by Mr. Norres, I putt on my
> armoure and wentt to the courte, where I founde all my

felowes armed in the halle, wiche they weare apoynted to kepe that daye. Old syr John Gage was apoynted withowte the utter gate, with sunie off the garde and his sarvantes and others with hym; the rest off the garde weare in the greate courte, the gattes standynge opune. Sir Rychard Southwell had the charge of the bakesydes, as the wood-eyarde and thatt waye, with vc men. The quene was in the galary by the gatehowse. Then came Knevett and Thomas Cobam, with a company of the rebelles' with them, thorow the gatehowse, from Westmester, uppon the sodein, wherewith syr John Gage and thre of the jugeis, thatt were menly armed in olde bryggantynes, weare so fryghtede thatt they fledd in att the gattes in suche hast thatt old Gage fell downe in the durte and was foule arayed; and so shutt the gates. Wheratt the rebelles' shotte many arow-es. By meanes of the greate hurliburli in shuttynge of the gattes, the garde thatt weare in the courte made as greate haste in att the halle doore, and wolde have cum into the halle amongst us, wiche we wolde not suffer. Then they wentt throungynge towardes the watergate, the kycheyns, and those ways. Mr. Gage came in amoungst us all durt, and so fryghted thatt he coulde nott speke to us; then came the thre jugeis, so fryghtede thatt we coulde nott kepe them owte excepte we shulde beate them downe. With thatt we issued owt off the halle into the courte to se whatt the matter was; where ther was none lefte butt the porters, and, the gattes beyng fast shutt, as we wentt towardes the gate, meanynge to goo forthe, syr Rycharde Southewell came forthe of the bake yardes into the courte. "Syr (saide wee) commaunde the gates to be opened thatt we maye goo to the quenes' enemyes', we wyll breake them opone eles; it is to mouche shame the gates shulde be thus shutt for a fewe rebelles'; the quene shall se us felle downe her enemys this daye before her face." "Masters," sayde he, and putt off his murianc off his heade, " I shall desyer yow alle as yow be jentyllmen, to staye yourselves heare thatt I maye go upe to the quene to known her plesure, and yow shall have the gates oponed; and, as I am a jentyllman, I wyll make spede." Uppon this we stayde, and he made a spedie returne, and brought us worde the quene was con-tentt we shoulde have the gates opened. "But her request is (sayde he) that yow wyll not goo forthe off her syght, for her only trust is in yow for the defence of her parsone this daye." So the gate was opened, and we marched before the galary wyndowe, wheare she spake unto us, requyrynge us, as we weare jentyllmen in whome she only trusted, thatt we wolde nott goo from thatt place. Ther we marched upe and downe the space off an ower, and then came a harrolde postynge to brynge newes that Wyatt was taken. Immediately came syr Mores Barkeley and Wyatt behynd hym, unto whome he dyd yelde att the Temple gate, and Thomas Cobam behynde ane other jentyllman.

Anone after we weare all brought unto the quenes' presentes, and every one kyssed her hande, off whome we hadde greate thanks, and large promises how goodc she wolde be unto us; but fewe or none off us gott any thynge, although she was very liberall to many others thatt weare enemys unto God's worde, as fewe off us weare. [Nichols, John Gough, 131-132]

When Wyatt arrived with his remaining force of less than one hundred men in front of the gate at Temple Bar they were stunned: no support. Having overcome numerous tumultuous conditions such as rain and cold during the long arduous marches, broken wheels on their artillery, desertions, bridges removed, opposition, skirmishes and battles, it was finally despair that had beaten them. Maurice Barkle, a knight not wearing any armor was riding by on his way to London and persuaded Wyatt and his men to surrender. With the Queen's forces all around and soon to overtake him and the size of his forces reduced to an ineffective number, Wyatt realized that his campaign had failed. He jumped onto the back of the knight's horse and Wyatt finally entered the heavily guarded city of London, as a prisoner.

CHAPTER 5. MARY, BLOODY MARY: THE AFTERMATH

When word arrived to the Queen of Wyatt's capture, she ordered the release Pembroke's forces at Saint James Field and each man given permission to return home. A proclamation was immediately issued in the city of London and the suburbs that anyone who attempted to hide the rebels involved with Thomas Wyatt would suffer the penalty of death, and to avoid such punishment, the guilty individuals should be brought before the Mayor or any of the Queen's justices. The result of the proclamation soon produced such an unexpected large number of rebels that the prisons in London could no longer hold them and churches were used to house some of the prisoners, but those became strained also.

Thomas Wyatt, William Kneuet, Thomas Cobham, two bothers named Mantel and Alexander Bret were escorted down the Thames River by Sir Henry Jeringham to the Tower where Sir Philip Denie received them at the bulwark. As Wyatt stepped from the barge and passed Denie, Denie said "Go traitor, there was never such a traitor in England." Wyatt stopped, turned to Denie and replied, "I am no traitor, I would thou shouldst well know thou art more a traitor than I, it is not the point of an honest man to call me so."

As the leaders of the rebellion arrived at the Tower gate, Sir Thomas Bridges the lieutenant of the Tower took in the brothers Mantel and told them, "Ah thou traitor, what hast thou and thy company wrought?" but both brothers held their heads down and said nothing in response. Next was Thomas Knevet who was escorted into the Tower by Master Chamberlaine.

Following Knevet was Alexander Bret brought in by Sir Thomas Pope who grabbed Bret by the shirt and said, "Oh traitor, how couldest thou find in thy heart to worke such a villanie, as to take wages, and being trusted over a band of men, to fall to her enemies, returning against her in battell." Bret replied, "Yea, I have offended that case."

Thomas Cobham followed with an escort by Sir Thomas Poines who said, "Alas Master Cobham, what wind headed you to worke such treason?" Cobham replied, "Oh sir, I was seduced."

The last to enter the Tower was Thomas Wyatt, escorted by Sir John Bridges, who reportedly grabbed Wyatt by the collar and said:

> "Oh thou villen and unhappy traitor, how couldest thou find in thy heart to work such detestable treason to the queen's maiestie, who gave thee thy life and living once already, although thou diddest before this time beare armes in the field against her, and now to yield her battle. If it were not but that law must passe upon thee, I would sticke thee through with my dagger." Wyatt stood with his arms along his side and with a grim look answered, "It is not maisterie now." [Holinshed, 1099]

Wyatt had on a shirt of mail with short sleeves and a velvet cassock trimmed in yellow lace with an empty sheath hanging at his side. He wore a pair of boots and a velvet hat with some bone work lace around it. Knevet, Cobham, and Bret were dressed similarly.

History has recorded several conflicting dates that Wyatt's trial was held on. Simon Renard informed the Emperor in a letter that the trial began on 8 February and John Nichols in *The Chronicle of Queen Jane* includes in chronological order the events from the period:

> The xv[th] daye of Merche (March) sir Thomas Wyat knight was arrayned at Westminster of treason and rebellion; ther sat in comyssyon as chefe the erle of Sussex, sir Edward Hastinges, maister Bourne the secretary, &c.

William Hamilton, in his *A Chronicle of England During the Reigns of the Tudors*, indicated:

> The xv of Marche Wyatt, capteyn of the rebels, was arregned at Westminster and there condemned of highe treason.

It should be noted that in Hamilton's accounts of the period he also indicated that Edward Courtenay the Earl of Devonshire was again committed to the Tower on the same day 15 March, but most early accounts place him in the Tower on 12 February the day Lady Jane Grey was executed. Given the speed that the rebel's trials, convictions, and executions were occurring coupled with Renard's reputation, it would seem logical that the Queen would want Wyatt to be tried and convicted as soon as possible and based on that, I have placed his trial date as recorded by Renard.

The following account of the trial of Thomas Wyatt the Younger was taken from the account recorded in Raphael Holinshed's 1586 chronicles though Mr. Holinshed has not included a date. Several early historians have indicated that Holinshed's account is the most accurate. Mr. Holished's record was compared with the complete trial record found in *Cobbett's Complete Collection of State Trials, London 1809* and found to have many differences. As with all the Holinshed references, we found this document difficult to transcribe as the original is from a 1586 edition and attempted to present the best copy possible.

Wyatt was brought from the Tower to Westminster where he stood trial on the charge of treason before the Earl of Sussex, Sir Edward Hastings and Sir Thomas Cornwallis acting as judges with a group of Wyatt's peers present. Wyatt was charged with leading a large force of armed men with ensigns displayed at Brainford where they openly declared war against the forces of the Queen with the intent to remove her from the throne.

The Council asked Wyatt whether he was guilty or not. Wyatt responded by asking if he might ask a question before he answered the question and the Council allowed him to do so. Wyatt asked if he confessed and pleaded guilty, would the court not be prejudicial to him and by his confession not be permitted to speak further on the matter. The court answered:

"Master Wyatt, ye shall have both leave and leasure to saie what you can."

"Then my lords, I must confess myself guiltie, and in the end the truth of my case must inforce me. I must acknowledge this to be a just plague for my sins, which most greevouslie I therefore have committed against God, who suffred me thus brutishslie and beastlie to fall into this horrible offense of the law.

Wherefore all you lords and gentlemen, with other here present, note well my words, lo here and see in me the same end which all other commonlie had, which have attempted the like enterprise from the beginning.

For peruse the chronicles through, and you shall see that never rebellion attempted by subjects against their prinse and countrie, from the beginning did ever prosper, or had ever better successe, except the case of king Henrie the fourth: who although he became a prince, yet in his act was but a rebel, for so must I call him: and though he prevailed for a time, yet was it not long but that his heirs were deprived, and those that had right againe restored to the Kingdome and crowne, and the usurpation so sharplie revenged afterward in his blood, as it well appeared, that the long delaie of Gods vengeance was supplied with more grievous plagues in the third and forth generation.

For the love of god all you gentlemen that be here present, remember and be twught as wll by examples past, as also by this my present infelicitie and most wretched case. Oh most miserable, mischiesous, bruthish and bestlie suspicus imaginations of mine! I was persuaded that by the marriage of the prince of Spaine, the second person of this realme, and next heire to the crowne, should have been in danger; and that I being a free borne man, should with my countrie have beene brought into the bondage and servitude of aliens and strangers. Which bruthish beastlie opinion when seemed to my reason, and wrought in me such effects, that it led me headlong into the practise of this detestable crime of treason.

But now being better persuaded, and understanding the great commoditie and honor which the realme should receive by this marriage; I should stand firme and fast in this opinion, that if it should please the queene to be merciful unto me, there is no subject in this land that should more trulie and faithfullie serve her highness than I shall; nor no sooner die at her graces feet in defense of her quarrel.

I served her highnesse against the duke of Northumberland, as my lord of Arundell can witness. My granfather served most trulie her graces grandfather, and for his sake was set upon the racke in the Tower. My father also served king Henrie the eight to his good contentation, and I also served him, and king Edward his son.

And in witness of my blood spent in his service, I carrie a name. I alledge not all this to set foorth my service by waie of merit, which I confess by dutie: but to decale to the whole world, that by abusing my wits, in pursuing my misadvised opinion, I have not onelie overthrowne my house, and defaced all the well doing of me and my ances-tors (if ever there were anie) but also have beene the cause of mine owen death and destruction. Neither doo I alledge this to justifie my selfe in anie point, neither for an excuse of mine offense: but most humblie submit my selfe to the queen's maiesties mercie and pitie, desireing you my lord of Susses, and you master Hastings, with all the rest of this honorable bench, to be meanes to the queen's highness for her mercie, which is the greatest treasure that maie be given to anie prince from God, such a vertue as God hath appropriate to himselfe, Which if her highness vouchsafe to extend unto me, she shall bestow it on him, who shall be most glad to serve truelie, and not refuse to die in her quarrel. For I protest before the judge of all judges, I never meant hurt against her highness person."

The queen's attorney said, "Maister Wiat you have great cause to be sorie, and repent for you fault, whereby you have not onlie undone you selfe and your house, but also a number of other gentlemen, who being true men might have served their prince and countrie: yet if you had gone no further, it might have beene borne withal the better.

But being not so contented to staie your selfe, you have so procured the Duke of Sufolk (a man soone trained to your purpose) and his two brethren also: by meanes whereof without the queen's greater mercie, you have overthrowne that noble house. And yet not so staied, your attempt hath reached as far as in you laie to the second person of the realme, in whome next to the queen's high-ness resteth all our hope and comfort, wherby her honor is brought in question and what danger will follow, and to what end it will come God knoweth: of all this you are the auther."

Wyatt replied, "As I will not in anie thing justifie my selfe, so I beseech you, I being in this wretched estate, not to overcharge me, nor to make me seeme to be that I am not. I am loth to touch anie person by name; but that I have written I have written."

The judge said, "Maister Wiat, maister attornie hath well moved you to repent your offenses, and we for our parts with you the same."

Sir Edward Hastings then addressed Wyatt, "Maister Wiat, doo ye remember when I and maister Cornwallis were sent unto you from the queens highnesse to demand the cause of your enterprise, and what you required? Were not these your demands, that the queenes' grace should go to the tower, and there remaine: and you to have the rule of the tower and her person, with the treasure in keeping, and such of her councell as you would require to be delivered into your hands, saieng that you would be trusted and not trust?"

Wyatt then confessed that all that Hastings had stated was true and then he addressed the queen's solicitor. "Your presumption was over great, and your attempt in this case hath purchased you perpetuall infamie, and shall be called W'iats rebellions as Wat Tilers was called Wat Tiler's rebellion."

Then the attorney addressed Wyatt, "Maister Wiat, were you not privie to a devise whereby the queene should have beene murthered in a place where she should walke? I doo not burthern you to confess this, for thus much I must saie on your behalfe, that you misliked that devise?"

Wyatt responded, "That devise was the devise of William Thomas, whome ever after I abhorred for that cause."

A member of the court then held a letter up for the members of the court to see. It was the letter that Wyatt, while in Southwark, had written to the Duke of Suffolk requesting that he should meet him at Kingston Bridge and from there accompany him to London. At first, Wyatt did not seem to remember any such letter, but when he was shown the letter; he confessed that he did write it.

A member of the court then asked several questions of Wyatt, one being why he refused that queen's pardon when it was offered to him. He responded,

"My lords, I confesse my fault and offense to be most vile and heinous, for the which first I aske God mercie, without the which I cannot challenge anie thing, such is my offense already committed. And therefore I beseech you to trouble me with no more questions, for I have delivered all things unto her grace in writing. And finallie here I must confess, that of all the voiages wherein I have served, this was the most desperate and painfull jorneie that ever I made. And where you asked whie I received not the queen's pardon when it was offered unto me; Oh un-happie man! What shall I saie? When I was entered into this divellish and desperate adventure, there was no waie but wade through with that I had taken in hand; for I had thought that other had beene as farre forward as my self, which I found farre otherwise. So that being bent to keepe promise with all my confederates, none kept promise with me; for I like a moile went through thicke and thin with this determination, that if I should come to anie treatie, I should seeme to betraie all my friends.

But whereto should I spend anie more words? I yeeld my selfe wholie unto the queen's mercie, knowing will that it is onlie in her power to make me (as I have deserved) an open example to the world with Wat Tiler; or else to make me participant of that pitie which she hath extended in as great crimes as mine; most humblie beseeching you all to be means for me to her highness for merrcie, which is my last and onelie refuge. The will of god be done on me."
[Holinshed 1103, 1104]

Based on the confession that Wyatt made and without further need for trial, the sentence of death by hanging, drawing, and quar-tering was passed by the court to be carried out on the Tower Hill on 11 April. Following Wyatt's trial, William Cobham, Anthonie Knevet (brother of William), George Harper, and several others were brought to the Tower.

Renard mentioned in his letter of 8 February to the Emperor that Edward Courtenay and William Somerset the Earl of Worcester showed no sign of fighting when Wyatt's forces were attacking and both distinguished themselves on their first field of battle by run-ning to court crying that all was lost and the rebels were winning the day. Renard seemed to believe that Courtenay's performance confirmed what the French Ambassador said about the rebellion being undertaken on Courtenay's behalf. Renard also mentioned that Courtenay had talked in a vain, foolish and dangerous tone to the Earl of Lennox saying that he (Courtenay) was as good a man as Pembroke and did not mean to obey him. Renard informed the Em-peror that Courtenay's actions angered the Queen who intended on consulting with the Council on what to do with him and Elizabeth.

On the same day, the Queen received information that Thomas, brother of the Duke of Suffolk, and James Croft were captured. Additionally, the Duke of Suffolk wrote and signed his confession, and in it he attributed his brother Thomas with motivating him to join the rebellion. He also mentioned that he attempted to persuade the Earl of Pembroke to join but he would have no part and refused to listen.

The Queen held a small ceremony to show her appreciation to those who served her, and she gave the Earl of Pembroke a diamond in Courtenay's presence, then told Pembroke that she would always remember his services. All present then cried, "Long live the Queen." After the ceremony, Wyatt was taken to prison as the Queen watched from one of her windows.

On 9 February, Henry Isley, who had evaded capture for a short time was brought to the Tower, with a total value in his possession, including the clothes on his back, of less than four shillings.

Monday, 12 February, began with the executions of Lady Jane Grey and her husband Guildford on the scaffold on Tower Hill at about 10:00 A.M. Guildford was executed first and after his body was removed, the lieutenant of the Tower led her to the scaffold, attended by her servants Mistress Tylney and Mistress Ellen, followed by Master Feckenham. From the platform, she recited a short speech she had prepared for the occasion:

> "Good people, I come hither to die. And by a law I am condemned to the same: the fact indeed against the Queens Highness was unlawful and consenting there unto by me. But touching the procurement and desire thereof by me on my behalf I do wash my hands thereof in innocence, before God and the face of you good Christian people this day. I pray you all good Christian people to bear me witness that I die a true Christian woman and that I look to be saved by none other means but only by the mercy of God. In the merits of the blood of his only son Jesus Christ, and I confess when I did know the word of God, I neglected the same and loved myself and the world and therefore this plague of punishment is happily and worthily happened unto me for my sins. And yet I thank God of his goodness that he has thus given me a time and respite to repent: and now good people while I am alive I pray you to assist me with your prayers" [Brown, 79].

After reciting the piece she had composed, she knelt down to pray and asked Master Feckenham, "Shall I say this psalm?" He replied, "Yes," and she repeated in English the psalm Miserere Mei, Deus.

She then said to Feckenham, "God will requite you, good sir, for your humanity, though your discourses gave me more uneasiness than all the terrors of my approaching death." After Lady Jane finished her devotions, she removed her gloves and handkerchief and gave them to her maid, Mrs. Ellen, and her book to Master Brydges, the lieutenant's brother. She then began to untie her gown, and the executioner stepped forward to assist her, but she requested him to let her alone and turned to her two gentlewomen who helped her, then gave her a handkerchief to cover her eyes with. Then the executioner knelt down in front of her and begged her forgiveness, which she granted, begging him in turn to dispatch her quickly.

As Lady Jane knelt down on the straw that covered the platform, she turned again to the executioner, saying, "Will you take it off before I lay me down?" He answered, "No, madam." She then tied the handkerchief over her eyes and feeling anxiously for the block and unable to locate it said, "What shall I do? Where is it, where is it?" One of the bystanders directed her to the fatal instrument on which she laid her neck and before the axe fell she said, "Lord, into thy hands I commend my spirit." The executioner removed her head with a single blow.

That day was called "Black Monday" and an unknown gentleman recorded the events that took place on that day which were later published in the Historical Memorials, Ecclesiastical and Civil, of events under the reign of Queen Mary I, by John Strype in a 1721 edition.

> Thus, this Black Monday began, with the Execution of this most Noble and Virtuous Lady and her Husband. On the same day, for a terrifying Sight, were many new Pairs of Gallows set up in London. As at every Gate one, two pair in Cheapside, one in Fleet Street, one in Smithfield, one in Holborn, one at Leadenhall, one at St. Magnus, one at Billingsgate, one at Pepper Alley Gate, one at St. George's, one in Barnsby Street, one on Tower Hill, one at Charing Cross, and one at Hide Park Corner. These gallows remained standing until Wednesday when men were hanged on every Gibbet, and some quartered also. In Cheapside six; at Aldgate one, hanged and quartered; at Leadenhall three; at Bishopgate one, and was quartered; at Moorgate one, and he was quartered; at Ludgate one and he was quartered; at Billingsgate three hanged; at St. Magnus three hanged; at

Tower Hill three hanged; at Holborn three hanged; at Fleet Street three hanged; at Paul's Churchyard four; at Pepper Alley Corner three; at Barneby Street three; at St. George's three; at Charing Cross four; whereof two belonged to the Court; at Hidepark Corner three, one of them named Pollard, a water bearer. Those three were hanged in chains. But seven were quartered, and their bodies and heads set upon the gates of London. [John Strype]

During the evening of the same day, Edward Courtenay was arrested and in his possession was several disguises and it was believed that he would have used them to escape capture by fleeing to France with Peter Carew. Courtenay was now to return to the very place he had already spent over half of his life, the Tower of London. The Queen issued his arrest warrant based on a confession Wyatt made after his arrest implicating Courtenay and Elizabeth in the rebellion. With Courtenay in confinement, the Queen would have one less matter to worry about.

The following day, Renard informed the Emperor that he received information that Peter Carew had arrived at the French court and immediately met with the French King and that Courtenay sent a servant to negotiate with the King on matters that were not clear but most likely had to do with preventing Philip from landing in England.

On 14 February, more of the rebels were executed; an account of the day is as follows:

> Bothe, one of the Queenes' footemen, one Vicars, a Yeoman of the Garde, great John Norton, and one Kinge, were hanged at Charinge Crosse. And three of the rebels, one called Pollarde, were hanged at the parke pale by Hide Parke, three allso in Fleet Street, one at Ludgate, one at Bishopsgate, one at Newgate, one at Aldgate, three at the Crosse in Cheape, three at Soper Lane ende in Chepe, and three in Smythfield, which persons hanged still all that daye and night tyll the next morninge, and then cutt downe. And the bodies of them that were hanged at the gates were quartered at Newgate, and the heades and bodies hanged over the gates where they suffered. [Hamilton, 112]

The ambassador Simon Renard wrote a letter to the Emperor in which he described that wherever he went in and around London he saw the gibbets and bodies of the hanged and the overwhelming stench was horrible.

The number of the executions of the rebels was in the hundreds and history has probably recorded only about half to two-thirds of all those who suffered for their involvement and it is understandable how Mary began to earn her nickname of "Bloody Mary" during this period.

On 15 February, ten more of the rebels were brought to Westminster where they would stand trial for their crimes. Further executions included:

> ....iii against St. Magnus Churche, iii at Billingsgate, iii at Ledenhall, one at Moregate, one at Creplegate, one at Aldrigegate, two at Paules, iii in Holborne, iii at Tower hill, ii at Tyburne, and at four places in Sowthwerke 14. And divers others were executed at Kingston and other places. [Hamilton, 112]

On a lighter note, during the morning of the same day many people in London noticed that in a clear sky, two suns were seen with one iris and it was thought to be a good omen and was interpreted as the union of the two kingdoms of England and Spain.

Later the same day the grim reality of executions continued with the two Knevet brothers and the two Mantel brothers and the day concluded as thirty-five more rebels executions occurred. Over the period of several weeks, an estimated two hundred additional executions occurred and half of which occurred in the county of Kent where they attempted to raise the people in rebellion. The Queen did this to provide an example to anyone who might think of attempting to do the same and what the outcome could be if they did.

On 17 February, the Duke of Suffolk was taken from the Tower to Westminster, where he was tried for committing the act of treason by participating in the rebellion with Thomas Wyatt. Suffolk was found guilty and sentenced to death by the Earl of Arundel, who served as the chief judge over the trial, and a group of his peers. The Duke most likely welcomed this punishment because it was his actions that had forced the execution of his daughter, Lady Jane.

On the same day, Alexander Bret, the captain who quit the Duke of Norfolk's forces to join Wyatt, was removed from the Tower to be taken to Kent for his execution. As they left the Tower, Bret embraced Lord Chamberlain and requested that he pass along a comment to Wyatt, then asked that all men pray for him. Unfortunately, history has not recorded what the comment was. Bret then said,

> "And I am wourthie of no lesse punishement then I do nowe go to suffer, for besyde myn offence I refused lyfe and grace iij. tymes when yt was offeryd; but I trust God

dyd all for the best for me, that my soule might repent, and therby after this lyfe (attain) to the more mercy and grace in his sight." [Nichols, 61-62]

The Queen issued two proclamations on the same day, the first informing all strangers who were not born within her highness's domains to leave within twenty-four days after the proclamation was issued with certain exceptions granted by the Queen, or suffer the forfeiture of their goods, imprisonment, and possibly death if they did not comply. The second proclamation was made in Cheapside by a trumpeter that if anyone hid or knew of the location of any of the rebels who escaped capture, to bring them, their names or their locations immediately to any of the Queen's officials.

The following day, the Emperor dispatched several letters to key individuals who served vital roles in the suppression of Wyatt's rebellion. All the letters contained the same beginning as that which was addressed to the Earl of Pembroke commending his valiant service rendered to the Queen in suppressing the rebels and furthermore stated that the Emperor and his son Philip would always be grateful for their actions. The letters closed with words tailored to those individuals.

On the same day, Bret and twenty-two others were delivered to the sheriff of Kent to be executed in various locations that had been determined by the Queen's Council.

On 23 February at about nine o'clock in the morning, the Duke of Suffolk was taken to the scaffold on Tower Hill where he recited a short speech:

> "Good people, this daie I am come hether to dye, being one whom the lawe hathe justlie condemned, and one who hathe no lesse deserved for my dysobedyence against the quenes' highenes, of whom I do moste humbly axe forgevenes, and I truste she dothe and will forgyve me."

> Then maister Weston, his confessor, standing by, saide, "My lorde, his grace hathe allredy forgeven and praieth for you."

> Then saide the duke, "I beseche you all, goode people, to lett me be an example to you all for obedyence to the quene and the majestrates, for the contrarie therof hath brought me [to this end b]. And also I shall most hartely desire you all to beare me witnes that I do dye a faythefull and true christian, beleving to be saved by non other but onely by allmightie God, thoroughe the passion of his son Jesus Christ And nowe I pray you to praie with me."

[Nichols, 63-64]

Suffolk knelt down with Weston then recited *Miserere mei Deus* and *In te, Domine, speravi*, the Duke one verse and Weston the other. Following this, the Duke tied a handkerchief around his eyes and held his hands towards heaven then laid his head down on the block, which was removed with one blow and fell on the same spot that his daughters' had.

On 24 February, Simon Renard informed the Emperor that Wyatt confessed that a French ambassador and another gentleman had a conversation with James Croft about preventing the marriage between Mary and Philip and placing Elizabeth on the throne and putting Mary to death. Renard also alleged that the French King offered Wyatt support in the form of money and men and that he would attack from Scotland. Certainly, the French would have been interested in joining Wyatt had his enterprise been successful though there were concerns that the King might launch a campaign against the Queen at any time.

Suspicions rose about the affairs of William Paget, who was a long time and well respected member of the Council, because he was opposing the Chancellor and several others and he had not attended a Council meeting for six days; and Wyatt was continually requesting to speak with him. Many believed that he had ties with Thomas Wyatt and his activities were watched closely.

In another letter to the Emperor, Renard included a list of the prisoners who were in the Tower because of their involvement with the last rebellion. The list included the Earl of Devonshire, Lord John and Thomas Grey brothers of the now executed Duke of Suffolk, Lord Cobham, Thomas Wyatt, Gawen Carew, Croft, George Harper, William Cobham, Alexander Bret (executed), Thomas Cobham, the Knevet and Mantell brothers, Cutbert Vaughan, Edward Fogge, and numerous other knights and gentleman.

On 1 March, it was reported that the trials of the rebels were progressing well and that the Earl of Devonshire confronted Wyatt in the presence of three witnesses. Wyatt maintained his deposition asserting that Courtenay was a party to the plot and acted on his behalf. Furthermore, Wyatt indicated that Courtenay was as much a traitor as he and of course, Courtenay denied any involvement. As those within the kingdom who were involved with Wyatt were now executed or waiting for punishment, more information became available which implicated the French in Wyatt's rebellion. Several prisoners came forward with information about Courtenay's involvement. Furthermore, they indicated that he had a cipher on his guitar that was to be used by Peter Carew and he conspired with the King of France and he had been ready to flee the country to France had Wyatt not dissuaded him and that Carew arranged a marriage between Courtenay and Elizabeth.

Because of Wyatt's confession, members of the Council interrogated Elizabeth and her answers were scrutinized. The son of the Lord Privy Seal who was under arrest in his father's house, confessed that he received letters from Wyatt addressed to Elizabeth during the rebellion and delivered them to the princess. This had the Queen and her Council very upset. Several Council members felt that Elizabeth and Courtenay should be executed as the evidence warranted the action.

As the punishment of the rebels continued with the large number of executions frequently occurring within the city and elsewhere coupled with the lingering tensions from the past rebellion, many of the citizens in London were in an uneasy state. On 9 March, an estimate of three hundred children gathered within the city and divided themselves into two groups, one group pretended they were the Queen and her forces and the other half pretended they were Thomas Wyatt and his forces. Both sides staged the confrontation as it happened a short time ago resulting in several of the children being wounded in their pretend skirmish and many of the children were arrested and placed in Guildhall until their punishment could be determined.

Another odd occurrence took place five days later when a large crowd gathered around a house in London and rumors spread quickly that an angel's voice could be heard from inside a wall in the house. When someone from the crowd said, "God save the queen," there was only silence, but when someone said, "God save Lady Elizabeth," the voice from inside the wall responded, "So be it." When someone from the crowd asked, "What is Mass?" the voice responded, "Idolatry." It did not take long for the Royal Guard to arrive and disperse the crowd of several thousand then arrested the homeowners. It was believed that they had hoped to stir the people against the Queen and gain sympathy for Elizabeth.

On the same day, Renard informed the Emperor that a spy arrived from Normandy with information that the King of France was preparing thirty large ships in Normandy and Brittany with troops and twenty were ready to attack England. Furthermore, Peter Carew was attempting to persuade the King that England would rather have the French than the Spaniards.

By now, Mary either had most of those involved in the rebellion in prison or executed except for two, Peter Carew and Elizabeth. Mary was unable to deal with Carew but she could Elizabeth. Mary sent several letters to her sister requesting her presence but Elizabeth indicated that she was still too sick to travel. The Queen sent several of her own physicians and three Council members to determine whether the princess was able to travel or not. They arrived late in the evening to find a sick and upset Elizabeth confined to her bed. After the doctors examined her, they determined that she could travel to London and after several requests to postpone the journey by the young princess they departed on a four-day journey. Upon their arrival in London, the visibly distressed princess was again questioned about her involvement with Thomas Wyatt and Peter Carew and though she denied all accusations, it was no use; her attendants were dismissed and she was told to prepare herself for imprisonment in the Tower of London.

The following day, two members of the Council arrived to take the princess to the Tower and she requested that she be allowed to write a letter to the Queen. The two men discussed the issue and she was allowed to write her letter before they departed. Elizabeth wrote several letters during this period, but I feel the following reflects the emotions she felt after a long and tedious trip while ill and facing the threat of confinement in the Tower, and even possibly her death:

> To the Queen.
>
> If any ever did try this olde saynge, that a Kinge's' worde was more than another man's othe, I most humbly besche your Majesty to verefie it in me, and to remember your last promis and my last demande, that I be not condemned without answer and due profe: wiche it semes that now I am, for that without cause provid I am by your Counsel frome You commanded to go unto the Tower; a place more wonted for a false traitor, than a tru subject. Wiche thogth I knowe I deserve it not, yet in the face of al this realme aperes that it is provid; wiche I pray God, I may dy the shamefullist dethe that ever any died, afore I may mene any suche thinge: and to this present hower I protest afor God (who shal juge my trueth, whatsoever malice shal devis) that I never practised, consiled, nor consentid to any thinge that migth be prejudicial to Your parson any way, or daungerous to the State by any mene. And therfor I humbly besche your Majestie to let me answer afore your selfe, and not suffer me to trust to your Counselors; yea

and that afore I go to the Tower, if it be possible; if not, afore I be further condemned. Howbeit, I trust assuredly, your Highnes wyl give me leve to do it afor I go; for that thus shamfully I may not be cried out on, as now I shalbe; yea and without cause. Let consciens move your Hithnes to take some bettar way with me, than to make me be condemned in al mens' sigth, afor my desert knowen. Also I most humbly beseche your Higthnes to pardon this my boldnes, wiche innocency procures me to do, togither with hope of your natural kindnes; wiche I trust wyl not se me cast away without desert: wiche what it is, I wold desier no more of God, but that you truly knewe. Wiche thinge I thinke and beleve you shal never by report knowe, unless by your selfe you hire. I have harde in my time of many cast away, for want of comminge to the presence of ther Prince: and in late days I harde my Lorde of Sommerset say, that if his brother had bine sufferd to speke with him, he had never sufferd: but the perswasions wer made to him so gret, that he was brogth in belefe that he coulde not live safely if the Admiral lived; and that made him give his consent to his dethe. Thogth thes parsons ar not to be compared to your Majestie, yet I pray God, as ivel perswations perswade not one sistar again the other; and al for that the have harde false report, and not harkene to the trueth knowin. Therfor ons again, kniling with humblenes of my hart, bicause I am not sufferd to bow the knees of my body, I humbly crave to speke with your Higthnis: wiche I wolde not be so bold to desier, if I knewe not my selfe most clere, as I knowe my selfe most tru. And as for the traitor Wiat, he migth paraventur writ me a lettor; but, on my faithe, I never received any from him. And as for the copie of my lettar sent to the Frenche Kinge, I pray God confound me eternally, if ever I sent him word, message, token, or lettar by any menes: and to this my truith I will stande in to my dethe. Your Highnes most faithful subject that hathe bine from the beginninge, and wylbe to my ende,

    ELIZABETH.

    I humbly crave but only one worde of answer from your selfe. [Ellis, Volume II, pg. 255-257]

Elizabeth traveled along the Thames River on Palm Sunday, 18 March, to arrive at the traitor's gate entrance to the Tower, where she refused to step ashore; and after several persuasions, she stepped onto the wharf and said looking up to heaven:

"Ohe Lorde! I never thought to have come in here as prysoner; and I praie you all, goode frendes and fellowes, bere me wytnes, that I come yn no traytour, but as true a woman to the que'ues majesty as eny is nowe lyving; and theron will I take my deathe."

And so going a lyttle further, she sayd to my lorde chamberlain, "What are all theis harnessyd men here for me?" and he saide, "No, madam."

"Yes (she said), I knowe yt is so; yt neded not for me, being, alas! but a weak woman."

Yt is saide that when she was in, the lorde trezerer and the lorde chamberlain began to lock the dores very stray-tlye, then the erle of Sussex, with weeping eyes, saide, "What will ye doe, my lordes? What mean ye therin? She was a kinges' daughter, and is the quenes' syster; and ye have no sufficient commyssyon so to do; therfore go no further then your comyssyon, which I knowe what ytis." [Nichols, 70-71]

Now locked inside the cold walls of the tower, it was a long time before she was allowed to have any exercise outside her walls of confinement.

On 22 March, Renard informed the Emperor he received infor-mation that Peter Carew left Normandy for Brittany and the King of France sent him to join the fleet there and furthermore a ship was captured in Cornwall with twenty Englishmen and some French-men on board sent by Peter Carew to reconnoiter the western coast. Though Wyatt and his followers were in prison, unrest was still prevalent in the realm and Renard reported that one-third of the kingdom still disapproved of the marriage and several conspira-cies had been discovered but no other details were available.

On 5 April, an event transpired involving eight to ten heretics who met in Essex and attempted to prevent the Earl of Oxford from attending a session of Parliament by blocking the road he was trav-eling along and attempting to persuade him to act as their leader. Eight of them were arrested and the Earl attended the session. An-other incident revealed on the same day involved a letter that was distributed around London that stated, "Stand firm and gather to-gether, and we will keep the Prince of Spain from entering the king-dom." The origin of the letter was never discovered.

The following account of an event in London on 8 April also portrays the attitude in London:

> Sunday the 8 of Aprill was a villanouse fact done in
> Cheape earlie or daye. A dead catt havinge a clothe lyke
> a vestment of the priest at masse with a crosse on it afore,
> and another behinde put on it; the crowne of the catte
> shorne, a peece of paper lyke a singinge cake putt betwene
> the forefeete of the said catt bownd together, which catt
> was hanged on the post of the gallowes in Cheape beyond
> the Crosse in the parishe of St. Mathewe, and a bottle
> hanged by it; which catt was taken downe at vi of the
> clock in the morninge and caried to the Bishop of London,
> and he caussed it to be shewed openlye in the sermon tyme
> at Paules' Crosse in the sight of all the audience there pres-
> ent. [Hamilton, 114]

The day of Wyatt's execution, 11 April arrived. In the morning, he requested that the lieutenant of the Tower permit him to confront Edward Courtenay also confined in the Tower over the Watergate. Wyatt was allowed to confront Courtenay in the presence of the lieutenant and sheriffs who acted as witnesses in a meeting that lasted about an hour and a half. When Wyatt entered Courtenay's chamber, one of two accounts (the second will be reviewed at the end of this chapter) indicate that he fell to his knees in front of the Earl and begged for his forgiveness because he had falsely accused him and the princess Elizabeth upon his capture in his conspiracy. There are no known fuller accounts of the conversation exchanged during the hour and a half they were together.

Wyatt left the Tower over the Watergate with a book in his hand and when he and his escorts arrived at a garden they encoun-tered the chamberlain and secretary Bourne and Wyatt spoke to them;

> "I praie you, sir, pray for me, and be a meane to the
> quene for my poore wife and chilldren; and yf yt might
> have pleased hir grace to have granted me my lyfe I wolde
> have trusted to have don hir such good servyce as shold
> have well recompenced myne offence; but, since not, I
> beseche God have mercy on me."
> [Nichols, 73]

Bourne gave no reply to Wyatt and continued to walk away, as Weston now led Wyatt by one arm and Lord Shandose by the other toward Tower Hill.

As Wyatt was standing on the scaffold, he requested again that each man pray for him. There are two accounts of what he said next;

I have included both. The first is from John Nichols in *The Chronicle of Queen Jane.*

> "Good people, I am come presently here to dye, being therunto lawfully and wourthely condempned, for I have sorely offended agaynst God and the quenes' majestic, and am sorry therfore. I trust God hath forgeven and taken his mercy apon me. I besyche the quenes' majesty also of forgevenes."

> "She hath forgeven you allredy," saith Weston. "And let every man beware howe he taketh eny thinge in hande against the higher powers. Unlesse God be prosperable to his purpose, yt will never take good effecte or successe, and therof ye may now lerne at me. And I pray God I may be the last example in this place for that or eny other like. And whereas yt is said and wysled abroade, that I shoulde accuse my lady Elizabeth's grace, and my lorde Courtney; a yt is not so, goode people, for I assure you neyther they nor eny other now." [Nichols, 73-74]

The second version is from a reference made by Mr. Nichols, quoted from Bayley's *History of the Tower:*

> *Verba Thome Wiet militis in hora mortit sue.* "Good people, I have confessyd before the quenes' majestyes' honorable counsayle alio those that toke parte with me, and were privaye of the conspiracye; butt as for mye ladye Elza yonder in holde or durance was previe of my rysing or commotyon before I began; as I have declared no lesse to the quenes counsaille. And this is most true."

> Then said Weston at those wordes, interrupting his tale, "Merke this, my masters, he sayeth that that which he bathe shewed to the counsell in wryting of my lady Elizabeth and Courtney ys true."

> And whether Mr. Wyat, being then amased at such interruptyon, or whether they on the scaftblde pluct him by the gown bake or no, yt is not well knowen, but without more talkc he tourned him, and put of his gown and untrussyd his pointes; then, taking the [earl of] Huntingdon, the lorde Hastinges, sir Gilesa Stranguesh, and many other by the handes, he plucked of his doblet and wasteote, unto his shirte, and knelyd downe upon the strawe, then laied his bed downe awhile, and rayse on his knees agaync, then after a fewe wourdes spoken, and his eyes lyft upp to

heaven, he knytt the handekersheve himself about his eyes, and a lyttel holding upp his hands sobdenly laid downe his hed, which the hangeman at one stroke toke from him. Then was he forthwith quarteryd apon the scatfolde, and the next day his quarters set at dyverse places, and his hed apon a stake apon the galloss beyond saynte James. Which his hed, as ys reported, remayned not there x dayes unstable awaye. [Nichols, 73-74]

History is not entirely clear about these details, but in the above account it is suggested that Wyatt was surprised by the interruption and did not speak further. Nevertheless, it has been recorded that Wyatt then undid his gown and momentarily held the hand of the Earl of Huntington and hands of several other gentlemen who were on the scaffold, then removed his doublet and waistcoat, leaving only his shirt, then knelt down on the straw. Wyatt laid his head down on the block, then rose back up on his knees again and after saying a few words, he raised his eyes toward heaven and tied a handkerchief over his eyes, then held his hands up before laying his head down on the block, which the executioner removed with one stroke. His body was then quartered and hanged on gibbets by chains at various locations around the city. Wyatt's head was placed on the gallows on Hay Hill beside Hyde Park, where Pollard and two others were hanged in chains. His head remained in that location for six days before it was stolen. Where his body and head ended up is not known but it is possible that some or all of his remains could have been buried near his father in the church of Sherborne.

Immediately after Wyatt's execution, the mayor received word of Wyatt's declaration while he was on the scaffold and of his conversation with his confessor. As the mayor sat down to dinner, two gentlemen who came from a session of Parliament where Wyatt's confession was discussed entered the mayor's chamber. One of the gentlemen informed the mayor that a contrary story was told in the House of Parliament. The gentleman told the mayor that an apprentice and a servant of the Queen were engaged in a conversation about Wyatt's confession while drinking in a local pub. Bishop Gardiner was informed of this conversation and immediately sent a man to bring the apprentice to the Star Chamber for questioning.

The apprentice was soon located and brought to the Star Chamber, where he stood and listened to Gardiner explain how the Queen had received her sister so tenderly and how she had freed Courtenay and restored his titles, only for them to repay her by conspiring treason against her with the traitor Wyatt that can be clearly seen by various letters. The Bishop then told the mayor that there were individuals in the city of London who stated that the Council provoked Wyatt to accuse Elizabeth and Courtenay, but no one was punished.

The mayor responded, "the partie is here, take them with you," then advised the Bishop that London was a whirlpool of evil rumors and to take caution for his action may have severe consequences. The lieutenant came forward swearing that what he was about to disclose was the truth then described what he witnessed while Wyatt confronted Courtenay in the Tower in the second account as Wyatt knelt down in front of him and begged that Courtenay should confess the truth and submit himself to the Queen's mercy.

There are no additional accounts of that interview in the Star chamber, or of Wyatt's confession. Many of the Council members and various other noblemen believed Wyatt's original accusation of Courtenay and Elizabeth's involvement, but without conclusive evidence, the princess and Courtenay would forever remain in the shadow of suspicion.

Thomas Wyatt the Younger was survived by his wife Jane. By her, they had several children including a son Henry who died in infancy; Charles who also died in infancy; Arthur who died without issue; Jane who married Charles Scott; Anne who married Roger Twisden; Mary who died without issue and George Wyatt who married Jane daughter of Sir Thomas Fainch. It is through George that the Wyatt name was carried on for many more generations.

CHAPTER 6. RETROSPECT

Those who recorded the events of Thomas Wyatt's rebellion had different motivations for doing so and probably a certain amount of bias occurred between the occurrence of the actual events and the words each writer chose to portray the events for history.

Two such contrasting differences are seen between the accounts given by the Ambassadors Simon Renard and Antoine de Noailles. However, both were French, served with the military, and were diplomats by necessity rather than by choice. The differences between the men are far more striking than the similarities and can be viewed in their correspondence. It has often been commented on that de Noailles spurred controversy with the way he reported events, often embellishing the facts.

One of the more influential if not most comprehensive of the known recorded sources of Wyatt's rebellion was by John Proctor master of the grammar school at Tunbridge Wells and published his account the following year. Proctor's account of Wyatt's rebellion has been described by several early historians as a "moral tale in the guise of a chronicle" written in a style that included the use of documents, proclamations issued in various locations, copies of speeches, and other accounts in a format that was widely accepted by chroniclers of the period.

Proctor was possibly Catholic and though there are indications that he set out to record the events of the rebellions as accurately as possible he also attempted to emphasize the moral implications that committing such an act could result in. Regardless of the motivations of the man, his account is the most vivid and gives a valuable insight into the rebellion. Notable historians such as Raphael Holinshed, Richard Grafton, John Stowe, John Strype, Frances Godwin, and others also contributed in providing insight into the events surrounding Wyatt's rebellion and when their opinions are all brought together, an image begins to form.

Thomas Wyatt the Younger was a well educated and intelligent man who spent a portion of his life serving in the military and distinguished himself numerous times in campaigns in and outside of England. Wyatt received the foundation of his military training from seasoned veterans who were both successful and unsuccessful in campaigns with Henry VII and his son Henry VIII. Wyatt's abilities as a soldier and leader reveal that his training and application of those tactics and skills gained him recognition and respect from his subordinates and peers, including the King.

Then why did Wyatt fail? Several factors contributed to the collapse of his campaign. Perhaps the most detrimental was the irrational actions of Peter Carew and his confederates by igniting the tinderbox in January before the planned date in March. Some early and later historians felt that if Edward Courtenay led the revolt, Carew may have succeeded, but Edward Courtenay had received no known formal military training and when Mary came to the throne in 1554, Courtenay had spent sixteen of his twenty-eight years imprisoned in the Tower of London not for crimes he committed but for his father's. There are no known records that suggest Courtenay was qualified to lead men especially in a military capacity and his limited education in those matters would have only provided a handicap. Had Courtenay showed up to support Carew, it would have been in name only as the Courtenay name was of a long and well respected lineage that first seated itself during the reign of Henry II (1154 to 1189). Courtenay certainly was unqualified to provide the military discipline and leadership that was critical in the success of any campaign or action of that type.

Several factors hindered Carew including the weather. January in England was often plagued with brutal cold, snow, sleet, rain, fog, frost, and short days that would have hindered those on the march. On the other hand, had he waited until the assigned date, the weather could have been more favorable. Based on the events that history has recorded, it appears that Carew took little or no time to prepare by securing support, issuing proclamations, and acquiring munitions and supplies needed for such a campaign. We have already reviewed the possible reason(s) that prompted Peter Carew into action, but these are only theories and no conclusive evidence is known to exist that would prove any of them. In Throckmorton's trial, a confession by Cutbert Vaughn indicated that Throckmorton was supplying intelligence from London to Carew and this might lend credence to a report from an unknown source indicating Philip would arrive before Candlemas Day, 2 February, prompting Carew into action. Whatever the reason, he jumped the gun.

With "the cat out of the bag," Thomas Wyatt most likely felt compelled to respond with action even though he had a couple of handicaps. He could have allowed the situation to cool down before launching again on a more favorable date before Philip arrived in England. As an experienced military leader, Wyatt should have known of the problems that could occur by launching a campaign at that time of the year; perhaps his confidence in securing a victory outweighed any concern.

There were a few more factors that contributed to failure as Wyatt marched to London. Wyatt spent some time at Rochester, perhaps too much, as any delay at all allowed the Queen to react better. While at Rochester, a report was made that Wyatt removed several pieces of artillery from the Queen's ships moored there. Had Wyatt considered using these ships?

It seems unlikely. Even if the tide had been favorable, and perhaps just as important, if qualified crews were available to handle such vessels, he could not have transported all of his army by ship. Nevertheless, two or three ships laden with artillery sailing down the Thames to London could have been a formidable threat, and not only to the Tower. The devastation those ships could have inflicted would have resulted in panic in London and might have provided a much different outcome. Perhaps Wyatt considered using the ships to, at the very least, cross the Thames River; it is perhaps best noted here that the Thames River was at its widest near Rochester and narrows the farther west one travels.

In a letter dated 8 February, Simon Renard wrote to the Emperor describing the events after Wyatt's capture. He mentioned that he was later told that a Venetian ship had come up the river to London and the captain gave five or six pieces of artillery to Wyatt. It seems likely that Renard was referring to London in general terms, not referring to the incident in Rochester. Renard also believed that the captain did so at the encouragement of the Venetian Ambassador, though his source was not sure enough to allow him to affirm this to the Emperor. No other account mentions what Renard told the Emperor.

However that may be, Wyatt marched, and along the way, he delayed several times, at Deptford Strand, Greenwich and South-wark. Those delays certainly allowed the Queen's forces to plan and prepare in reaction to the impending threat, and to convert many whose sentiments were against a marriage of their Queen to a for-eigner and who might have been inclined to support Wyatt's cause by any means.

Mary must be given a great deal of credit for her reactions. The half-Spanish Queen lost popularity when she announced her choice for a husband, but she responded to Wyatt's insurrection with a level of skill one would expect from a seasoned monarch. She re-mained calm and made clear decisions even when those around her believed all was lost. Perhaps Mary's most noteworthy tactic was when she addressed her subjects at Guildhall. That speech re-minded many that her actions were something that the great Henry would have done; and many, if only for a short period, forgot that she was half-Spanish. The Queen's speech changed the attitudes of many who listened and transformed hostility into cheers of sup-port; this would prove fatal when Wyatt finally entered the city hoping to find much needed backing.

Suffering from desertions, Wyatt finally entered London only as one force instead of many as originally planned. Wyatt hoped for additional reinforcements from the Duke of Suffolk, whose rath-er miserable attempt to raise support is surprising given his past military experience. He was a member of the Order of the Garter and during the reign of Edward VI served as a member of the Privy Council. As a reward for his services, he was made Duke of Suffolk on 11 October 1551. It would be safe to speculate that Suffolk was ill-prepared to undertake such a campaign on short notice, or was not fully committed to the cause, resulting in a minor contribution to Wyatt's failure. Unfortunately, Suffolk's actions not only con-demned himself, but his daughter Jane Grey, who otherwise might have been released after serving a short period in the Tower.

Finally, the last factor contributing to the failure of Wyatt's re-bellion was Wyatt himself. After finally entering London, he was advised that Pembroke's forces had positioned themselves in two different locations around St. James field, but instead of reacting defensively with his remaining forces in a manner that would be most effective, he continued to march through them, obsessed with seizing the Tower. And had Wyatt abandoned his artillery when the wheels broke, instead of taking the precious time to repair them in the cold and difficult night, he might yet have entered London with little opposition as perhaps Pembroke had not yet fully positioned his forces and ordnance.

After encountering Pembroke's men, Wyatt's forces were split and fled in different directions. Instead of allowing time for those who could reassemble to do so, he obstinately continued toward Ludgate, hoping that it would be open to him; but not only was it closed, it was well defended. Captain Bret's advice to Wyatt about being caught in a city with few means of egress certainly seems applicable now; and with no way to escape the Queen's forces that outnumbered and surrounded him, Wyatt gave up.

Analyzing his mistakes after the fact is easy. However, this is a man who could have spent the remainder of his life in relative luxury, perhaps as his father had done, in ambassadorial duties or serving the Queen in some capacity; but he stood firm on his morals in a cause that he strongly believed in, and that, by any definition, is commendable in itself.

Though some praise is due, he was nevertheless a traitor to his Queen and let many of his followers down in the end; and that was perhaps the worst punishment that he could have received. Nevertheless, Thomas Wyatt did have a few redeeming qualities that should not be overlooked. While he was in Southwark, some of his men ransacked the house of the Bishop of Winchester and this action upset Wyatt considerably. Wyatt took precautions to prevent such a thing from happening by lecturing his men on maintaining discipline and insisted that plundering would not be tolerated. Wyatt did not want to give an impression that they were common criminals and he disciplined those who ransacked the Bishop's house severely. He forced no one to join him; all did so at their own choice and believed that Wyatt was a solution to a problem.

Some speculation exists between historians as to whether Wyatt would have seized the crown for himself after Mary was locked in the Tower, but nothing is known to exist that would confirm that. Wyatt is quoted as saying that he wanted the Queen locked in the Tower and that he would replace certain members of the Privy Council with those of his own choosing. Some historians regard that statement as being arrogant enough to suggest he would pursue the crown itself; we cannot rule out the possibility. But Wyatt was also well quoted as saying that he would place Elizabeth and Courtenay on the throne, possibly hoping that the new Queen would grant him a notable position or reward him for his actions.

When Wyatt was reconnoitering the London side of the London Bridge late in the night, he startled a man and a couple others that were warming themselves by coals. Wyatt spared their lives even though one of them could have yelled out giving away Wyatt's presence. When Wyatt was in France during the 1545 campaign, he was given charge of three hundred hackbuttiers (a soldier armed with a firearm):

> "[C]oming to a gate on the first bridge he went into the door, which he [Wyatt] brake open and himself being the first man that entered, slew one of their watchmen upon the said bridge, took other twain of them and set his hackbutters in the braye about the castle." [Nott, 188]

Wyatt clearly could have done the same to those on the bridge, but he did not, probably because they were his own countrymen: an act of compassion.

During his march to London, Wyatt acquired several prisoners, all of whom were cared for and none executed, even though a couple took advantage of Wyatt's compassion by escaping, which they had promised not to do. Furthermore, though the castle that Lord Cobham attempted to defend suffered damage and it was reported that a couple of his men were killed in the skirmish, Wyatt let Cobham live and did not destroy the castle. Most certainly had Wyatt acted as a renegade in any respect, history would have recorded it.

Soon after Wyatt became a prisoner, he may have implicated the princess Elizabeth and Courtenay in a desperate attempt to receive leniency by disclosing such important information. The extent to which Elizabeth and Courtenay might have been involved remains a great mystery. It seems highly probable that both knew of the plot but would not have participated in any direct way. Though Elizabeth was questioned more than Courtenay, she continually denied any knowledge or involvement. The life of Edward Courtenay is certainly intriguing because several references are made to altered or missing documents from the period that might have proven his knowledge or involvement in the plot. During Throckmorton's trial, a confession by Cutbert Vaughn suggested that the information had leaked out by Courtenay's tailor. Some intriguing information remains about Elizabeth also, but if either was involved, the evidence has been carefully erased from history.

Many suffered for their beliefs or hopes including two of the principle leaders of the rebellion: Henry Grey the Duke of Suffolk on 23 February, and Thomas Wyatt on 11 April. The third, Peter Carew, escaped the same fate.

It has been suggested that Carew received intelligence that he was to be apprehended by any means through Edward Courtenay who was a relative of his, though rather distant. Carew dispatched several letters to the sheriff but after receiving no useful information from those inquiries, Carew sent a letter to the sheriff informing him that he was going to London to confess his actions. However, this was only a diversion and he quickly departed to a friend's house to spend the night. Carew then sent one of two of his associates to Exeter for money and the other to Weymouth to secure a small sailing vessel.

Dressed like a servant, Carew departed to Weymouth with his possessions and money. On the night before, his wife had a dream that he would drown while at sea. As he was stepping onboard the small vessel, he slipped and fell in the sea but was rescued by someone standing near by. They soon set out for France but encountered a terrible storm and forced to return to Weymouth but no one would set foot on land because they were now wanted men. As soon as the weather permitted travel and with a good wind, they set out again this time arriving at Rouen and from there straight to the court of France.

Though he was well received, accepting certain amenities offered to him would have been an admission of guilt to treason and that he would not do. He departed to Venice where he hoped to seek sanctuary in the city through an alliance established earlier in England but this proved almost fatal when Carew narrowly escaped an assassination attempt made by the same alliance and he quickly departed for Strasburg, Germany where he joined other Englishmen who fled England for religious reasons.

Meanwhile, his wife who was traveling with King Philip made several requests to the King to pardon her husband as she received only a cold reception in England with her requests. She was eventually successful and Philip dispatched a letter to Mary on 16 March 1556:

> (translated from Spanish)
>
> Most serene Queen, my very dear and beloved wife,
>
> I have already informed you how I had received the two pardons of Pedro Caro [Peter Carew]. I have desired one of them to be given to him, and have sent the other to your Highness in order that it may be cancelled. And inasmuch as his wife is now proceeding to your kingdom to obtain the execution and fulfilment of that grace and mercy which

your Highness has shown to her husband, I affectionately entreat of you to give orders that her desire may be fully complied with, and that the said lady may not receive any detriment for having remained in this country some days longer than the time prescribed by your Highness, since the delay has been owing to her having waited until I could write to you about her affairs and her husband;— which I have been unable to do until now. May our Lord preserve and prosper the royal person and estate of your Highness as I desire. From Brussels, the 16th day of March, 1556.

I kiss the hands of your Highness.

I The King. [Maclean, 183-184]

When Carew received word of his wife's accomplishment, he departed Strasburg to Antwerp because he was informed that Sir William Paget and Sir John Cheke had a message from the Queen to the King regarding him. Tricked, Carew soon found himself bound, blindfolded, and en route to England where the Constable of the Tower had already received word of their arrival and met Carew at the Tower. Carew was imprisoned in the Tower without a bed, but his wife quickly protested the conditions in which her husband was being kept. He soon had a bed to sleep on and she was allowed to visit him.

Peter Carew stood trial for treason and after several appearances before the Council where he defended himself with great skill, he was acquitted of all charges of treason and after paying a fine that his grandfather left behind at the time of his death, he was given liberty. The register of the Privy Council indicated that he was set free on 1 December 1556. Soon after, Carew regained the favor of the Queen and remained in court for several years, eventually retiring in Ireland, where he died on 27 November 1575 in Ross. His body remained in his house until 15 December, when he was taken to Waterford and buried with honors.

While reviewing material for this project I experienced a problem similar to what I faced with *The Shadow of the White Rose, Edward Courtenay Earl of Devon 1526-1556*; altered or missing documents. Of course, the majority of these involved Edward Courtenay, Elizabeth, Peter Carew, Nicholas Throckmorton, Thomas Wyatt the Elder and Thomas Wyatt the Younger, pretty much in that order.

Most intriguing are numerous references to certain letters that Courtenay left behind when he died. As I wrote in *The Shadow of the White Rose*, there is a short trail that began on 17 November 1556 in which the Council of Ten in Venice instructed the bailiff of Padua to wrap the casket (box) containing Courtenay's writings in way that would hide the contents for transportation and to perform this task cautiously and secretly. Three days later the Council of Ten voted unanimously on a motion to hire a carpenter that possessed certain qualifications and swear him to silence; then they would open the sealed casket and review all the letters inside, and later the carpenter would return the casket to the state it was in before it was opened. By 26 November, all of the letters contained in the casket were reviewed. The Council of Ten then placed a small cross on each of the letters they reviewed, then returned them to their bundles. Others were returned to their linen covers, stitched closed and placed back in the casket as they were first found so as to it appear that they were undisturbed; then the casket was closed and, in the presence of the retinue of Courtenay, sealed with his official seal.

Rawdon Brown, editor of the *Calendar of State Papers and Manuscripts. Relating to English Affairs Existing in the Archives and Collections of Venice,* indicated that of the thirty-two drafts of letters to and from Courtenay he reviewed, which at the time were preserved in the Venetian archives, dating 8 May 1555 to 22 February 1556, not one of those letters contained a cross. Based on that evidence, one could speculate that the letters were either personal or political in nature, and possibly included correspondence to or from the French King expressing a desire to place Courtenay and Elizabeth on the throne and suggesting his involvement in Wyatt's rebellion.

Perhaps the Council of Ten seized the letters by the request of the Bishop of Lodeve, then French Ambassador in Venice. The Republic of Venice would have had less motive than the French to commit such an act of state larceny by opening a sealed container.

On 21 June 1557, Doctor Wotton wrote to Queen Mary in what is the last known mention of certain letters. Wotton described an interview with a gentleman named Lant, who had some ties with the French and told a correspondent of Doctor Wotton that he had in his possession certain letters that once belonged to Courtenay. Furthermore, he was later questioned about them and denied that he ever said such a thing or ever had been in possession of letters of the late Courtenay.

There are no further indications or suggestions as to where any of the letters went, who received them, how many there actually were or additional information as to their whereabouts or the disposition of the letters marked by the Council. They were most likely destroyed forever, possibly to protect Courtenay's name and those of anyone else who was mentioned in the letters and their intrigues.

Those missing and altered documents concerning Elizabeth are certainly intriguing, as are the others. If Elizabeth or Courtenay had any involvement in Wyatt's rebellion, the evidence seems to have been obliterated. It is clear that certain individuals were careful to allow history to reflect only certain events; yet we may always wonder whether perhaps some of these letters or documents lie in an obscure collection of manuscripts yet to be discovered.

APPENDIX I. WYATT FAMILY ANCESTRAL CHART

For the most part, taken from *The Works of Henry Howard Earl of Surrey and of Sir Thomas Wyatt the elder.* By George Fredrick Nott, London, 1818-16

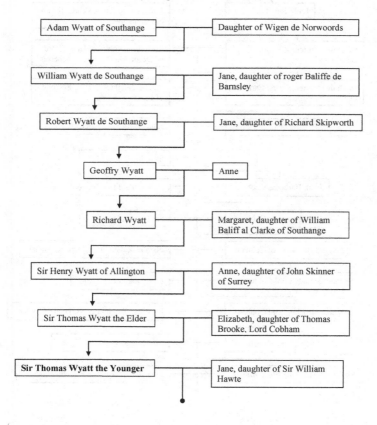

Adam Wyatt of Southange	Daughter of Wigen de Norwoords
William Wyatt de Southange	Jane, daughter of roger Baliffe de Barnsley
Robert Wyatt de Southange	Jane, daughter of Richard Skipworth
Geoffry Wyatt	Anne
Richard Wyatt	Margaret, daughter of William Baliff al Clarke of Southange
Sir Henry Wyatt of Allington	Anne, daughter of John Skinner of Surrey
Sir Thomas Wyatt the Elder	Elizabeth, daughter of Thomas Brooke, Lord Cobham
Sir Thomas Wyatt the Younger	Jane, daughter of Sir William Hawte

Wyatt Family Ancestral Chart.
For the most part derived from *The Wyatt Family of England and America with special reference to the descendants of John Wyatt of Morgan County Illinois.* .By Arah-Dean G. Finch, Nov. 1929
Table 2

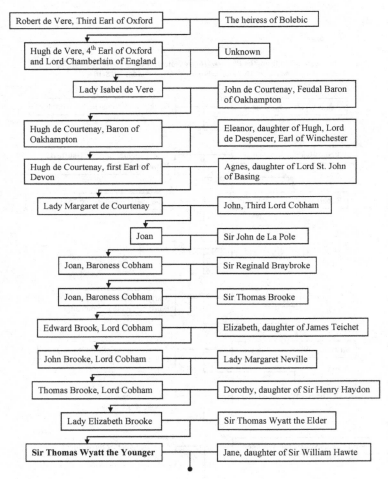

Robert de Vere, Third Earl of Oxford	The heiress of Bolebic
Hugh de Vere, 4th Earl of Oxford and Lord Chamberlain of England	Unknown
Lady Isabel de Vere	John de Courtenay, Feudal Baron of Oakhampton
Hugh de Courtenay, Baron of Oakhampton	Eleanor, daughter of Hugh, Lord de Despencer, Earl of Winchester
Hugh de Courtenay, first Earl of Devon	Agnes, daughter of Lord St. John of Basing
Lady Margaret de Courtenay	John, Third Lord Cobham
Joan	Sir John de La Pole
Joan, Baroness Cobham	Sir Reginald Braybroke
Joan, Baroness Cobham	Sir Thomas Brooke
Edward Brook, Lord Cobham	Elizabeth, daughter of James Teichet
John Brooke, Lord Cobham	Lady Margaret Neville
Thomas Brooke, Lord Cobham	Dorothy, daughter of Sir Henry Haydon
Lady Elizabeth Brooke	Sir Thomas Wyatt the Elder
Sir Thomas Wyatt the Younger	Jane, daughter of Sir William Hawte

Wyatt Family Ancestral Chart: Royal Line.
For the most part derived from *The Wyatt Family of England and America with special reference to the descendants of John Wyatt of Morgan County Illinois.* By Arah-Dean G. Finch, Nov. 1929
Table 3

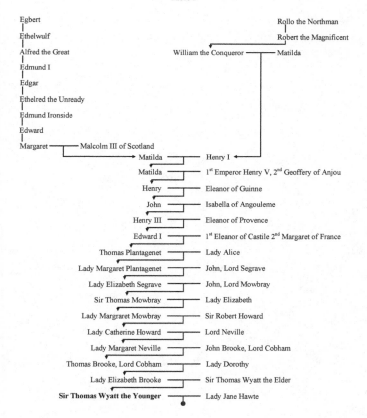

Egbert
Ethelwulf
Alfred the Great
Edmund I
Edgar
Ethelred the Unready
Edmund Ironside
Edward
Margaret ——— Malcolm III of Scotland

Rollo the Northman
Robert the Magnificent
William the Conqueror ——— Matilda

Matilda ——— Henry I
Matilda ——— 1st Emperor Henry V, 2nd Geoffery of Anjou
Henry ——— Eleanor of Guinne
John ——— Isabella of Angouleme
Henry III ——— Eleanor of Provence
Edward I ——— 1st Eleanor of Castile 2nd Margaret of France
Thomas Plantagenet ——— Lady Alice
Lady Margaret Plantagenet ——— John, Lord Segrave
Lady Elizabeth Segrave ——— John, Lord Mowbray
Sir Thomas Mowbray ——— Lady Elizabeth
Lady Margraret Mowbray ——— Sir Robert Howard
Lady Catherine Howard ——— Lord Neville
Lady Margaret Neville ——— John Brooke, Lord Cobham
Thomas Brooke, Lord Cobham ——— Lady Dorothy
Lady Elizabeth Brooke ——— Sir Thomas Wyatt the Elder
Sir Thomas Wyatt the Younger ——— Lady Jane Hawte

APPENDIX II. A TREATISE ON THE MILITIA

Thomas Wyatt the Younger composed a treatise during the time he served as a captain for the forces of Edward VI, as a result of his growing concerns over threats to the English from rivals like the French and also because of signs of domestic unrest. The treatise was presented to the Protector Somerset and the Council who approved it in principle, but it was never put into practice.

Based on Wyatt's terms in the work, such as 'the northern men' (The Pilgrimage of Grace) and several others, it is possible to date his work between January and June of 1549.

The treatise consists of eight closely-written folios in the handwriting of Thomas Wyatt the Younger, now bound together giving the appearance of one continuous work. It is clear that the work is incomplete and fragments of the complete work are missing. It is possible that these missing elements are a result of Wyatt's later attainder when his possessions were seized. The breaks in the work presented here are an approximation of the original folio breaks.

The composition and partial implementation of the treatise certainly adds weight to Wyatt's reputation as a competent military leader.

A special thank-you to the Royal Historical Society, University College, London for allowing this to be reproduced.

A Treatise on the Militia,
by Sir Thomas Wyatt the Younger

For havinge of the harnes whear thei want w [Page torn] which m[ay] doe noe hurt. Item that no man gent nor other sholde have in his house anie feilde weapon, but onlie *harneys* for his houshold servan[ts]. Item that thei goe not the tyme of their assemble oute of th[e] muster-inge place above a mile in order and armour, unles it be to the delyveri[n]ge of their weapons. Item that this chiefe Captain shall have towardes his reward because he co-meth from his provision from home fortie pounds by yere which should be gathered by the rate of the Attres' after the value paide to the Lorde. So when his yere is run oute to retorne holme and a nother to come, and in like sort to doe his office, and to have for his labour, and as this Shere is ordered so order all the rest accordingly. Wherby within short space I dare warrant that ye shall not nede either for invasion or for defence to seke for anie other souldiers then theis, nor so good can youe have for money as thei that fight for manie respectes more thein for money, for which thinge onlie the hired multitude dothe anie thinge wor-thie praise: and all this without the Kinges' charge nether for the armoure, nether for waginge ether of Captein or souldier, yet might ye nevertheles if ye wodde spare our owne nacion and fight and followe the warres, have the hired soldiers, as longe as ye might have them comodiou-slie, and yet doe it with suertie of your self seing ye are able to matche with them that youe hyre.l All whiche thinges considered withoute cause is this fonde feare and more is the evident harme that wolde come where we bye other wise ordered then the hurt wolde be of *that we feare* tho that came to pas that we feare. For as we be at this pres-ent nether Religious nor unreligious is able to hold oute the comyn Enemie. But [by] the other waie arminge bothe sides and tho that followed which I cannot devise howe it sholde, Theare ware yet hope of agreament for that we be all of one country, no multitude is so unreasonable but that thei will heare reason tolde them especiallie at a grave mans mouthe -a man of estimacion, whose name and pres-ence *presentment* wear reverent by an unspotted life, and so to come to a good conclusion a hundreth waies. And also who soever shulde assaile us thear, it wear the next waie to set us agreved against him for everie man takithe the outward Enemie for the Common Enemie of the whole, and so shall we by the means of armoure make them some plaie, but this waie being unarmed our diversitie of Religion is like to the travaile between the Ratt and the Frogg. The frogge labored to Carrie the rate over the marishe, the whiche thinge to bringe to pas she devised to tie the one end of a stringe unto her legg, and the other to be fastned unto the rattes neck, and by that meanes to have holpen him over the water. Which the Kite espyinge hovered untill the knot was knit, and suddenlie Carried them both awaye. I fear me mutche we make our selfes in like estate.

For men saie that weapon worne biddes peace and whiche beinge drawen showeth reason whi, wheare as the naked man is sone appeased and suerlie we

shall nether withe mariage nor withe money get no freindes or reputacion, nor stand so fast agrounde of libertie as by meanes of our armoure, for then shuld retorne the auncient fear of us unto our auncient enemise, when thei shall see our ancient vartue alyve againe. Then shold our olde freindes be our fast freindes, when the[y] might make some accompt of our strength, wherby we shuld be able to succer them, or defend them and yet stand fast assured of our selfes for the estimacion that we nowe have standes onlie in monie and in the situacion of our Countrey beinge so sett in the sea. As for our monie, thoughe we wear better stored therewith then we be, yet that without Armoure cannot defende it selfe, so it is nothinge whear is no armoure, no more then marchantes tho thei be monied, yet standethe there monie at the princes discression wear thei be, so is the reputacion that men have of merchantes equall with oures in that point. And as for thother that we have the seas to keape us, howe insufficient it is agenst an obstinat emperour fyers and prowde of his late victorious wonne with his armid souldiers,l or against a frenche kinge that fereth no other ill negbor but us, god knowes, for to the one in money we be not to be compayred with the other in men & monie bothe not one prince Christened is able to compare muche les we. The one hathe meanes to hier souldyers alwaies of the Swyzeres, the other hathe manie stronge nacions at his commandement, bothe which thinges we wante. And then what cause we have to trust suche mens' curtisyes, wer we be certeine of the ones malice as we that have a good plege thereof by Bullyon beinge . in our handes,z & beinge uncerteine of the others good will withe whome what our countrie will freindshipp showed him is able to doe, we may hope but assuredlie knowe not. This wot I well, that we take in hand to set up the Religion that he pulleth doune,' suerlie unto an ambicious mynd there is no better title, Then nedes of Religion as most part of men well call it. Nor better ministers of our mischif there b the supersticious Spayniard, no better procurers thereof then the malicious flemynge envious of our welthe and ease whose

merchantes profit in the comanndinge of us, how can a man then trust in suche cases whear honnor ritches, spoile, praie, and also revenge provoketh our mischif and speciallie our ill provessieon of defence.

What ruined thief is he that wold not step out of his bushe to leape on our naked man laden with golde. Wel I see noe wheare noe sewertie and also no remdie, but at youre' Lordshipes handes, and synes the suertie and remedie is in our fist, happie is that man that god hathe lent suche a fortune unto, and happie that as bothe maie and will therto knowethe the waie to doe his countrie good, and happie that kinge because he is younge, when he bathe suche a protector, that of an unarmed nacion shall restore unto him without his troble a people armed able to defende him, wherein youe shall verifie your self of protectorship with nothing more lyvelie then in this Doinge. For howe can ye defend and have not the meane and if ye defend not, so lese youe your name, and the thinge ye professed which if youe save upright by your provicion, more shall your honor be not onlie to defend, but that youe have also the defens wheare was none before. To the performance whereof to the bringinge in of so mouche welthe and honor and savegard unto us all, yet have youe lesure yet have youe space. So loose noe tyme for gods sake bringe in this armie whilst we may have it, procure workmen of suche occupacion to dwell with us to oure commoditie. Folowe occasion offered whiles ye maie. She is painted unto its balde passing quickly bye without holde to fasten on her but on the topp before which lost she is gonne, repentannce followethe and waling is to late. Howe be that there is another thinge to be answered, and because som seeme to make Reason to the contrary of this *that is saide* I must somewhat *shewe* saye to *first* theire reason that *in this saieng* saye unto me that it weare well to be armed it weare well to be exercised *but the worlde* but the worlde is channged saie thaie, Religion that hathe of longe tyme bene rooted ys suppressed and the hated trewethe is mayntained. The worlde is stirred therewith and therefore saie they my frende wot you well what you saie these be grave matters will you putt fier and towe togeether, will you displease men and then gyve weapon into there handes. Ye maie chaunce to make suche a blase as will peradventure fier the whole house. In apparaunce suerly this is a greate affraie. But whoe considerethe the thinge never shall finde more apparannce then trothe more feare then cause and this I saie tho you wolde suppose suche mallyce in the multytude, yet when it is waied what men without heddes are able to doe and synce it is knowene that heddes sufficient for the same there is none, me thinkethe the matter full annswered for takeng awaie the occasion of every harme and the harme nether increasethe nor tackethe Roote, for I see not why men sholde not nowe beinge unarmyd venture againest unarmed men.

Ensample of the northern men when all the Realme was a like ill armed and therefore I suppose that yf theare weare any so greate hardynes in mens' hartes it wolde nowe be don as well as then. Which for that it is seene they dare not, in likewiese I praie you whie sholde not the same feare holde them in quiet thoe they weare armed. For as mooche feare shold armed men gave unto armed men as unarmed men to unarmed men beside on the one side is the kinge his aucthority all the nobilyty and gentlemen of any credit unlesse it be suche as no harme is to be feared at their handes either by their symplicitie or litle knowlege, and towchinge the people alone, of themselves either they stirr not or yf theie doe there fury falethe with a lytle delaie of tyme and a while endured dothe clayme of it selfe. Without ordre they rise without ordre they are quieted and all there blase ys soone up soone downe, and yf so be they doe proceede and doe as dyd the blacksmithe it is alwaies seene that like disordered sheepe they com to the feelde and like Calves are they knoked downe. And surly it is not the least matter to wynne mens' hartes to showe what trust they are putt in when we dare put armour on their backes, in that there is no mistrust of that. They maie intend noe cause to feare the men tho they intended that,' and nevertheles so might there weapons be governed so might there exercises be had under suche heades as sholde be appointed that it weare a thinge unpossible any discorde to followe there by. The place of exercises appointed the tyme apointted of gatheringe togeather sometyme on this holyday, sometyme on that the cyrcuite of parishes appointed that shold gather togeather the captayns appointed and the weapons delivered unto them. Let them tell me nowe by there' ...... As he bathe geven unto them. Nevertheles as towchinge suche names as bene bokid thoe theie weare elect and appointed by the prince and right ripe advisers of his counsaile yet if any of the princes pryncipall Captaines maye finde by industrious examynacion that suche as be appointed to them doe lacke good will and desire to serve as men of warr they maie Right justly refuse them. So that upon the refusall other maie be provided. Howe be it to make the matter more perfect ye shall understand that the prince with his lyvetenaunte and Counsailours must before the saide pryncipall captaines be dispatched from them as before is saide, choose and appointe suche a noomber of sufficient men as they shall thinke necessarye and meete to be Commissioners to take the muster of all suche horssemen armed footemen and archers on foote as beene appointed to fynishe the noombers whiche beene before expressed. Also the saide Commissioners must be appointed by there Commissions in which shieres of the prynces Realme they shall execute there aucthorytye. Also when suche Comissioners be founde oute and appointed they are to be sworne in the prynces' presence dewly and trewly to followe the fourme of such instruccions as shall then be delivered unto them and to the intent that the nature of the saide instruccion maie appeere to followe the ordinary purpose I shall here follow[ing] under correccion shewe suche a fourme of the same as me seemethe is to be admitted for thinges convenient. First when the saide commissioners doe come into the shire which is comitted to there charge by the prynces Commission thoughe so be that by vertewe of the same they maie lefully Calle before them all suche temporall persons abiding in the same shires as be of convenient age, that is to witte betwene threescore and xvi. Yet in no wiese they ought to ellect any person of them but suche as they perceave to be not onely personable and actyve but moste specially suche as shewe them selfes desiereous and well willing to serve there prynce as men of warr. And furthermore thowghe the musters taken, the commissioners shall finde suche as shall appeere to be bothe personable and actyve, also seme well willinge and desierous to serve.

Yet and they maie knowe that the same personages be purvied of wyves and children landes or farmes above xx sterrling the yeare they are rather to be refused then taken for suche it is likenoughe that suche as be so provided will when they have a while endured the contynuall travaille and perill that is to be suffered in an army call righte lightly to remembrannce the differrence of sleepinge under an hedge and in a bedd which their wyves weare wont to make. In so muche that they have wished them selfes to be at home in there smoky houses and because suche holowe folke cannot well keepe there owne counsaille, they faile not to be the occasion that many another growe to be of the same opynion, where upon there failethe not to followe aswell danngerous perill to the Army as dyshonour and muche forlorne cost to the prynce. Wherefore yf the saide comissioners intend to execute there Comission in ordinary manner and dewe fourme, it is right meete that in all places where men be assembled to muster they cause a well spoken man yf they will not doe the feate them selfes to stand upp and declare unto the saide assemblie, that they by the princes highe commaundement and sufficiently aucthorised by his commission be comme thether not onely to choose vew and admitt all suche for soldiours as be of convenient age also personable and actyve, but rather and chiefely all suche as they perceave to be joyefull and desierous to serve there prynce as men of warr for his ordinary wages which shalbe well and suerly paied them. And furthermore it is Right meete that the saide speaker shewe unto them the intended bountye of the prynce unto all those that shall serve him dewly and trewly in the warres that is to wytt, they shall not onely by that meane obtaine favour lande and avansement to landes and ryches, but also the highe rewarde of nobylitie to them and to there heires forever. All which beinge declared unto them in ordynary manner maie not faile (yf they be men) to anymate and encorrage them to serve and suffer all suche labour travill, perill and paine with pacyence as is meete for men of warr which desire to be decorate with nobilitie honour lande and glorie.

Wherefore the saide declareacion made with suche frutefull exhortacion added to the same as shalbe thought meete the commissioners ought to ordre them selfes as hereafter shalbe specified in this treaty in place and tyme covenient for the same. For I will nowe retoorne agame to the prins beinge accompayned with his lyve tenante, also the fyve pryncipall Captaines with the Residewe of his Counsailours. For suerly those beinge togeathere and at the termes of consultacion before mencioned, it is meete that the Prynce by there moste ripe and deliberat Coun-saile choose fyve pryncipall officers which beene so meete & necessary to mynister' fyve pryncipall offices in tharmye that in no wiese any of them maie be myssed or forborne, of the whiche the firste and moste pryncipall is to be called the highe and pryncipall marsshall of the Armye,l and the second is to be called the principall master or governour of the ordynannce or Artillery and the thirde is to be called the principall treasaurer of tharmy, and the forthe is to be called the pryncipall comptrouler and the f wethe is to be called the pryncipall purveiour not onely of all manner of vittiall, but also of all suche other necessary thinges as beene meete for an Armye except all suche as appertaine to the ordynannce and artillery as hereafter it shall appeere in particuler manner in place convenient. Wherefore when the saide fyve pryncipall officers shalbe dewly ellecte and chosen, they are to be sent for, so that in the prynces pres-ence theye maye be sworne and instructe aswell to observe as to followe the saide instruccions proceedinge from his highenes pleasure to every of them in particuler manner. And for the conclusion of the premisses in as muche as concearnethe the thinges afore towched, ye shall under-stand that the Prince with his counsailors ought to sett them in suer termes vi or viii monethes at the leaste before suche tyme as the armye shalbe appointed to sett forward.

For at the self same tyme it is Requisite that suche a sufflciente some of Threasure be delivered to the pryncipall Threasorour of the warres hand as shalbe thoughte sufficient for all suche provisions as are to be made in tyme aswell for the Artillery and monicions as for all provisions belonging to the charge of the principall purveiour. Wherefore there must be chosen by the prince and his counsaile a substanciall and upright man to take charge as Threasorour of the artillery. Unto whom the before mencioned principall Threasorour of the Army must deliver of suche Threasour as he bathe receaved a sufficient porcion to thintent that provision maie be made and all thinges provided in tyme. Also the saide principall threasorour must deliver another sufficient porcion of suche Threasour as he hathe receaved to the pryncipall purveiour of victualles' and of all other necessary thinges to thintent that the saide pryncipall purveiour maie purvey all manner of thinges belonginge to his charge in convenient tyme. Also the prince and his counsayle must appointe a sufficient man to be a comptrowler of the Artillery whose office is to comptrowle all manner of thinges whiche are to be purveied for the artillery. And nowe yf I have shewed you howe many pryncipall officers & other which are to be elected and pointed by the prince him self and his counsaile, I shall here hereafter followinge shewe what under officers the saide fyve principall officers aught to choose by the knowlege & consent of the princes lyvetenaunte. And furste I will [begin] with the chief marsshall: which marshall ought to choose fowre substanciall and wiese men being knightes to occupie and take charge under him as knightes marshalles' in the fower partes of the army before appointed to be under the leadinge and charge of fowre Ligates. Also he muste choose other fowre sufficient men being Squieres to occupie under him as provost of marshalles'. Also he must choose fowre Cyvilions to heere and determyne all causes as well crymynall as personall accordinge to Right equity without hate or amyty, wrathe or mercy. In the saide fowre partes also he muste purveye iiii discreete men to be clarkes of the marckett in the saide iiii partes of the Army.

And likewiese he must purvey iiii sufficient men to be scowtemasters on horssebacke in the saide iiii partes of the Army having the charge of suche Scowtewatche as is to be kept by nighte. Also he must purvey iiii sufficient men which are to be called forage masters because all provision and distribucion of forage shalbe comitted to them. And furthermore he muste provide iiii sufficient & suer men to have charge of purveyeng and governinge of all suche guydes and spies as are meete to be had in all the iiii partes of the Army and for conclusion you shall understande that all the persons aforenamed ought to be ellecte personages in somuche that it is muche necessary that every of those be well languaged, at the leaste that he be not to learne in the language of the contrie in the whiche the prince en-tendethe to make warr. And most specially in the highe marshall himself, oughte not onely to be well languaged but also well learned in the science of Geographie and if suche one maie be found.

Also the saide highe marshall beinge an Earle ought to have the place of the first Earle of tharmy.l And if so be that a man learned in the science cannot be founde of the saide estate, it is meete that the prince emongst other thinges doe straightlye commannde him that he provide to have suche a Clarck alwaie neere him as is knowene to be connynge and ripe in the saide science of Geography. Also ye shall understand that he which is to be principall master of Artyllery ought to be a viscont or a baron either of auncient or lifte up to one of those degrees by the prince for that purpose and the same beinge sworne and instructe as is before saide muste by the consent and knowlege of the lyvetenante provyde and appointe iiii sufficient and skillfull men to be masters of Artillery under him in the iiii partes of the Armye. For likewise as the whole Arme[y] is appointed to be devided unto iiii severall partes Right so the whole Artillery with all the munycions belonginge to the same is to be devided into iiii equall partes. Also the saide pryncipall master of Artillery havinge joyned unto hym a sufficient man to be (Sv) Threasorour of the Artillery and another to be comptrowler by the prynces appointement, and havinge as afore is saide by the know-lege and consent of the lyvetenaunte fowre sufficient men beinge squieres to be masters of the Artillery under him to have the charge of the iiii partes of Thartillery he must in likewise provide suche a noomber of *[master]* gonners and other ordinary gonners as may sufficiently wielde the saide Artillery. And likewiese he must provide all suche Artificers of all sortes as beene meete not onely to associate the same but also to satisfie unto all suche necessities as maie [be] founde or chance to the army. Also he must provide him self of all manner of officers as beene sufficient and meete not onely to satisfie all necessityes under him but also of suche as must have the charge to admynister Justice emongst all suche as belongethe to the Artillery under him in the Army. Wherefore the premisses considered the principall master of the artillery beinge a Baron is to be accepted for the principall Baron of the Army. Also the pryncipall Threasorour of the Warres ought to be a baron of auncientie or lifte up to that degree for that purpose by the prynce. Whoe beinge sworne, also instructe of the princes pleasure concerninge his charge and that he have receaved a parte of the princes Threasour into his handes yn time as is before mencioned he must by the knowlege and consent of the princes lyvetenante provide iiii sufficient men to occupie under him as Theasorours in the iiii partes of the army. Also the principall comptrowler beinge a knighte also sworne and dewly instructe of the princes pleasure concerninge his charge must by the knowlege and consent of the saide lyvetenante provide iiii sufficient men to comptrowle under him in the saide iiii partes of the army. Also the principall purviar beinge also a knight sworne and instructe of the princes pleasure concerninge his charge also provided of monney in sufficient manner must by the knowlege and consent of the lyvetenante *he must choose other* provide iiii substancyall men to occupie under him in the iiii partes of the army as purviours & mynisters of all suche bredd and drinck as is to be spente in the army. Also by the knowlege and consent of the lyvetenante he must choose other iiii sufficient men to purvey and mynister under him in the saide iiii partes of the army all suche victualles' as longe to boocherye and in likewiese for all suche victualles' as longe to the powltery. Other iiii suffycient men must be purvied and appointed to. provide and mynister the same under him [in] the saide iiii partes of the Armye. Also he must purvey iiii to provide and mynister in the iiii partes of the Army all suche butter fisshe egges cheese and mylcke as is to be spent in the army.

Also he must provide iiii sufficient men by the like knowlege and consent to occupy under him in the iiii partes of
the army as purviours and mynisters [of] all suche clothe
wollen and lynnen. Also all suche garmentes reddy made
as beene meete to foornishe the necessities of the Army at
all pointes. Also he muste provide iui sufficient [men] to
be purveiours under him of all suche horsses and mares as
shalbe meete to foornishe the armye at all needes aswell for
the sadell as for drawght and carriage in all the iiii partes
of the Army. Also he must provide iiii sufficyent men to be
purveiours and distributers of all such cartes and wagyns
as shall suffice to foornishe to the carriage of all victualles'
and luggage as longithe to the armye and as for towchinge
suche drawght horsses Cartes and waggyns as must serve
for the artyllerye and such municion as dothe depende and
belonge to the same muste be purveied by suche one as
the chiefe master of Artillery shall appointe, to the intent
that yf all thinges goe not handsomly forward eche shall ne
maie laye faulte in any other but in him selfe and in suche
as he shall appointe. Also thowghe in this treaty there is
no mencion made of the eleccion of a sufficient man to be
a principall captaine of pioners, beinge of suche noomber
as is meete to foornishe suche an armye as is before appointed: yet ye shall understand that in the tyme when the
prince hathe his Counsailours abowte him and also hathe
his lyvetenante present, it is meet that the prynce and they
doe determyne not only (6v) the noomber of pyoners but
to ellecte and choose a substanciall and an expert man beinge a knighte to be chiefe captaine of pioneres.

Also when suche one is founde oute and chosen, it is
meete that he be sworne and instructe in the princes presence. And nowe that in the premisses I have declared the
manner and fourme of a princes consultacion which en-
tendethe to make an outwarde warr: Also shewed how
many and what manner of men the Princes Lyvetenante
and principall Captaines of the Army ought to be and
howe many inferiour Captaines of all sortes beene meete
to have charge and the leading of the noombers of suche
horssemen, armed footemen and archers on foote, as beene
before mencyoned aswell in grosse noomber as in particuler parte. Also [I] have partly shewed howe the Comissioners of musters ought to be electe sworne and instructe,

and furthermore howe they oughte to demeane them self-es when the people is assembled to muster before them. Also howe that the prince beinge accompanied with his lyvetenaunte, pryncipall captaines and counsailours must electe and choose the fyve principall officers before ap-pointed, also a captaine of Pioners. I will nowe retoorne againe to shewe further howe the Comissioners of musters ought to proceede in there charge: that is to wytte when they have the personages before them which be assembled to muster. And that suche declareacion and exhortacion is made and used unto them as is before towched, it is meete that before any of the saide personages be admitted and booked, that suche as beene weaponed with bowes be de-vided from suche as be weopned with pikes and holberdes: so that beinge in suche manner devided the commissioners maie see all suche as shoote with there longe bowes shoote before them one after another. And in like manner all suche as shoote with Crossebowes and handgonnes' and that muster of shootinge taken the saide Commissioners ought not onely to consider there personages and feate of shootinge but also to question with every of them as well to feede there myndes of appetite and desire to serve as to knowe howe they be purvied of wyves and children landes in farme or otherwiese, to thintente that none be writ-ten in theire bookes such as either lacke good will or be charged with wyves or children also with landes and Fer-mes above the Some of xxs sterrlinge by the yeare.

Also it is meete that all suche as shalbe booked for Ar-chers be not onely nymble shooters but also men of greate corrpulensl for suerly it is meete that all suche as shallbe appointed to use longe bowes, Crossebowes & hand-gonnes' in an armye be cleene and lighte men, for by mean of there quick channgeinge of the placis they shall righte often molest and greeve there enemyes without any greate dannger to them selfes. And one the other partie when the Comissioners shall vewe and take muster of all suche as be weapned withe halberdes and pikes they are to be cho-sen by there Fatness. So that withe the largenes of there personages they appeere to be lighte and nymble in hand-leng of there weapons. And furthermore that of them selfes theie be gladd and desierous to serve there prince in hope and truste of the rewarde and promocion before spoken of and principally that they shewe them selfes desierous and gladd as is premised. And when the Commissioners have used them selfes in all shieres Comitted to there charge and that they have founde out as many able personages aswell archers as weopned with pikes and halbardes as was appointed they must shewe unto the saide persons to what place also what daie they shall resorte unto the saide place where the generall musters shalbe made where they shalbe appointed unto suche captaines as shall have the leadinge and charging of them. And furthermore the saide personages must be warned, that when they shall appeere at the generall musters every suche as be appointed for ar-chers be purvied of a good Coate of leather on there bodies, or of suche a lighte coate of fence as shall not lett them to shoote before them nymbly when neede shall Require. Also they must be purvied of good lighte scoolles' for there heddes and splyntes for there least Armes. Also they are to be purvied of good swoordes and shorte daggers.

And furthermore every of the saide archers must be purvied of a good bowe meete for his shootinge and of a good sheafe of Arrowes, bothe of them being well cased with leather. Also every of them must be purvied of three good bowstringes which must also be cased, that they nei-ther take wete or be fraied in the carriage for and they ap-peere at the before mencioned generall musters lackinge any of the thinges before mencyoned they shall not onely be Crossed but also greveously punyshed for there offenc-es, specially yf theie be not purvied of sufficient monney to provide with all suche thinges as they lacke. For suche a man is no more woorthy to be admitted for a soldiar yf he lack any piece of harnes or necessary weapons, then is the labourer in any Crafte lackinge suche tooles as he must nedes occupye. Also they must geve like warninge to all suche as they have chosen and appointed to be weap-oned with pikes and halberdes. So that at the generall musters they faile not to be armed on the hedd armes and body with good and strong harnes, also girte with good swoordes and shorte daggers. And furthermore that those that bene appointed to beare pikes be purvied of stronge and handsom pikes, and they that be appointed to beare halbardes that they be purvied of stronge halberdes upon payne before lymitted yf they be not purvied of money as is before expressed. And the premisses thus performed the said Comissioners have satisfied sufficiently to there charge. Wherefore I will nowe retoorne to shewe howe the Lyvetenaunte and the fyve pryncipall Captaines before mencioned ought to use them selfes after the lyvetenaunte is departed from the prynce and his Counsaile.

For thowghe it is afore expressed that in the prynces presence fewe or all bookes sholde be made and delivered to the fyve principall captaynes conteynenge the names of all suche Earles Barons knightes and squieres as must have charge under them, yet it [is] not only meete that the lyvetenannte have the saide fyve principall Captaines afore him to see that the saide bookes be perfecte, But also the Comissioners of musters must bringe before them there bookes of the whole noomber of archers pikes and halberdes by them admitted and booked to thintent that he maie devide all the saide bowes pikes and holberdes unto iiii equall partes and to cause there names to be written into iiii severall bookes which himself ought to deliver to the iiii principall Captaines of the partes otherwiese called legates to the intent that when theie weare possessed of the saide bookes theie maie devide and make other bookes out of the same in suche manner and fourme as shalbe shewed in tyme convenient, for when the saide fyve captaines principall be departed from the lyvetenaunte to goe about there particuler busynes, ye shall knowe howe the moste principall of those fyve whoe is ordeyned to be moste principall captaine of horsemen ought to use himself with the booke that was delivered unto him, for m that booke there was wrytten no moo names but of iiii Earles to be Standerdes viii barons to be banners xvi knightes to be penoners and xxxii squieres to be Eittoners of horssemen. Wherefore he beinge possest of the saide booke must first calle unto him the saide iiii Earles viii barons and xvi knightes to the intent that he maie suerly knowe what noomber of horssemen he and they maie make of there owne and furthermore yf amonge them the whole noomber of horssemen cannot be well foornished the xxxii squieres must be called foorthe so that it maie be knowene what horssemen maie be made emongest them also. Yf it be seene to the principall captaine of horssemen that the whole noomber of horssemen cannot be foornishe[d] up by them he must by an aucthority geven unto him by the prynce or lyvetenante provide the rest upon the ordinannces that are made for the mayntenance of the horssemen. And when he is fully foornished of his whole noomber which risethe to iiii thowsand iiii xvi besydes the Earles Barons knightes and squieres before mencioned.

Of which horssemen there must one thowsand xxiiii of men of armes one thowsand xxiiii speares one thowsand xxiiii dymylaunces and one thowsand xxiiii archers one horsseback he must devide them into iiii equall partes So that in every party there [are] iicUxxiiii men of Armes iilxxiiii speares iiclxxiiii dymilaunces iiClxxiiii archers on horseback which great noomber being devided into iiii equall parties and wrytten into iiii severall bookes one of them is to be delivered to the first earle which is appointed to the first standerde of horssemen and likewiese the other three bookes are to be delivered in order to the other iii Earles which be pointed the iind the iiird the iiiith standerdes of horssemen: And that donne the said iiii Earles must be swoorne in the principall captaines presence and also are to be instruct by him by severall wntmges & by woorde of mowthe howe every of them oughte to devide and ordre all suche horssemen as be named in the iiii bookes delivered unto them. And furthermore when the saide iiii Earles have receaved the saide bokes also be sworne and instructed as is before saide, he that is the fyrst of the fowre Earles havinge appointed unto him by booke ii barons to be banerers and iiii knightes to be penoners and viii Squieres to be Eytoneres to have the leadinge of a thowsand xxiiii horssemen of all sortes he muste call before him the saide ii barons and deliver unto them in ii severall bookes the names of all suche knightes and squieres also of men of Armes speares dymilannces and Archers on horsseback as bene equally demded & weare delivered unto him by one booke from the principall captaine. And when the saide Barons have receaved the before mencioned bookes they must be sworne in the Standardes presence and by him instructe aswell by writing as by woorde of all suche thinges as the first standard received by instruccion of his pryncipall captaine. And that don he that first of those two barons havinge named in his book ii knightes iiii squieres to have the leading of vexii horssemen of suche sortes as is before expressed he muste calle before him the ii knightes that be appointed to be penoners and deliver two bookes unto them the names of all suche squieres and horssemen equally devided as he receaved of thearle his standard in one booke. So that every of the saide Knightes which are to be called the first and the second penoners shall have named in every of the saide ii bookes.....

[the remainder of the page is blank]

APPENDIX III. THE TRIAL OF NICHOLAS THROCKMORTON

This chapter contains a literal transcription of the trial of Nicholas Throckmorton as recorded in *The First and Second volumes of Chronicles collected by Raphael Holinshed in 1586*. The transcript was compared with the record in *Cobbett's Complete Collection of State Trials, London 1809* and, as with the trial of Thomas Wyatt the Younger, many differences were noted.

This record is a rare example of a court proceeding from a Renaissance English Tudor-period court. I feel it is an integral part of the history of Thomas Wyatt because of Throckmorton's involvement, and furthermore, because of the various confessions of others regarding the rebellion Thomas Wyatt led.

The order of the arreignement of Nicholas Throckmorton knight, in the Guildhall of London the seventeenth daie of Aprill (Tuesday) 1554, expressed in a dialog for the better understanding of every mans part.

The names of the commissioners. Sir Thomas White knight lord mayor of London, the earle of Shrewsburie, the earle of Derbie, sir Thomas Bromlese knight lord chief justice of England, sir Nicholas Hare knight master of the rolles, sir Francis Englefield knight master of the court of wards and liberties, sir Richard Southwell knight one of the priviy councel, sir Edward Walgrave knight one of the privy councell, sir Roger Holmeseie knight, sir William Postman knight one of the justices of the kings bench, sir Edward Sanders knight one of the justices of the common pleas; master Stanford and master Dier sergeants, master Edward Griffin attourne generall, master Senhall and Peter Tichbourne clearks of the crowne.

First after proclamation made and the commission read, the lieutenant of the Tower, Master Thomas Bridges, brought the prisoner to the barre; then silence was cammanded, and Sendall said to the prisoner as followeth.

Sendal. Nicholas Throckmorton knight hold up thy hand, thou art before this time indicted of high treason, and that thou then and there didst falelie and traitorouslie and conspire and imagine the death of the queens maiestie, and falselie and traitorouslie didest levie warre against the queene with her realme and also thor wast adherent to the queen'ed enemies within her realme, giving to them aid and comfort, and also falselie and traitorouslie diddest conspire and intend to depose and deprive the queene of her royall estate and so finallie dethrone her, and also thou diddest falslie and traitorouslie devise and conclude to take violentilie the tower of London, of all which treasons and everie of them in maner, forme art thou giltie or not gilite?

Throckmorton. Maie it please you my lords and maisters, which be authorized by the queens commission to be judges this daie, to give me leave to speake a few words, which dooth both concerne you and me, before I answer to the indicetment, and not altogether impertinent to the matter, and then plead to the indictment.

Bromleie. No, the order is not so, you must first plead whether you be guiltie or no.

Throckmorton. If that be your order and law, judge accordinglie to it.

Hare. You must first answer to the matter where with you are charged, and then you maie talke at your pleasure.

Throckmorton. But things spoken out of place, were as good not spoken.

Bromleie. These be but delaies to spend time, therefore answer as the law willeth you.

Throckmorton. My lords I praie you make not too much hast with me, neither thinke not long for your dinner, for my case requireth leasure, and you have well dined wen you have doone justice trulie. Christ said, blessed are they that hunger and thirst for righteousnesse.

Bromleie. I can forebare my dinner as well as you, and caare as little as you peradventure.

Shrewsburie. Come you hither to checke us Throckmortone; we will not be so used, no no, I for mine owne part have forborne my breakfast, dinner, and supper to serve the queene.

Throckmorton. Yea my good lord I know it right well, I meant not to touch your lordship, for your service and pains is evidentlie knowne to all men.

Southwell. Master Throckmorton, this talk needeth not, we know what we have to doo, and you would teach us our duties, you hurt your matter: go to, go to.

Throckmorton. Master Southwell, you mistake me, I meant not to teach you, nor none of you, but to remember you of that I trust you all be well instructed in; and so I satisfie my selfe, with (?) I shall not speake, thinking you all know what you have to doo, or ought to know: so I will answer to the indidement, and doo plead not guiltie to the whole, and to everie part therof.

Senhall. How wilt thou be tried?

Throckmorton. Shall I be tried as I would, or as I should?

Bromleie. You shall be tried as the law will, and therefore you must saie by God and by the countrie.

Throckmorton. Is that you law for me? It is not as I would, but with you will have it so. I am pleased with it, and doo desire to be tried by faithfull just men, which more feare God that the world.

Then the intrie was called. The names of the iurors. Lucar, Low, Young, Whetston, Martin, Painter, Besooike, Banks, Barscarfeld, Calthrop, Knightleie, Cater. What time the arrurnie went forthwith to master Crolmeleie, and shewed him the shiriffes returne, who being acquainted with the citizens, knowing the corruptions and dexteriteis of them in such cases, noted certeine to be challenged for the queene (a rare case) and the same men being knowne to be sufficient and indifferent, that no exceptions were to be taken to them, but onelie for their upright honesties: notwithstanding, the atturnie prompting sergeant Dier, the said sergeant challenged one Bacon, and an other citizen peremptosilie for the queene. Then the prisoner demanded the cause of the chalenge; the sergeant ansered; We need not to shew you the cause of the chalenge for the queene. Then the inquest was furnished with other honest men, that is to saie, Whetson and Lucar, so the prisoner used these words.

Throckmorton. I trust you have not provided for me this daie, as in times past I knew an other gentleman occuping this wofull place was provided for. It chanced one of the justices upon gelossie of the prisoners acquitall, for the goodness of his cause, said to an other of his companions a justice, when the jurie did appeare: I like not this jurie for our purpose, they seeme to be too pitifull and to charitable to condemne the prisoner. No no, said the other judge, I warrant you, they be picked fellowes for the nonce, he shall drinke of the same cup his fellowes have donne. I was then a looker on of the pageant as others be now here: but now wo is me, I am a plaier in that woful tragedie. Well, for these and suchother like the blacke ore hath of late troden on some of their feet: bit my trust is, I shall not be so used. Whilest this talke was, Cholmeleie consulted with the atturnie about the jurie, which the prisoner espied, and then said as here insueth; Ah ah master Cholmeleie, will this soule packing never be lest?

Cholmeleie. Whie what doo I, I prate you n. Throckmorton? I did nothing I am sure, you do picke quarrels to me.

Throckmorton. Well maister Cholmeleie if you doo well, it is better for you, God help you.

The jurie then was sworne, and proclemation made, that whoso-ever would give evidence against sir Nicholas Throckmrton knight, should come in and be heard, for the prisoner stood upon his deliv-erance, whereupon sergeant Stanford presented himself to speake.

Throckmorton. And it may please you master sergeant and the others my maisers of the queenes' learned councell, like as I was minded to have said a few words to the commissioners, if I might have had leave for their better remembrance of their duties in this place of justice, and concerning direct indifferencie to be used towards me this daie: so by your patience I doo thinke good to saie some what to you, and to the rest of the queenes' learned counsell, appointed to give evidence against me. And albeit you and the rest by order be appointed to give evidence against me, and iterteined to set foorth the despositions and matter against me; yet I praie you remember I am not alienate from you, but that I am your christian brother; neither you so charged, but you ought to consider equite; nor yet so provileged, but that you have a dutie of God appointed you how you shall doo your office; which if you exceed, will be greevouslie required at your hands. It is lawful for you to use your gifts which I know god hath largelie given you, as your learning art and eloquence, so as thereby you doo not seduce the minds of the simple and unlearned jurie, to credit matters otherwise than they be. For masster sergeant, I know how by persuasions, in forcements, presumptions, applieng, implieng, inferring, coniecturing, deducing of arguments, wresting and exceeding the law. The circumstances, the depositions and confessions that unlearned men may be inchanted to thinke and judge those that be things indiffernet, of at the woorst but oversights to be great tresons; such power orators have and such ignorance the unlearned have. Almightie God by the month of his prophet dooth concluded such advocates be curssed, speaking these words: Curssed be he that dooth his office craftlie, corruptilie, and maliciouslie. And consider also, that my blood shall be required at your hands and punished in you and yours, to the third and fourth generation. Notwithstanding, you and the justices excuse alwaies such erronious dooings, when they be after called in question by the verdict of the twelve men: but I assure you the purgation serveth you as it did Pilat, and you wash your hands of the bloodshed, as Pilat did of Christs, and now to your matter.

Stanford. And it please you my lords, I dought not to proove evidentlie and manifestlie, that Throckmorton is worthlie and rightlie indicted and arreigned of these treasons, and that he was a principall deviser, procurer, and contriver of the late rebellion; and that Wiat was but his minster. Now saie you Throckmorton, did not you send Winter to Wiat into Kent, and did devise that the tower of London should be taken, with other instructions concerning Wiats rebellion.

Throckmorton. Maie it pleasse you that I shall answer particularlie to the matters obiected against me, in asmuch as my memorie is not good, and the same much decaied since my greevous disquietnesse: I confess I did saie to Winter that Wiat was desirous to speack with him, as I understand.

Stanford. Yea sir, and you devised togither of the taking of the tower of London, and of the other great treasons.

Throckmorton. No, I did not so, proove it.

Stanford. Yes sir, you met with Winter sundrie times as shall appeare, and sundrie places.

Throckmorton. That granted, prooveth no such matter as is supposed in the indictment.

Stanford read Winter's confession which was of this effect, that Throckmorton met with Winter one daie in the tower street and told him, that sir Thomas Wiat was desirous to speake with him, and Winter demanded where Wiat was, Throckmorton answered at his house in Kent, not farre from Gillingham, as I heard saie, where the ships lie, then they parted at that time, and shortlie after, Throckmorton met with Winter, unto whome Winter said; Master Wiat dooth much as dailie he heareth thereof, dooth see dailie deiverst of them arrive here, scattered like souldiors; and therefore he thinketh good the tower of London should be taken by a fleight, before the prince came, least that peeve be delivered to the Spaniards. How saie you Throckmorton to it? Throckmorton answered; I mislike it for diverse respects. Even so doo I, said Winter. At another time Throckmorton met me the said Winter in Paules', when he had sent one to my house, to seeke me before, and he said to me, you are admerall of the fleet that now goeth into Spaine. I answered Yea. Throckmorton said, when will your ships he redie? I said within ten daies. Throckmorton said, I understand you are appointed to conduct and carried the lord privie seale into Spaine, and considering the danger of the Frenchmen, which you saie arme them to the sea apace, me thinke it well doone, you put my said lord and his traine on land in the west countrie to avoid all dangers. Throckmorton said also, that Wiat changed his purpose for taking the tower of London. I said I was glad of it, as for the Frenchmen, I care not much for them. I will so handle the matter, that the queens ships shall be (I warrant you) in safegard. Another time I met with master Throckmorton, when I cane from the emperours' ambassadors, unto whome I declared that the emperour had sent me a faire chaine, and shewed it unto Throckmorton, who said; for this chaine you have sold your countrie. I said it is neither French king nor emperour that can make me sell my countrie, but I will be a true Englishman. Then they parted. This is the summe of the talke bewixt Throckmorton and Winter.

Stanford. Now my masters of the jurie, you have heard my saiengs confimed with Winters confession. Now saie you throckmorton, can you denie this. If you will, you shall have Winter say it to your face.

Throckmorton. My lords, shall it please you that I shall answer.

Bromieie. Yea, saie your mind.

Throckmorton. I may trulie denie some part of this confession, but bicause there is nothing materiall greatlie, I suppose the whole be true, and what is herein desposed, sufficient to bring me within the compasse of the indictment.

Stanford. It appeareth that you were of counsell with Wiat, in as much as you sent Winter downe to him, who uttered unto him diverse traitorous devises.

Throckmorton. This is but coniecturall, yet with you will construe it so maliciouslie, I will recompt how I sent Winter to Wiat, and then I praie you of the jurie judge better than master sergeant dooth. I met by chance a servant of master Wiats, who demanded of me from Winter, and shewed me, that his master sould gladlie speake with him: and so withut anie further declaration, desireed me if I met Winter to tell him master Wiats mind, and where he was. Thus much for the sending downe of Winter.

Attournee. Yea sir, but how saie you to the taking of the tower of London, which is treason?

Throckmorton. I answer, though Wiat thought meet to attempt so dangerous an enterprise, and that Winter informed me of it, you cannot pretend Wiats devise to be mine, and to bring me within the compasse of treason. For what maner of resoning or proofe is this, Wiat would have taken the tower, Erge Throckmorton is a traitor? Winter dooth make my purgation in his owne confession, even now red as it was by master sergeant, though I saie nothing: for Winter dooth avow there, that I did much mislike it. And bicause you shall the better understand that I did alwaies not allow these master W'iats denises, I had there words to Winter, when he informed me of it; I thinke master Wiat would no Englishman hurt and this enterprise cannot be doone without the hurt and sloughter of both parties. For I know him that hath the charge of the peece, and his brother, both men of good service, the one had in charge a peece of great importance, Bullongne I meane, which was stoutlie assailed, and notwithstanding he made a good account of it for his time: the like I am sure he will doo by this his charge. Moreover, to account the taking of the tower, is verie dangerous by the law. These were my words to Winter. And besides, it is verie unlike that I of all men would confederate in such a matter against the lieutenant of the tower, whose daughter my brother hath married, and his house and mine alied togither by marriage sundrie times within these few years.

Hare. But how saie you to this, that Wiat and you had conference togeither sundrie times at Warners house and in other places?

Throckmorton. This is a verie generall charge to have conference, but whie was it not as lawful for me to confer with Wiat as with you, or anie other man? I then knew no more by Wiat, than by anie other. And to proove to talke with Wyatt was lawful and indifferent, the last die that I did talke with Wiat, I saw my lord of Arundell, with other noble men and gentlemen, talke with him familiarlie in the chamber of presence.

Hare. But they did not conspire nor talke of anie sturre against the Spaniards as you did pretend, and meant it against the queen, for you, Crofts, Rogers, and Warner did oftentimes devise in Warners' house about your traitous purposes, or else what did you so often there?

Throckmorton. I confesse I did mislike the queen's mariage with Spaine, and also the coming of the Spaniards hither, and then me thought I had reason to doo so: for I did learne the reasons of my misliking of you master hare, master Southwell, and other in the parlement house, there I did see the whole consent of the realme against it; and I a hearer, but no speaker, did learne my mislikeing of those matters, confirmed by manie sundrie reasons amoungst you: but as concerning anie sturre or upose against the Spaniards, I never made anie, neither procured anie to be made and for my much resort to master

Wiat, but to shew my freendship to my verie good lord the marquesse of Northhampton, who was lodged there when he was inlarged.

Stanford. Did not you Throckmorton tell Winter that Wiat had changed his mind for the taking of the tower, wherby it appeared evidentlie that you knew of his doings?

Throckmorton. Truelie I did not tell him so. But I care not greatlie to give you that wepon to plaie you withall, now let us see what you can make of it.

Stanford. Yea sir, that prooveth that you were privie to W'iats mind in all his devises and treasons, and that there was sending betwixt you and Wiat from time to time.

Throckmorton. What master sergeant? Dooth this proove against me, that I knew Wiat did repent him of an evil devised enterprise? Is it to know Wiat's repentansed sinne? No, it is but a veniall sinne, if it be anie, it is not deadlie. But where is the messenger of message that Wiat sent to me touching his alteration, and yet it was lawful inough for me to heare from Wiat at that time, as from anie other man, for anie act that I knew he had doone.

Dier. And it may please you my lords, and you my masters of the jurie, to proove that Throckmorton is a principll doore in this rebellion, there is yet manie other things to be delared: among other, there is Crofts confession, who saith, that he and you, and your complicied, did manie times devise to all his determinations, and you shewed him that you would go into the west countrie with the earle of Devon, to sir Peter Caroe, accompanied with others.

Throckmorton. Master Crofts is yet living, and is heere this daie, how happeneth it he is not brought face to face to instisie this matter, neither hath beene of all this time? Will you know the truth? Either he said not so, or he will not abide by it, but honestlie hath reformed himself. And as for knowing his devises, I was so well acquainted with them, that I can name none of them, nor you neither as matter knowne to me.

Attorneie. But whie did you advise Winter to land my lord privie seale in the west countrie?

Throckmorton. He that told you that my mind was to land him

there, dooth partlie tell you a reason whie I said so, if you would remember as well the one as the other: but bicause you are so forgetfull, I will recite wherefore. In communication betwixt Winter and me, as he declared to me that the Spanirds provided to bring their prince hither, so the Frenchmen preparred to interrpt his arrivall: for they began to arme to the sea, and had alreadie certeine ships on the west coast (as he heard). Into who, I said, that peradventure not onelie the queen's ships under his charge might be in jeopardie, but also my lord privie seale, and all his traine; the Frenchmen being well preparred to meet with them, and therefore for all events it were good you should put my said lord in the west countrie in case you espie anie jeopardie. But what dooth this proove to the treasons, if I were not able to give convenient reasons to my talke?

Stanford. Marie [exclamation] sir now commeth the proofe of your treasons, you sall heare what Cutbert Vaughan saith against you.

Vaughans confession was read by Stanford. Then sergeant Stanford did read Vaughans confessions, tending to this effect. That Vaughan coming out of Kent, met with Throckmorton at master Warners house, who after had had doone commendations from Wiat to him, desired to know where Crofts was. Throckmorton answered either at Arundell' house where he lodged, or in Paules'. Then Vaughan desired to know how things went at London, saieng; Master Wait and we of Kent doo much mislike the marriage with Spaine, and the coming of the Spaniards for diverse respeas: howbeit, if other countries mislike then as Kent dooth, they shall be but hardlie welcome, and so they parted. Shortlie after Throckmorton met with Vaughan in Paules', unto whome Throckmorton declared with sundrie circumstances, that the Westerne men were in as readiness to come forwards, and that sir Peter Carow had sent unto him even now, and that he had in order a good band of horsemen, and an other of footmen. Then Vaughan demanded what the earle of Devonshire would doo? Throckmorton answered he will mar all, for he will not go hence, and yet sir Peter Caroe would meet him with a band, both of horsemen and footmen, by the waie at Andever for his safegard, and also he should have beene well accompainied from hence with other gentlemen, yet all this will not moove him to depart hence. Moreover, the said erle hath (as is said) discovered all the whole matter to the chancellor, or else it is come out by his tailor, about the trimming of a shirt of male, and the making of a cloke. At another time, Vaughan saith, Throckmorton shewed him that he had sent a post to Sir Peter Caroe, to come forward with as much speed as might be, and to bring his force with him. And also Throckmorton aduised Vaughan to will master Wiat to come forward with his power: for now was the time, in as much as the Londoners would take his part if the matter were presented to them. Vaughan said also, that Throckmorton and Warner should have ridden with the said earle westward. Moreover the said Vaughan deposed, that Throckmorton shewed him in talke of the earle of Pembroke, that the said earle would not fight against them, though he would not take their parts. Also Vaughan said, that Throckmorton shewed him that he would ride downe into Barkeshire to sir Francie Englfields, house, there to meet his eldest brother, to moove him to take his part. And this was the sum of Cutbert Vaughans' confession.

Stanford. How saie you? Doth not here appeare evident matter to proove you a principall, who not onelie gave order to sir Peter Caroe and his adherents, for their rebellious acts in the west countrie, but also procured Wiat to make his rebellion, appointing him and the others also, when they should attempt their enterprise, and how they should order their dooings from time to time. Besides all this evident matter, you were speciallie apointed to go awaie with the earle of Devon as one that would direct all things, and give order to all men. And therefore Throckmorton with this matter is so manifest, and the evidence so apparent, I would advise you to confess you fault and submit you selfe to the queenes' mercie.

Bromleie. How saie you, will you confess the matter, and it will be best for you?

Throckmorton. No, I will never accuse my selfe unjustlie, but in as much as I am come hither to be tried, I praie ye let em have the law favourablie.

Attourneie. It is apparent that you laie at london as a factor, to give intelliegence as will to them in the west, as to Wait in Kent.

Throckmorton. How proove you that, or who dooth accuse me but thim condemned men?

Attourneie. Whie will you denie this matter? You shall have Vaughan justifie his whole confession here before your face.

Throckmorton. It shall not need, I know his unshamfastnesse, he hath advowed some of thie untrue talke before this time to my face, and it is not otherwise like, considering the price, but he will doo the same againe.

Attourneie. My lord and masters, you shall have Vaughan to justifie this heere before you all, and confirme it with a booke oth.

Throckmorton. He that hath said and lied, will not being in this case strike to sweare and lie.

Then was Cutbert Vaughan brough into the open court.

Sendal. How saie you Cutbert Vaughan, is this your own confession, and will you abide by all that is here written?

Vaughan. Let me see it and I will tell you.

Then his confession was shewed him

Attorneie. Bicause you of the jurie the better may credit him, I praie you my lords let Vaughan be sworne.

Then was Vaughn sworne on a booke to saie nothing but the truth.

Vaughan. It may please you my lords and masters, I could have beene will content to have chose seven years imprisonment, though I had been a free man in the law, rather than I would this daie have given evidence against sir Nicholas Throckmorton; against whome I beare no displeasure: but with I must needs confess my knowledge, I must confess all that is there written is true. How saie you master Throckmorton, was there anie displeasure betweene you and me, to moove me to saie aught against you?

Throckmorton. None that I know, how saie you Vaughn, what acquaintance was there betweene you and me, and what letters of credit or token did you bring me from Wiat, or anie other, to moove me to trust you?

Vaughan. As for acquaintance, I knew you as I did other gentelmen: and as for letters, I brought you none other but commendations from master Wiat, as I did to diverse other of his acquainteance at London.

Throckmorton. You might as well forge the commendations as the rest: but if you have doone with Vaughan my lords, I praie you give me leave to answer.

Bromleie. Speakee and be short.

Throckmorton. I speake generallie to all that be here present, but speciallie to you of my jurie, touching the credit of Vaughns' depositions agains me, a condemned man, and after to matter: and note I praie you the circumstance, as somewhat materiall to induce the better. First I praie you remember the small samiliaritie betwixt Vaught and me, as he hath advowed before you, and moreover, to procure credit at me hand, brought neither letter nor token from Wiat, nor from anie other to me, which he also hath confessed here: and I will suppose Vaughan to be in as good condition as anie other man here, that is to saie, an uncondemned man; yet I referre it to your good judgement, whether it were like that I knowing onelie Vaughans' person from an other man, and having nine other acquaintance with him, would so frankelie discover my mind to him in so dangerous a matter. How like (I saie) is this, when diverse of these gentlemen now in captiviey, being my verie familiars, could not depose anie such matter aginast me, and nevertheless upon their examinations have said what they could and though I be no wise man, I am not so rath as to utter to an unknown man (for so I may call him in comparison) a matter so dangerous for me to speake, and him to heare. But bicause my truth and his falsehood shall the better appeare unto you, I will declare his inconstancie in uttering this his evidence. And for my better credit, it may please you master Southwell, I take you to witnesse, when Vaughan first insinued this his unjust accusation against me before the lord Paget, the lord Chamberleien, you master Southwell, and other, he referred the confirmation of this his surmised matter, to a letter sent from him to Sir Thomas Wiat, which letter dooth neither appeare, not anie testimonie of the said master Wiat against me touching the matter; for I doubt not sir Thomas Wiat hath been examined of me, and hath said what he could directlie or indirectlie. Also Vaughan saith that young Edward Wiat could confirme theis matter, as one that knew this pretended discourse betwixt Vaughan and me, and there upon I made sute that Edward Wiat might either be brought face to face to me, or otherwise be examined.

Southwell. Master Throckmorton you mistake your matter, for Vaughan said, that Edward Wiat did know some part of the matter, and also was privie of the letter that Vaughan sent sir Thomas Wiat.

Throckmorton. Yea sir, that was Vaughan last shift, when I charged him before the master of the horse and you with his former allegatins thouching his witness, whome when he espied would not doo so lewdie as he though, then he appeareth neither his first nor his last tale to be true. For you know master Bridges, and so dooth my lord your brother, that I desired twice or thrice Edward Wiat should be examined and I am sure, and most assured he hath beene willed to saie what he could, and here is nothing deposed by him against me, either touching anie letter of other conference. Or where is Vaughans' letter sent by sir Thomas Wiat concerning my talke?

But now I will speake of Vaughans' present estate in that he is a condemned man, whose testimonnie is nother worth by anie law. And bicause false witnesse is mentioned in the gospell, treating of accusation, hearke I praie you what S. Jerome saith, expounding that place. It is demanded whie Crofts accusers be called false witness, which did report Christs' words not as he spake them. They be false witness saith S. Jerome, which doo ad, alter, [unclear], or doo speake for hope to avoid death, or for malice easilie gather he cannot speake truelie of me, or in the case of another man'slife, where he hath hope of his owne by accusation. Thus much speaketh S. Jerome of false witness. By the eivil law there be manie exceptions to taken against such testimonies: but bicause we be not governed by that law, neither have I my trial by it, it shall be superfluous to trouble you there with, and therfore youshall heare what your owne law dooth saie. There was a statue made in my late souereigne lord and master his time, touching accusation, and there be the words.

Be it enacted that no person nor persons shall be indicted, arreigned, condemned, or convicted for anie offense of treason, petit treason, misprision of treason, for which the same offendor shall suffer anie pains of death, imprisonment, losse or forfeiture of his goods, lands, and unlesse the same offendor be accused by two sufficient and lawfull withnesses of shall willinglie without violence confesse the same. And also in the fixt yeare of his reigne, it is thus ratidied as insueth.

That no person nor persons shall be indicted, arreigned, condemned, convicted or attainted of the treasons or offenses aforesaid, or for anie other treasons that now be, or hereafter shall be; unlesse the same offendor or offendors be therof accused (if they be then living) shall be brought in person before the said partie accused, and avow and maintain what they have to saie against the said partie, to proove him giltie of the treason or offense conseined in the bill of indictment laid against the partie arreigned, unlesse the said partie arreigned shall be willing without violence to confesse the same. Here note (I praie you) that our law dooth require two lawfull and sufficient accusers to be bought face to face, and Vaughan is but one, and the same most unlawful and insufficient. For who can be more unlawfull and insufficient, than a condemned man, and such one as knoweth to accuse me is the meane to save his owne life? Remember (I prai you) how long and how manie times Vaughns' execution hath beene respited, and how often he hath beene conjured to accuse (which by Gods grace he withstood untill the last houre) what time perceiving there was no waie to live, but to speake against me or some other (his former grace being taken awaie) did redeeme his life most unijustlie and shamefullie, as you see.

Hare. Why should he accuse you more than anie other, seeing there was no displeasure betwixt you, if the matter had not beene true?

Throckmorton. Bicause he must either speake of some man, or sufer death, and then he did rather choose to hurt him whom he least knew and so loved least, than anie other well knowen to him, whome he loved most. But to you of jurie I speake speciallie, and therefore I praie you not what I saie. In a matter of lesse weight than reiall of life and land, a man maie by the law take exceptions to such as he impaneled, to trie the controversies betwixt the parties: as for example. A man maie chalenge that the shiriffe is his enimie, and therefore hath made a parciall returne; or bicause one of the jurie is the shiriffe my adversaries servant: and also in case my adversaries villen or bondman be impaneled, I may lawfullie chalenge him, bicause the adversarie part hath the use of his bodie for servile office: much more I may of right take exception to Vaughans' testimonie, my life and all that I have depending therupon, and the same Vaughan being more bound to the queenes' highnesse my adversarie (that wo is me therefore) but so the law dooth here so terme her maiestie, than anie villen is to his lord: for her highnesse hath not onlie power over his bodie, lands and goods, but over his life also.

Stanford. Yea, the exceptions are to be taken against the jurie in that case, but not against the witness or accuser and therefore your argument serveth litle for you.

Throckmorton. That is not so, for the use of the jurie, and the witnesse and the effect of their dooings dooth serve me to my purpose, as the law shall discusse. And thus I make my comparison. By the civill law the judge dooth give sentence upon the depositions of the witnesse and by your law the judge dooth give judgement upon the verdict of the jurie; so as the effect is both one, to finish the matter, triall in law, as well by the depositions of the witness, as by the juries verdict, though they varie in forme and circumstance: and so Vaughans' testimonie being credited, may be the materiall cause on my condemnation, as the jurie to be induced by his depositions to speake their verdict, and so finallie ther upon the judge to give sentence. Therefore I may use the same expectations against the jurie, or anie of them, as the principall meane that shall occasion my condemnation.

Bromleie. Why do you denie, that everie part of Vaughans' tale is untrue?

Attournie. You may see he will denie all, and saie there was no such communication betwixt them.

Throckmorton. I confess some part of Vaughan' confesson to be true, as the name, the places, the time, and some part of the matter.

Attournie. So you of the jurie may peceive the prisoner dooth confess some thing to be true.

Throckmorton. As touching my sending to sir Peter Carow, of his sending to me, or concerning my advise to master Wiat to stur of to repaire hither, or touching the earle of Devonshire parting hence, and my going with him, and also concerning the matter of the erle of Pembroke, I doo advow and saie that Vaughan hath said untrulie.

Southwell. As for my lord of Pembroke, you need not excuse the matter, for he hath shewed himselfe cleer in these matters like a noble man, and that we all know.

Hare. Why what was the talke betwixt Vaughan and you so long in Paules', if these were not so, and what meant your oft meetings?

Throckmorton. As for our meetings, they were of no act purpose, but by chance, and yet no oftener than twise. But sithence you would know what communication passed betwixt us in Paules' church, I will declare. We talked of the incommodities of the marriage of the queene with the prince of Spaine, and how grievios the Spaniards would be to us here. Vaughan said, that it should be verie dangerous for anie man, that trulie professed the gospell to live here, such was the Spaniards crueltie, and especiallie against christian men. Whereunto I answered it was the plague of God justlie come upon us, and now almightie God dealt with us as he did with the isrealites, taking from them for their unthankefulnesse ther godlie kings, and did send tyrants to reigne over them. Even so he handled us Englishmen, which had a most godlie and vertuous prince to reigne over us, my late souereigne lord and master king Edward, under whome we might both faselie and lawfullie profess Gods word, which with our lewd dooings, demeanor, and living, we handled so irreverentilie, that to whip us for our faults he would send so stranger, yea such verie tyrants to exercise great tyrannie over us, and did take a waie the vertouous and faithfill king from amongst us: for everie man of everie estate did colour his naughtie affections with a pretense of religion, and made the gospell a stalking horse to bring their evill desires to effect. This was the summe of our talke in Paules, somewhat more dilated.

Stanford. That it may appeere yet more avidentlie how Throckmorton was a principall dooer and counsellor in this matter, you shall heare his owne confession of his owne handwriting.

The clerk began to read, Throckmorton desired master

Stanford to read it, and the jurie well to marke it. Then master Stanford did read the prisoners owne confession to this effect: that Throckmorton had conference with Wiat, Caroe, Crofts, Rogers, and Warner, as well of the queens marriage with the prince of Spaine, as also of religion, and did particilarlie confer with everie the forenamed, of the matters aforesaid. Moreover, with sir Thomas Wiat the prisoner talked of the brute [rumor] that the Westernen men shuld much mislike the coming of the Spaniards into the realme, being reported also that they intended to interrupt their arrival here. And also that it was said, that they were in consultation about the same at Exceter. Wiat also did saie, that sir Peter Caroe could not bring the same matter to good effect, not that there was any man so meet to bring it to good effect, as the erle of Devonshire, and speciallie in the west parts, insomuch as they drew not all by one line.

Then Throckmorton asked how the Kentishmen were affected to Spaniards? Wiat said; the people like them evill inough, and that appeered now at the coming of the count of Egmount, for they were readie to stur against him and him traine, supposing it had bin the prince. But said Wiat, sir Robert Southwell, maister Baker and maister Noile, and their [unclear], which be in good credit in some places of the shire, will for other malicious respects hinder the liberite of their countrie. Then Throckmorton should saie; though I know there hath been an unkindnesse betwixt maister Southwell and you for a monie matter, wherein I travelled to make you freends, I doubt not, but in so honest a matter as thei is, he will for the safegrd of his countrie joine with you, and so you may be sure of the lord Aburgauennie and his force. Then Wiat said, it is for another matter than for monie that we disagree, wherein he hath handled me and others verie doublie and unneighborlie, howbeit, he can doo no other, neither to me, nor to anie other man and therefore I forgive him.

Item, with sir Peter Caroe, Throckmorton had conference touching the impeachment of the landing of the said prince, and touching prouision of armour and munition as insueth, that is to sai, that sir Peter Carow told Throckmorton that he trusted his countriemen would be true Englishmen, and would not agree to let the Spaniards to governe them.

Item, the said sir Peter Caroe said, the matter importing the French king, as it did, he thoght the French king would worke to hinder the Spaniards coming hither, with whome the said sir Peter did thinke good to practise for armour, munition, and monie.

Then Throckmorton did advise him to beware that he brough ani Frenchmen into the realme forceablie, inasmuch as he could as evill abide the Frenchmen after that fort as the Spaniards. And also Throckmorton thought the French king unable to give aid to us, by meanes of the great consumption in their owne warres. Maister Caroe said; as touching the bringing in of the Frenchmen, he meant it not, for he loved neither parite, but to seve his owne countrie, and to helpe his countrie from bondage: declaring further to Throckmorton, that he had a small barke of his owne to worke his practise by and so he said, that shortlie he intended to depart to his owne countrie, to understand the devotion of his countrimen.

Item, Throckmorton did saie, he would for his part hinder the coming in of the Spaniards as much as he could by persuasion.

Item, to sir Edward Warner, he had and did become his owne estate, and the tyrannie of the time extended upon diverse honest persons for religion, and wished it were lawfull for all of each religion to live safelie acording to their conscience; for the law will be intollerable and the clergies discipline now maie rather be resembled to the Turks tyrannie, than to the teaching of christien religion.

This was the summe of the matter which was read in the foresaid confession, as maters most greevous against the prisoner.

Then Throckmorton said, sithence maister sergeant you have read and gathered the place (as you thinke) that maketh most against me, I praie you take the pains, and read further, that hereafter whatsoever become of me, my words be not perverted and abused to the hurt of some others, and especiallie against the great personages, of whom I have beene sundrie times (as appeareth by my answers) examined, for I perseive the net was not cast onelie for little fishes, but for the great ones.

Stanford. It shall be but losse of time, and we have other things to charge you withall, and this that you desire dooth make nothing for you.

Dier. And for the better consirmation of all the treasons obiected against the prisoner, and therein to proove him guiltie, you for the jurie shall heare the duke of Suffolks' depositions against him, who was a prisoner, amounting to this effect, that the lord Thomas Greie did informe the said duke, that sir Nicholas Throckmortone was privie to the whole devises against the Spaniards, and was one that should go into the west countie with the earle of Devonshire.

Throckmorton. But what dooth the principall authour of thie matter saie against me, I meane the lord Thomas Greie who is yet living? Why be not his depositions brought against me, for so it ought to be, if he can saie anie thing? Will you know the truth? Neither the lord Thomas Greie hath said, can saie, or will saie anie thing aginst me, notwithstanding the duke his brothers confession and accusation, who hath affirmed manie other things besides the truth. I speake not without certeine knowledge: for the lord Thomas Greie being my prison-felow for a small time, informed me, that the duke his brother had misreported him in manie things, amongst others in matters touching me, which he had declared to you maister Southwell, and other the examinors not long ago. I am sure if the lord Thomas could, or would have said anie thing, it should have beene here now. And as to the dukes confession, it is not materiall: for he dooth referre to the matter to the lord Thomas report who hath made my purgation.

The attourneie. And it please you my lords, and you my maisters of the jurie, besides these matters touching Wiat's rebellion, sir Peter Caroe's treasons and confederating with the duke of Suffolke, and besides the prisoners conspiracie with the earle of Devonshire, with Crofts, Rogers, Warner and sundrie others in sundrie places, it shall manifestlie appeare unto you, that Throckmorton did conspire the queenes' maiesties death, with William Thomas, sir Nicholas Arnold, and other traitors intending the same, which is the greatest matter of all others, and most to be abhored. And for proofe hereof, you shall heare what Arnold saith.

Then was sir Nicholas Arnold confession read, saieng that

Throckmorton shewed to him, riding betwixt Hinam and Crosselaund in Glocestershire, that John Fitzwilliams was verie much displease with William Thomas.

Attourneie. William Thomas devised, that John Fitzwilliams should kill the queene, and Throckmorton knew of it, as appeareth by Arnold confession.

Throckmorton. First I denie that I said anie such thing to maister Arnold, and though he be an honest man, he may either forget himselfe, or devise meanes how to unburthen himselfe of so weightie a matter as this is; for he is charged with the mater as principail. Which I did perceive when he charged me with his tale, and therfore I doo blame him the lesse, that he seeketh how to discharge himselfe, using me as a witness, if he could so transferre the devise to William Thomas. But trulie I never spake anie such words unto him. And for my better declaration, I did see John Fitzwilliams here even now, who can testifie, that he never shewed me of any displesure betwext them, and as I know nothing of the displeasure betwixt them, so I know nothing of the cause: I pray you my lords let him be called to despose in this matter what he can.

Then John Fitzwilliams drew to the barre, and presented himselfe to depose his knowledge in the matter in open court.

The atturnie. I praie you my lords suffer him not to be sworne, neither to speake, we have nothing to doo with him.

Throckmorton. Why should he not be suffered to tell truth? And why be ye not so well contented to heare truth for me as untruth against me?

Hare. Who called you hither Fitzwilliams, or commanded you to speake? You are a verie busie officer.

Throckmorton. I called him, and doo humblie desire that he maie speake, and be heard as well as Vaughan; or else I am not indifferentlie used, especiallie seeing maister attourneie dooth so presse this matter against me.

Southwell. Go your waies Fitzwilliams, the court hath nothing to doo with you: peradventure you would not be so readie in a good cause.

Then John Fitzwilliams departed the court, and was not suffered to speake.

Throckmorton. Sithence this gentlemans' declaration may not be admitted, I trust you of the jurie can perceive, it was not for anie thing he had to saie against me, but contrariwise that it was feared he would speake for me. And now to maister Arnolds depositions against me, I saie I did not tell him anie such words, so as if it were materiall, there is but his yea and my naie. But bicause the words be not sore strained against me, I praie you maister atturneie why might not I have told maister Arnold, that John Fitzwilliams was angrie with William Thomas, and yet know no cause of the anger? It might be understood, to disagree oftentimes. Who dooth confesse that I know anie thing of William Thomas devise touching the queens death? I will answer, No man for maister Arnold dooth mention no word of that mater, but of the displeasures bewixt them. And to speake that, dooth neither prove treason. Is here all the evidence against me that you have to bring me within the compassed of the indictment?

Stanford. Me thinke the matters confessed by others against you, togither with your owne confession, will weie shrewdlie. But how saie you to the rising in Kent, and Wiat's attempt against the queen's roiall person at her palace.

Bromleie. Why doo you not read Wiat's accusation to him, which dooth make him partener to his treasons?

Southwell. Wiat hath greevouslie accused you, and in manie things that others have confirmed.

Throckmorton. Whatsoever Wiat hath said of me in hope of his life, he unsaid it at his death. For since I came into this hall, I heard one saie (but I know him not) that Wiat upon the scaffold did not onelie purge my ladie Elizabeth her grace, and the erle of Devonshire, but also all the gentlemen in the tower, saieng they were all ignorant of the sturre and commotion. In which number I take my selfe.

Hare. Not withstanding he said, all that he had written and confessed to the councell, was true.

Throckmorton. Naie sir, by your patience, maister Wiat said not so, that was maister doctors addition.

Soutwell. It appeareth you have had good intelligence.

Throckmorton. Almightie God provided that revelation for me this daie since I cam hither: for I have bin in close prison these eight and fiftie daies, where I heard nothing but what the birds told me, which did flie over my head. And now to you of my jurie I speake speciallie, whome I desire to marke attentiuelie what shall be said. I have beene indicted, as it appeareth, and now am arreigned of compassing the queen'ed maiestries death, of levieng was against the queene, of taking the tower of London, of deposing and depriving the queene of her roiall estat, and finallie to destroie her, and of adherence to the queenes' enimies. Of all which treasons, to prove me guiltie, the queen's learned councell hath given in evidence these points materiall; that is to saie: for the compassing or imagining the queenes' death; and the destraction of her roiall person, sir Nicholas Arnolds depositions, which is, that I should saie to the said sir Nicholas in Glocestershire, that maister John Fitzwilliams was angrie with William Thomas.

Whereunto I have answered, as you have heard, both denieng the matter: and for the proofe on my side, doo take exceptions prove nothing concerning the queens death. For levieng of warre against the queene, there is alleged my conference with sir Thomas Wiat, sir James Crofts, sir Edward Rogers, sir Edward Warner. Against the mariage with Spaine, and the coming of the Spaniards hither, which talke I doo not denie in fort as I spake it, and ment it: and notwithstanding the malicious gathering this daie of my conference, proveth yet no levieng of warre. There is also alleged for proofe of the same article, sir James Crofts confession, which (as you remember) implieth no such thing, but generall talke against the mariage with Spaine. And of my departing westward with the earle of Devon, which the said James dooth not avow, and therefore I praie you consider it as not spoken. There is also for proofe of the said article, the duke of Suffolks' confession, with whome I never had conference; and therefore he avouched the tale of his brothers mouth, who hath made my purgation in those matters; and yet if the matter were proved, they be not greatlie materiall in law. There is also alleged for the further proofe of the same article, and for deposing and depriving the queene of her roiall estate, and for my adhering to the queens enimies, Cutbert Vaughans' confession, whose testimonie I have sufficientlie disprooved by sundrie anthorities and circumstances, and principallie by your owne law, which dooth require two lawfull and sufficent witnesses to be brought face to face. Also for the taking of the tower of London, there is alleged Winters depositions, which uttereth my misliking, when he uttered unto me sir Thomas Wiat's resolution and devise for attempting of the said peece. And last of all, to inforce these matters, mine owne confession is ingreeved against me, wherein there dooth appeare neither treason, neither concelement of treason, neither whispering of treason, nor procurement of treason.

And forsomuch as I am come hither to be tried by the law, though my innocencie of all these points materiall obiected, be apparent to acquite me, where to I doo principallie cleane: yet I will for your better credit and satisfactions, shew you evidentlie, that if you would beleeve all the despositions laid against me, which I trust you will not doo, I ought not to be attainted of the treason comprised within my indictment, considering the statute of repeals of the last parlement, of all treasons, other than such as be declared in the five and twentith yeare of king Edward the third, both which statutes, I pray you my lords, maie be read here to the inquest.

Bromleie. No sir, there shall be no bookes brought at your desire, we doo all know the law sufficientlie without booke.

Throckmorton. Doo you bring me hither to trie me by the law, and will not shew me the law? What is your knowledge of the law to these mens' satisfactions, which have my triall in hand? I praie you my lords, and my lords all let the statutes be read, as well for the queene as for me.

Stanford. My lord chiefe justice can shew the law, and will, if the jurie doo doubt of anie point.

Throckmorton. You know it were indifferent that I should know and heare the law whereby I am adjvdged, and for asmuch as the stature is in English, men of meaner learning than the justices can understand it, or else how should we know when he offend?

Hare. You know not what belongeth to your case, and therefore we must teach you: it apperteineth not to us to provide bookes for you, neither sit we here to be taught of you, you should have taken better heed to the law before you had come hither.

Throckmorton. Because I am ignorant, I would learne, and therefore I have more need to see the law, and partlie as well for the instructions of the jurie, as for my own satisfaction, which mee thinke were for the honor of this presence. And now if it please you my lord chiefe justice, I doo direct my speech speciallie to you. What time it pleased the queenes' maiestie, to call you to this honorable office, I did learne of a great personage of her highnesse privie councell, that amongst other good instructions, her maiestie charged and injoined you to minister the law and justice indifferentlie without respect of persons. And not withstanding the old error amongst you, which did not admit anie witnesse to speake, or anie other matter to be heard in the favor of the adversarie, her maiestie being partie; her highnesse pleasure was, that whatsoever could be brough in favor of the subject, should be admitted to be heard. And moreover that you speciallie and likewise all other justices, should not persuade themselves to sit in judgement otherwise for her highnesse, than for her subject. Therefore this maner of indifferent proceeding being princilallie injoined by Gods commandement, which I had thought partlie to have remembered you and others here in commission, in the beginning, if I might have had leave; and the same also being commanded you by the queene's own mouth: me thinke you ought of right to suffer me to have the statutes read openlie, and also to reject nothing that could be spoken in my defense; and in thus doing, you shall shew your selves woorthie ministers, and fit for so woorthie a misresse.

Bromleie. You mistake the matter, the queene spake those words to maister Morgan chiefe justice of the common pleas: but you have no cause to complaine, for you have beene suffered to talke at your pleasure.

Hare. What would you doo with the statute booke? The jurie dooth not require it, they have heard the evidence, and they must upon their conscience trie whether you be guiltie or no, so as the booke needeth not; if they will not credit the evidence so apparent, then they know what they have to doo.

Cholmleie. You ought not to have anie books read here at your appointment, for where dooth arist anie doubt in the law, the judges sit here to informe the court, and now you doo but spend time.

The attornie. I pray you my lord chiefe justice repeat the evidence for the queene, and give the jurie their charge, for the prisoner will keepe you here all daie.

Bromleie. How saie you? Have you anie more to saie for your self?

Throckmorton. You seeme to give and offer me the law, but in verie deed I have onelie the forme and image of the law, nevertheless, with I cannot be suffered to have the statutes red openlie in the booke, I will by your patience gesse at them as I maie, and I praie you to helpe me if I mistake, for it is long since I did see them. The statute of repeale made the last parlement, hath these words: be it enacted by the queene, that from henceforth none act, deed, of offense, being by act of parlement or statute made treason, petit treason, of misprision of treason, by words, writing, printing, ciphering, deeds, or otherwise whatsoever, shall be taken, had deemed, or advineged treason, petit treason: but onelie such as be declared of expressed to be treason, in or by an act of parlement made in the five and twentith yeare of Edward the third, touching and concerning treasons, and the declaration of treason, and none other. Here may you see, this statute dooth referre all the offenses aforsaid, to the statute of the five and twentith yeare of Edward the third, which statute hath these words thouching and concerning the treasons that I am indicted and arreigned of, that is to saie: Whosoever dooth compasse of imagine the death of the king, or levie warre against the king in his realme, or being adherent to the kings enimies within this realme, or elsewhere, and be therfor probablie attainted by open deed by people of their condition; shall be adjudged a traitor. Now I praie you of my jurie which have my life in triall, note well what things at this daie be treasons, and how these treasons must be tried and decerned; that is to say, by open deed, which the lawes dooth at some time terme. And now I aske notwithstanding my indictiment, which is but matter alleged, where dooly appeare the open deed of anie compassing of imagining the queen's death? Or where dooth appeare anie open deed of being adherent to the queens enimies, giving to them aid and comfort? Or where dooth appeare anie open deed of taking the tower of London?

Bromleie. Why doo not you of the queenes' learned councell answer him? Me thinke, Throckmorton, you need not have the statutes, for you have them meetlie perfectlie.

Stanford. You are deceived to conclude all treasons in the statute of the five and twentith yeare of Edward the third, for that statute is but a declaration of certeine treasons, which were treason before at the common law. Even so there didth remaine divers other treasons at this daie at the common law, which be expressed by that statut, as the judges can declare. Nevertheless, there is matter so licient alleged and prooved against you, to bring you within the compasse of the same statute.

Throckmorton. I praie you expresse those matters that bring me within the compassed of the statute of Edward the third. For the words be these: and be thereof attainted by open deed: by people of like condition.

Bromleie. Throckmorton you deceive your selfe, and mistake these words; by people of their condition. For thereby the law dooth understand the discovering of your treasons. As for example, Wiat and the other rebels, attainted for their great treasons, alreadie declare you to be his and their adherent, in as mind as diverse and sundrie times you had conference with him and them about the treason, so as Wiat is now one of your condition, who (as all the world knowith) hath committed an open traitourous fact.

Throckmorton. By your leave my lord, this is a verie strange and singilar understanding. For I suppose the meaning of the law-makers did understand these words: but people of their condition; for the state and condition of those persons which should be on the inquest to trie the partie arreigned, guiltie or not gultie, and nothing to the betraieng of the offense by another mans act, as you saie. For what have I to doo with Wiat's acts, that was not nigh him by one hundred miles?

The atturnie. Will you take upon you to still better [understand] of the law than the judges? I doubt not but you of the jurie will credit as it becommeth you.

Cholmleie. Concerning the true understanding of these words: By people of their condition, my lord chiefe justice here hath declared the truth, for Wiat was one of your condition, that is to saie, of your conspiracie.

Hare. You doo not denie, Throckmorton, that there hath beene conference and sending betweene Wiat and you: and he and

Winter dooth confesse the same, with others, so as it is plaine;
Wiat may be called one of your condition.

Throckmorton. Well, seeing you my judges rule the understanding
of there words in the statute, by people of your condition,
thus strangelie against me: I will not stand longer upon them.
But where dooth appeare in me an open deed whereunto the
treason is speciallie referred?

Bromleie. If three of foure doo talke, devise, and conspire togither of
a traitorous act to be doone, and afterwards one of them dooth
commit treason, as Wiat did, then the law dooth repute them,
and everie of them as their acts, so as Wiat's acts doo implie
and argue of your open deed, and so the law dooth terme it
and take it.

Throckmorton. These be marvellous expositions and wonderfull
implications, that another mans act whereof I was not privie,
should be accounted mine: for Wiat did purge me that I knew
nothing of his strirre.

Hare. Yea sir, but you were a principall procurrer and contriver
of W'iats rebellion, though you were not with him when he
made the stirre. And as my lord hare hath said, the law alwaies
dooth procure treason, or anie other man to commit treason,
of a traitorous act, as you did Wiat and others: for so the
overt act of those which did it by your procurement, shall in
this case be accounted your open deed. We have a common
case in the law, if one by procurement should disseize you of
your land, the law holdeth us both wrong dooers and giveth
remedie as well against the one as the other.

Throckmorton. For Gods sake applie not such constructions
against me, and though my present estate dooth not move you,
yet it were well you should consider your office, and thinke
what measure you give to others, you your selves I saie shall
assuredlie receive the same againe. The state of mortall life is
such, that men know full little what hangeth over them. I put
on within these xij moneths such a mind, that I most wofull
wight was as unlike to stand here, as some of you that sit there.
As to your case last recited, wherby you would conclude; I
have remembered and learned of you maister Hare, and you
maister Stanford in the parlement house, where you did sit
to make lawes, to expound and explane the ambiguities and

doubts of law sincerelie, and that without affections. There I saie I learned of you, and others my maister of the law, this difference betwixt such cases as you remembered one even now, and the statute whereby I am to be tried. There is a maxime of principle in the law, which ought not to be violated, that no penall statute maie, ought, or should be construed, expounded, extended, of wrested, otherwise than the simple words and nude letter of the same statute dooth warrant and signifie. And amongest diverse good and notable reasons by you there in the parlement house debated (maister sergeant Stanford) I noted this one, whie the said maxime ought so be inviolable. You said, considering the private affections manie times both of princes and ministers within this realme, for that they were men, and would and could erre, it should be no securitie, but verie dangerous to the subject, to refer the construction and extending of penall statutes to anie judges equitie (as you termed it) which might either by feare of the higher powers be seduced, or by ignorance and follie abused: and that is an answer by procurement.

Bromleie. Notwithstanding the principall (as you alledge it) and the precisenesse of your sticking to the bare words of the statute, it dooth appeere and remaine of record in our learning, that diverse cases have beene adjvdged treason, without the expresse words of the statute, as the queenes' learned councell there can declare.

The attornie. It dooth appeare the prisoner did not onelie intise or procure Wiat, Caro, Rogers, and others, to commit their traitorous act, and there dooth his open facts appeere, which Vaughans' confession dooth witness, but also he did mind shortlie after to affect at himself with those traitors: for he minded to have departed with the earle of Devonshire westward.

Throckmorton. My innocencie concerning these matter I trust sufficientlie appeereth by my former answers, notwithstanding the condemned mans unjust accusation. But because the true understanding of the statute is in question, I sai procurement, and speciallie by words onelie, is without the compasse of it, and that I doo learne and proove by the principle which I learned of maister Stanford.

Stanford. Maister Throckmorton, You and I maie not agree this daie in the understanding of the law, for I am for the queene, and you are for your selfe: the judges must determine the matter.

Bromleie. He that dooth procure another man to commit a felonie or a murder, I am sure you know well enough the law dooth adjvdge the procurer there a felon or a murtherer; and in case of treason it hath beene alwaies so taken and reputed.

Throckmorton. I doo and must cleame to my innocencie, for procured no man to commit treason: but yet for my learning I desire to heare some case so ruled when the law was as it is now. I doo confesse it, that at such time there were statutes provided for the procurer, counsellor, aider, abetter, and such like, as there were in king Henrie the eights time; you might lawfullie make this cruell construction, and bring the procurer within the compasse of the law. But these statutes being repealed, you ought not now so to doo: and as to the principall procurer in felonie and murther, it is not like as in treason; for the principall and accessaries in felonie and murther be triable and punichable by the common law: and so in those cases the judges maie use their equitie, extending the determination of the fault as they thinke good: but in treason it is otherwise, the same being limited by statute, which I saie and advow is restreined from anie judges construction, by the maxime that I recited.

Stanford. Your lordships doo know a case in Richard the thirds time, where the procurer, to conterfeit false monie, was judged a traitor, and the law was as it is now.

Hare. Maister sergeant dooth remember you Throckmorton of an experience before our time, that the law hath beene so taken: and yet the procurer was not expressed in the statute, but the law hath beene alwaies so taken.

Throckmorton. I never studied the law, whereof I doo much repent me: yet I remember, whilest penall statutes were talked of in the parlement house, you the learned men of the house remembered some cases contrarie to this last spoken of. And if I missreport them, I praie you helpe me. In the like case you speake of concerning the procurer to counerfeit false monie at one time the procurer was judged a felon, and at another time neither felon nor traitor: so as some of your predecesors adjvdged the procurer no traitor in the same case, but leaned to their principall, though some other extend their constructions too large. And here is two cases with me, for one against me.

Bromleie. Because you relie upon the principall, I will remember where one taking the great seale of England from one writing, and putting it to another, was adiudged a traitor in Henri the forths time, and yet his act was not within the expresse words of the statute of Edward to third. There be diverse other such like cases that maie be alledged and need were.

Throckmorton. I praie you my lord chief justice call to your good remembrance, that in the selfe same case of the seale, justice Spilman, a grave and well learned man, since that time, would not condemne the offendor, but did reproove that former judgement by you last remembered, as erronoius.

Stanford. If I had though you had beene so well furnished in booke cases, I would have beene better provided for you.

Throckmorton. I have nothing but I learned of you speciallie maister sergeant, and of others my maisters of the law in the parlement house and therefore I maie saie with the prophet *salutem ex inimicis nostris.*

Southwell. You have a verie good memorie.

The attornie. If the prisoner maie avoid his treasons after this maner, the queenes' suretie shall be in great jeopardie. For Jacke Cade the blacksmith, and diverse other traitors, sometime alledging the law for them, sometime they meant no harme to the king, but against his councell, as Wiat, the duke of Suffolke and these did against the Spaniards, when there was no Spaniards within the realme. The duke and his brethren did mistake the law, as you doo, yet at length did confess their ignorance, and submitted themselves: and so were you best to doo.

Throckmorton. As to Cade and the blacksmith, I am not so well acquainted with their treasons as you be: but I have read in the chronicle, they were in the field with a force against the prince, whereby a manifest act did appeere. As to the duke of Suffolkes' dooings, they apperteine not to me. And though you would compare my speech and talke against the Spaniards to the dukes acts, who assembled a force in armies, it is evident they differ much. I am sorie to ingreeve anie other mans dooings, but it serveth me for a peece of my defense, and therefore I wish that no man should gather evill of it: God forbid that words and acts be thus confounded.

The attornie. Sir William Stanleie used this shift that the prisoner useth now; he said he did not levie warre against king Henrie the seaventh, but said to the duke of Buckingham, that is a good quarrel he would aid him with five hundred men; and neverthelesse Stanleie was for those words atteined, who (as all the world knoeth) had before that time served the king verie faithfullie and trulie.

Throckmorton. I praie you maister attorneie doo not conclude against me by blind contraries. Whether you alledge Stanl'ies case trulie or no, I know not. But admit it be as you saie, what dooth thei proove against me? I promised no aid to maister Wiat nor to anie other. The duke of Buckingham levied warre against the king, with whome Stanleie was conferdrate so to doo as you saie.

The attornie. I praie you my lords that be the queene's commissioners, suffer not the prisoner to use the queenes' learned councell thus, I was never interrupted thus in my life, nor I never knew anie thus suffered to talke, as this prisoner is suffered; some of us will come no more at the barre and we be thus handled.

Bromleie. Throckmorton you must suffer the queenes' learned councell to speake, or else we must take order with you, you have had leave to talke at your pleasure.

Hare. It is prooved that you did talke with Wiat, against the coming of the Spaniards, and devised to interrupt their arrival: and you promised to doo what you could against them: where upon Wiat being incoraged by you, did levie a force, and attemped warre against the queenes' roiall person.

Throckmorton. It was no treason nor procurement of treason, to talke against the coming hither of the Spaniards, neither was it treason for me to saie I would hinder their comming hither as much as I could (understanding me rightlie as I meane it) yea though you would extend it to the worst, it was but words, it was not treason at this daie as the law standeth. And as for Wiat's dooing, they touch me nothing; for at his death when, it was not time to report untruelie, he purged me.

Bromleie. By sundrie cases remembered here by the queenes' learned councell (as you have heard) that procurement which did appeare none otherwise but by words and those you would make nothing, hath beene of long time, and by sundrie well learned men in the lawes adjudged treason. And therefore, your procurement being so evident as it is, we maie lawfullie saie it was treason, because Wiat performed a traitorous act.

Throckmorton. As to the said alleaged forpresidents against me, I have recited as manie for me, and I would you my lord chiefe justice should incline your injudgements rather after the example of your honourable predecessors, justice Markam, and others, which did enchure corrupt judgements, judging directlie and sincerelie, after the law and the principles in the same, than after such men as swarving from the truth, the maxime, and the law, did judge corruptlie, maliciouslie, and affectionatlie.

Bromleie. Justice Markam had reason to warrant his dooings: for it did appeare, a merchant of London was arreigned and slanderouslie accused of treason for compassing and imagining the king's death, he did saie he would make his sonne heire of the crowne, and the mechant meant it of a house in Cheapside at the sign of the crowne, but your case is not so.

Throckmorton. My case dooth differ I grant, but speciallie bicause I have not such a judge: yet there is an other cause to restreine these your strange and extraordinarie constructions: that is to saie, a provide in the latter end of the statute of Edward the third, having these words: Provided alwaies, if anie other case of supposed treason shall chance hereafter to come in supposed treason shall chance hereafter to come in question of triall before anie justice, other than is in the said statute expressed, that then the justice shall forbeare to adjudge the said case, untill it be shewed to the parlement to trie whether it should be treason or felonie. Here you are restreined by expresse words to adjudge anie case, that is not manifestie mentioned before, and untill it be shewed to the parlement.

Postman. That provison is understood of cases that maie come in traill which hath beene in use, but the law hath alwaies taken the procurer to be a principall offendor.

Sanders. The law alwaies in cases of treason dooth account all principals and no accessaries as in other offenses, and therefore a man offending in treason, either by covert act of procurement, whereupon an open deed hath insued, as in this case, is adjudged by the law a principall traitor.

Throckmorton. You adjudge (me thinke) procurement verie hardlie, besides the principall, and besides the good proviso, and besides the good example of your best and most godlie learned predecessors, the judges of the realme, as I have partlei declared, and notwithstanding this grievios racking and extending of this word procurement, I am not in the danger of it, for it dooth appeare by no desposition that I procured neither one or other to attempt anie act.

Stanford. The jurie have to trie whether it be so or not, let it weie as it will.

Hare. I know no meane so appareant to trie procurement as by words and that meane is probable inough against you, as well by your owne confession, as by other mens' depositions.

Throckmorton. To talke of the queenes' marriage with the prince of Spaine, and also the coming hither of the Spaniards, is not to procure treason to be doone: for then the whole parlement house, I meane the common house did procure treason. But with you will make no difference betwixt words and acts, I praie you remember a statute made in my late souereigne lord and masters time, king Edward the first, which apparantlie expressed the difference. These be the words: Whosoever dooth compasse of imagine to depose the king of his roiall estate by poem preaching, express words or saiengs, shall for the first offense loose and forfet to the king all his and their goods and cattels, and also shall suffer imprisonment of their bodies at the king's will and pleasure. Whosoever and for the second offence shall loose and forfet to the king the whole issues and profits of all his or their lands, tenements and other hereditanients, benefices, prebends, and other spirituall promotions. Whosoever and for the third offense, shall for tearme of life or lives of such offendor of offendors, and shall also forfet to the king's maiestie, all his or their goods and cattels, and suffer during his or their lives perpetuall imprisonment of his or their bodies. But whosoever and by writing, ciphering, or act and shall for the first offense be adjudged a traitor, and suffer the paines of death. Here you maie perceive how the whole realme and all your judgements hath before this understood words and acts deverselie and apparantlie. And therfore the judgements of the parlement did assigne diversitie of punishments, bicause they would not confound the true understanding of words and deeds, appointed for compassing and imagining by word, imprisonments: and for compassing and imagining by open deed, paines of death.

Bromleie. It is agreed by the whole bench, that the procurer and the adherent by deenied alwaies traitors, when as a traitorous act was committed by anie one of the same conspiracie: and there is apparent proofe of your adhering to Wiat, both by your owne confession and other waies.

Throckmorton. Adhering and procuring be not all one, for the statute of Edward the third dooth speake of adhering, but not of proccuring; and yet adhering ought not to be further extended, than to the queenes' enimies within her realme, for so the statute dooth limit the understanding. And Wiat was not the queenes' enimie, for he was not so reputed when I talked with him last, and our speech implied no enimie, neither tended to anie treason, or procuring of treason: and therefore I praie you of the jurie note, though I argue the law, I alleage mine innocencie, as the best part of my defense.

Hare. Your adhering to the queenes' enimie within the realme, is evidentlie prooved: for Wiat wass the queenes' enimie within the realme, as the whole realme knoweth it, and he hath confessed it both at his arreignment and at his death.

Throckmorton. By your leave, neither Wiat at his arreignement nor at this death, did confess that he was the queenes' enimie when I talked last with him; neither was he reputed nor taken in foureteene daies after, until he assembled a force in armes, what time I was at your house master Englefield, where I learned the first intelligence of W'iats stirre. And I aske you who dooth depose that there passed anie maner of advertisement betwixt Wiat and me, after he had discovered his dooings, and shewed himselfe an enimie? I had beened so disposed, who did let me that I did not repaire to Wiat, or to send to him, or to the duke of Suffolk either, who was in mine owne countrie, and thither I might have gone and conveied my self with him, unsuspected for my departing homewards.

Englefield. It is true that you were there at my house, accompainied with others your brethren, and to my knowledge, ignorant of these matters.

Bromleie. Throckmorton, you confessed you talked with Wiat and others against the coming of the Spaniards, and of the taking of the tower of London, whereupon Wiat levied a force of men against the Spaniards he said, and so you saie all: but in deed it was against the queene, which he confessed at length: therefore Wiat's acts doo proove you counsellor, and procurer, howsoever you would avoid the matter.

Throckmorton. Me thinke you would conclude against me with a mishapen argument in logike, and you will give me leave, I will make an other.

Stanford. The judges sit not here to make disputations, but to declare the law, which hath beene sufficientlie doone, if you would consider it.

Hare. You have heard reason and the law, if you eill conceive it.

Throckmorton. Oh mercifull God, oh eternal father, which seeth all things, what maner of proceedings are these? To what purpose serveth the statute of repeale the last parlement, where I heard some of you here present, and diverse other of the queenes' learned councell, grievouslie inveie against the cruell and bloodie lawes of king Henry the eight, and against some lawes made in my late souereign lord and master time, king Edward the first. Some termed them Dracos lawes, which were written in bloud: some said they were more intollerable than anie laws that Dionysius or anie other tyrant made. In conclusion, as manie men, so manie bitter termes and names those lawes had. And moreover, the preface of the same statute dooth recite, that for words onelie, manie great personages, and others of good behaviour, have beene most cruellie cast awaie by these former sanguinolent thirtie lawes, with manie other suggestions for the repeale of the same. And now let us put on indifferent eies, and thoroughlie consider with our selves, as you the judges handle the constructions of the statute of Edward the third, with your equitie and extentions, whether we be not in much woorse case now than we were when those cruell laws yoked us. These lawes albeit they were grievous and captious, yet they had the verie propertie of a law after saint Paules' descrption. For these lawes did admonish us, and discover our sinnes plainlye unto us, and when a man is warned, he is halfe armed. These lawes, as they be handled, be verie baits to catch us and onlie prepared for the same, and no laws: for at the first sight they ascerteine us we be delivered from our old bondage, and by the late repeale the last parlement, we live in more securitie. But when it pleaseth the higher powers to call anie mans life and saiengs in question, then there be constructions, interpretations, and extentions reserved to the justices and judges aquite, that the partie triable, as I am now, shall find himselfe in much woorse case than before when those cruell lawes stood in force. Thus our amendment is from Gods blessing into the warme sunne. But I requre you honest men which are to trie my life, consider there opinions of my life, judges be rather agreeable to the time, than to the truth: for their judgements be repugnant to their owne principle, repugnant to their godlie and best learned predecessors opinions, repugnant I saie to the proviso in the statute of repeale made in the last parlement.

The attornie. Master Throckmorton quiet your selfe, and it shall be the better for you.

Throckmorton. Master atturnie, I am not so unquiet as you be, and yet our cases are not alike: but bicause I am so tedious to you, and have long troubled this presence, it maie please my lord chiefe justice to repeat the evidence wherewith I am charged, and my answers to all the objections, if there be no other matter to laie against me.

Then the chiefe justice remembered particularlie all the depositions and evidences given against the prisoner, and either for want of good memorie, or good will, the prisoners answers were in part not recited: whereupon the prisoner craved indifferencie, and did helpe the judges old memorie with his owne recitall.

Sendall. My masters of the jurie, you have to inquire whether sir Nicholas Throckmorton knight, here prisoner at the barre, be giltie of these treasons, or anie of them, whereof he hath beene indicted and this daie arreigned, yea or no. And if you find him giltie, you shall inquire what lands, tenements, goods, and cattels he had at the daie of his treasons committed, of anie time since: and whether he fled for the treasons or no, if you find him not giltie.

Throckmorton. Have you said what is to be said?

Sendall. Yea for this time.

Throckmorton. Then I praie you give me leave to speake a few words to the jurie. The weight and grauitie of my cause hath greatlie occasioned me to trouble you here long, with anie prolix oration: you perceive not withstanding this daie great contention betwixt the judges and queenes' learned councell on the one partie, and me the poore and wofull prisoner on the other partie. The triall of our whole controversie, the triall of my innocencie, the triall of my life, lands, and goods, and the destruction of my posteritie for ever, dooth rest in your good judgements. And albeit manie this daie have greatlie inveied against me, the finall determination thereof is transferred onelie to you. How grievous and horible the shedding of innocents bloud is in the fight of almightie God, I trust you doo remember. Therefore take heed (I saie) for Christs' sake, doo not defile your consciences with such heinous and notable crimes. They be grievouslie and terriblie punished, as in this world and vale of miserie upon the childrens' children to the third and forth generation, and in the world to come with everlasting fire and damnation. Lift up your minds to God, and care not too much for the world, looke not backe to the fleshpots of Aegypt, which will allure you from heavenlie respects, to worldlie securitie, and can thereof neither make you anie suertie. Believe I prai you, the queene and her magistrats be more delighted with favourable equite, than with rash crueltie. And in that you be all citizens, I will take my leave of you with S. Paules' farewell to the Ephesians, citizens also you be, whom he tooke to record that he was pure from sheding anie bloud, a speciall token and doctrine left for your instruction, that everie of you maie wash his hands of innocents bloud shed, when you shall take your leave of this wretched world. The holie ghost be amongest you.

Sendall. Come hither sergeant, take the jurie with you, and suffer no man to come at them, but to be ordered as the law appointeth, untill they be agreed upon their verdict.

Throckmorton. It may please you my lords and maisters which be commissioners, to give order that no person have accesse or conference with the jurie, neither that any of the queen'es learned councell be suffered to repaire them, or to talke with anie of them, untill they present themselves here in open court, to publish their verdict.

Upon the prisoners sute on this behalfe, the bench gave order that two seargeants were sworne to suffer no man to repaire to the jurie, untill they were agreed according unto order. Whereupon then the prisoner was by commandement of the bench withdrawne from the barre, and the court adjourned untill three of the cloke at afternoone, at which houre the commissioners returned to the Guildhall, and there did tarie untill the jurie were agreed upon the verdict. And about five of the clocke, their agreement being advertised to the commissioners, the said prisoner, sir Nicholas Throckmorton was againe brought to the barre, where also the jurie did repaire; and being demanded whether they were agreed upon their verdict, answered universallie with one voice, Yea. Then it was asked who should speake for them: they answered, Whetston the foreman.

Sendall. Nicholas Throckmorton knight, hold up thy hand.

Throckmorton. Then the prisoner did so upon the summons.

Sendall. You that be of the jurie, looke upon the prisoner.

Jurie. The jurie did as they were injoined.

Sendall. How saie you, is maister Throckmorton knight there prisoner at the bar, giltie of the treasons whereof be hath bene indicted and arriegned in maner and forme, yea or no?

Whetston. No.

Sendall. How saie you, did he flie upon them?

Whetston. No, we find no such thing.

Throckmorton. I had forgotten to answer that question before, but you have found according to truth: and for the better warrantie of your dooings, understand that I came to London, and so to the queenes' councell unbrought, when I understood they demanded for me: and yet I was almost an hundred miles hence, where if I had not presumed upon my truth, I could have withdrawne my selfe from catching.

Bromleie. How saie you the rest of you, is Whetstons verdict all your verdicts?

Jurie. The whole inquest answered Yea.

Bromleie. Remember your selves better, have you considered substantially the whole evidence in fort as it was declared and recited; the matter dooth touch the queenes' highness, and your selves also, take good heed what you do.

Whetston. My lord, we have throughlie considered the evidence laid against the prisoner, and his answers to all these matters, and accordinglie we have found him not giltie aggreeable to all our consciences.

Bromleie. If you have doone well, it is the better for you.

Throckmorton. It is better to be tried, than to live suspected. Blessed be the Lord God of israell, for he hath visited and redeemed his people, and hath raised up a mightye saluation for us in the house of his servant David. And it may please you my lord cheefe justice, forsomuch as I have bene indicted and arreigned of sundrie treasons, and have according to law put my triall to god and my countrie, that is to saie, to these honest men which have found me not giltie, I humblie beseech you to give me such benefit, acquitall and judgement, as the law in this case dooth appoint.

When the prisoner had said these words the commissioners consulted togither.

Throckmorton. Maie it please you my lord cheefe justice to pronounce sentence for my discharge?

Bromleie. Whereas you doo aske the benefit that the law in such case dooth appoint, I will give it you; to wit, that where you have beene heere this daie before the queenes' commissioners and justices arreigned of the said treasons, whereunto you have pleaded not giltie, and have for triall therein put your selfe on god and your countrie, and they have found you not giltie, the court dooth award that you be cleerlie discharged paieng your fees. Notwithstanding master lieutenant take him with you againe, for there are other matters to charge him withall.

Throckmorton. It maie please you my lords and masters of the Q. highnesse privie councell, to be on my behalfe humble sutors to her maiestie, that like as the law this daie (God be praised) hath purged me of the treasons wherewith I was most dangerouslie charged: so it might please her excellent maiestie to purge me in her privat judgement, and both forgive and forget my overrath boldnesse, that I used in talke of her kighness marriage with the prince of Spaine, matter too far above my capacitie, and I verie unable to consider the gravitie thereof, a matter impertinent for me a privat person to talke of, which did apperteine to her highness privie councell to have in deliberation. And if it shall please her highness of her bountifull liberalitie, to remit my former oversights, I shall thinke my selfe happie for triall of the danger that I have this daie escaped, and maie thereby admonish me to eschue things above my reach, and also to instruct me to deale with matters agreeable to my vocation. And God save the queen's maiestie, and grant the same long to reigne over us. And the same Lord be praised for you the magistrats, before whome I have had my triall this daie indifferentlie by the law, and you have proceeded with me accordinglie and the grace of God be amongst you now and ever.

There was no answer made by anie of the bench to the prisoners sute, but the atturnie did speake these words.

The atturnie. And it please you my lords, forsomuch as it seemeth these men of the jurie which have strangelie acquited the prisoner of his treasons wherof he was indicted, will foorthwith depart the court. I praie you for the queene, that they, and everie of them maie bee bound in recognisance of five hundred pounds a peece, to answer to such matters as they shall bee charged with in the queenes' behalfe, whensoever they shall be charged or called.

Whetston. I praie you my lords be good to us and let us not be molested for discharging our consciences trulie. We be poore merchantmen, and have great charge upon our hands, and our livings doo depend upon our travels, therefore it maie please you to appoint us a certeine day for our appearance, for perhaps some of us maie be in forren parties about our businesse.

Thus much for Sir Nicholas Throckmorton arreignement, wherein is to be considered, that the repealing of certeine statute in the last parlement, was the chief matter he had to alledge for his advantage: whereas the repealing of the same statutes was meant notwithstanding for an other purpose (as before you have partlie heard) which statutes, of the effect of the chiefe branches of them have beene since that time againe revived, as by the bookes of the statutes it maie better appeare, to the which I referre the reader. [Holinshed, 1104-1117]

Note: Though acquitted of the charge of treason, Nicholas Throckmorton may have known of Thomas Wyatt's intentions; but as with Edward Courtenay, Throckmorton may have backed out, realizing that it would not be a successful campaign, before his reputation was damaged beyond salvation.

APPENDIX IV. OFFICERS OF STATE

Officers of State during the majority of the period of this book

Governor of King Edward VI and Protector of the realm.
1546-7. Edward Seymour, Earl of Hertford, declared Protector by the Privy
Council 31 Jan. 1546-7; created Duke of Somerset on the 16th of the
following month.

Great Master of the Household (afterwards Lord Steward and President of the Council.
1544. William Paulet, Lord Seynt John of Basing; created Earl of Wiltshire
19 Jan. 1550-1.

1549-50. John Dudley, Earl of Warwick; created Duke of Northumberland
11 Oct. 1551.

1553. Henry Fitzalan, Earl of Arundel; re-appointed by Queen Elizabeth in
1558; resigned in 1564.

Lord Chancellor, or Lord Keeper.
1544. Sir Thomas Wriothesley, received the great seal as Lord Keeper 22
April, and as Lord Chancellor 3 May 1544; surrendered it 6 March
1546-7.

1546-7. William Paulet, Lord Seynt John, appointed Lord Keeper 7 March
1546-7, resigned 23 Oct. 1547.

1547. Richard Lord Rich, received the seal 23 Oct. 1547; surrendered it 21
Dec. 1551.

1551. Thomas Goodrick, Bishop of Ely; received the seal as Lord Keeper 22 Dec. 1551; as Lord Chancellor 19 Jan. 1551-2; surrendered it 20 July, 1553.

1553. Stephen Gardyner, Bishop of Winchester; constituted Lord Chancellor 23 Aug. 1553, died 12 Nov. 1555.

1555-6. Nicholas Heath, Archbishop of York; received the seal 1 Jan. 1555-6; surrendered it 18 Nov. 1558.

1558. Sir Nicholas Bacon, received the seal as Lord Keeper 22 Dec. 1558; died 20 Feb. 1578-9.

Lord Treasurer.
1546-7. Edward Seymour, Earl of Hertford; patent 10 Feb. 1 Edward VI.

1549-50. William Paulet, Earl of Wiltshire; patent 1 Feb. 4 Edward VI. Created Marquess of Winchester 12 Oct. 1551. Patent of re-appointment by Queen Mary in 1553; re-appointed by Queen Elizabeth, and died in this office in 1571-2.

Lord Privy Seal.
1543. John Lord Russell, appointed by patent 3 Dec. 34 Henry VIII. Reappointed by patent 21 Aug. 1 Edward VI. Created Earl of Bedford; died 14 March 1554-5.

1555. Edward Stanley, Earl of Derby.

1555-6. William Lord Paget, pat. 29 Jan.

Lord Great Chamberlain of England.
1546-7. John Dudley, Viscount Lisle; created Earl of Warwick and made Lord Great Chamberlain on King Edward's accession.

1549-50. William Parr, Marquess of Northampton by patent 4 Feb. 1549-50.

Earl Marshal of England.
1546-7. Edward Seymour, Duke of Somerset; patent 17 Feb. 1 Edward VI.

1551. John Dudley, Duke of Northumberland; patent 20 Apr. 5 Edward VI.

1553. Thomas Howard, Duke of Norfolk; died 25 Aug. 1554.

1554. Thomas Howard, Duke of Norfolk (grandson of the preceding).

Lord Admiral.
1542. John Dudley, Viscount Lisle, patent 27 June, 34 Henry VIII.; he resigned this office for that of Lord Great Chamberlain, the latter being relinquished by the Duke of Somerset when made Protector and Earl Marshal.

1547. Thomas Lord Seymour of Sudeley; patent 30 Aug. 1 Edward VI; attainted and beheaded 1548-9.

1548-9. John Dudley, Earl of Warwick, patent 28 Oct. 3 Edward VI.

1550. Edward Lord Clinton and Say, by patent 14 May, 4 Edward VI.

1553-4. Lord William Howard, by patent 10 March, 1 Mary; created Lord Howard of Effingham 11 March, 1553-4.

1557-8. Edward Lord Clinton and Say, by patent 13 Feb. 4 and 5 Phillip and Mary; continued by Queen Elizabeth, created Earl of Lincoln in 1572, and died Lord Admiral in 1585.

Lord Warden of the Cinque Ports.

1540. Sir Thomas Cheney, Knight of the Garter. Patent 32 Henry. VIII., died 20 Dec. 1558.

1558. William Lord Cobham, died Lord Warden in 1596.

Lord Chamberlain of the Household.

154-. Henry Earl of Arundel.

15--. Thomas Lord Wentworth; died 3 March 1550-1.

1551. Thomas Lord Darcy of Chiche, Knight of the Garter April 3, 1551, Thomas Darcy made Lord Darcy of Chiche, and Lord Chamberlain for maintenance whereof he had given 100 marks to his heirs general, and 300 to his heirs males.

1553. Sir John Gage, Knight of the Garter; died 18 April 1556.

1556. Sir Edward Hastings, appointed 25 Dec. 1557, created Lord Hastings of Loughborough, Jan. 19, 1557-8.

1558. William Lord Howard of Effingham.

Treasurer of the Household.

1541. Sir Thomas Cheney, Knight of the Garter, 20 Dec. 1558.
1560. Sir Thomas Parry.

Comptroller of the Household.

1542. Sir John Gage..

1547. Sir William Paget, Knight of the Garter, resigned on being summoned to parliament as Lord Paget of Beaudesert 3 Dec. 1550.

1550. Sir Anthony Wingfield, Knight of the Garter, died 15 Aug. 1552.

1552. Sir Richard Cotton; appointed Aug. 27, 1552.

1553. Sir Robert Rochester, appointed by Queen Mary on her accession, Aug. 1553.

1557. Sir Thomas Cornwallis; appointed 25 Dec. 1557.

1558. Sir Thomas Parry; made Treasurer in 1560.

1560. Sir Edward Rogers; he died Comptroller in 1565.

Vice-Chamberlain and Captain of the guard.

154-. Sir Anthony Wingfield, Knight of the Garter, made comptroller Dec.1550.

1550. Sir Thomas Darcy. Promoted to be Lord Chamberlain 1551.

1551. Sir John Gates. Vice-Chamberain and Captain of the Guard. Sent prisoner to the Tower: 25 July, 1553.

1553. Sir Thomas Jerningham, appointed 31 July, 1553, promoted to be Master of the Horses, 25 Dec.1557.

1557. Sir Henry Bedingfeld, appointed 25 Dec. 1557.

1558. Sir Edward Rogers; afterwards Comptroller in 1560.

1560. Sir Francis Knollys.

Cofferer of the Household.

1547. Sir Edmond Peckham (among the council nominated in the patent of the protectorship). Still in office 1553, and probably to the death of King Edward.

1557. Sir Richard Freston. Died Jan. 1557-8

1558. Michael Wentworth Esquire. Died Oct. 1558.

Master of the Horses.

1539-40. Sir Anthony Browne, Knight of the Garter; appointed 12 March 1539-40; died 6 May, 1548.

1548. Sir William Herbert, created Earl of Pembroke 10 Oct. 1551.

1552. John Dudley, Earl of Warwick; sent prisoner to the Tower 25 July 1553.

1553. Sir Edward Hastings, appointed July 1553; promoted to be Lord Chamberlain.

1557. Sir Henry Jerningham, appointed 25 Dec. 1557.

1558. Lord Robert Dudley.

Lord Chamberlain to the Prince of *Spain*

1554. Sir John Williams, Lord Williams of Thame, 8 April, 1554.

Master of the Prince of Spain's Horses.

1554. Sir Anthony Browne 8 April 1554; created Viscount Montagu 27 Sept. following.

Constable of the Tower of London.

1540. Sir John Gage, Knight of the Garter, patent. 32 Henry VIII.

Lieutenant of the Tower of London.

154-. Sir John Markham; removed by the Council of Warwick's party in Oct. 1549.

1549. Sir Leonard Chamberlain, Sir John Markham, again.

1551. Sir Arthur Darcy.

1553. Sir James Crofts?

1553. Sir John Brydges.

1556. Sir Robert Oxenbridge.

1559 and 1561-2 Sir Edward Warner.

APPENDIX V. RELEVANT CORRESPONDENCE

This appendix contains correspondence relating to and or about Thomas Wyatt the Younger, and though they do not fit in with the main body of the book, they shed additional light on the subject and are included here. The first three letters were written during the time Thomas Wyatt the Younger served in Boulogne while he was a member of the council.

Letter I. From the Council at Boulogne to the King

It may like your most Excellent Majesty,

That whereas Sir Thomas Palmer hath declared unto us your Majesty's contentation upon our humble suit, t' appoint some worthy man to be his Lieutenant for the more surety of the piece in his absence, and the discharge of our duties for all events; We have thought it good, most humbly to recommend unto your Highness Mr. Crofts, late Water Bailiff of this town, and in the consideration of th' abatement of superfluous charges, discharged by Mr. Southwell, and me the Earl of Surrey; assuring your Highness that his service hath been such, both for his diligence and hardiness, that he meriteth to be recommended most humbly to your Highness for one of the most worthy gentlemen of this town: beseeching your Majesty to be his good and gracious Lord, and that the rather, at our humble intercession it may please your Highness to admit him to that place; and that your Majesty will think that no other private affection than the service of your Highness causeth us to make this motion; which maketh us bold to be suitors to your, Majesty, to th' intent every other by the preferment of him may be encouraged to serve well. And thus we pray to God to preserve your most excellent Majesty. From your Highness's Town of Boulogne, this 10th of February, 1546. Your Majesty's most humble and obedient Servant and Subjects,

H. SURREY. John Brygate, Thomas Wyatt, Thomas Palmer, Rauf Ellerker, Richard Wyndebanck [Nott, 204]

Letter II. From the Council of Boulogne to the King.

It may like your most excellent Majesty to be advertised; that whereas this bearer, Sir Richard Wingfield, was taken prisoner in the great service that was done unto your Majesty what time the Frenchmen were repulsed in their camisado out of Base Boulogne; and hath remained ever since in th' enemy's hands by the space of seventeen months; he is now returned ransomed so high, that scarce all that the poor Gentleman hath to be sold will suffice to redeem him. We are [therefore] so bold, trusting in the natural clemency of your Highness, most humbly to recommend his service unto your Majesty, [if] it may please the same to shew your most gracious favour towards him; which shall encourage all others your Highness's subjects to adventure their lives in the service of so noble and thankful a Prince, as never yet left acceptable service unrewarded. And thus we pray to God to preserve your most excellent Majesty. From your Highness' town of Boulogne, this 8th of March, 1545.

Your Majesty's most humble, and obedient servants, and subjects,

H. Surrey, John Bryggys, Hugh Powlett, Thomas Wyatt, Rychard Caundysche, Rauf Ellerker, Thomas Palmer, Rychard Wyndebancke

To the King's most excellent Majesty. [Nott, 213]

Letter III. The Earl of Surrey to Mr. Secretary Paget.

It may like you to understand; that I have received your letters of the thirteenth of this present, wherein you require to know our numbers, and what supplement of men of war we desire; wherein I cannot speak unless I touch Rogers' charge; that is to say, the strength of the pieces.

At such time as there was hope of the reforming of the Castle Brays, at the first reducing of the Base Town into a Citadel, in respect only of landing of the victuals, when it was concluded to finish the Young Man to be a cavalier over the same, there was a plan devised by me and penned by Mr. Southwell, for the winter garrison in such season as th' enemy could not keep the field, to th' intent his Majesty's charges might be aleived, and the victual spared until the year should open: at which time it was thought his Majesty would resolve with what numbers his pieces might be defended. According to the said plat, I and Mr. Southwell, by th' authority of our commission, in the month of January (for sooner we could not cass the rest for lack of money) established in the High Town and Castle five ensigns of three hundred men a piece; whereof four ordinary, and one extraordinary; in the Citadel three ensigns; and in th' Old Man three: which could never yet amount unto the number of five hundred; not only for lack of men (for many come over hither daily) but for lack of lodging. Wherein how often I have desired Rogers' help, who hath th' only charge of all his Majesty's fortifications, works, and reparations here, I have good witness; and yet nothing redressed, save that th' expectation of the summer maketh the soldiers the better content them with their misery. And for th' extraordinary ensign within the High Town, it was reserved, upon a letter that I have to shew from my Lords of the Council, that I should cass no able men strangers, or English, for the better furniture also of the Castle Bray, yet unfurnished; and to supply the wants of th' Old Man, for any sudden attempt as occasion should serve, albeit the fortress were not able to lodge them.

And now, Mr. Secretary, as one that neither dare keep silence, nor meddle in those things that are excluded out of my charge, I can do yet no less in discharge of my duty but revoke my consent from the plat of this garrison devised by me; considering that the Young Man is dampned; and in place thereof another work devised of more travail and charge, and as me seemeth of more danger, and less defence. Most humbly now referring unto his Majesty what numbers shall suffice for the surety of the pieces in all seasons; whereas I durst not take upon me to speak for the summer garrison, so the fortifications being now altered, I cannot think the winter garrison by me devised meet. Beseeching you to think that if the zeal that I bear to his Majesty's service did not touch me, I would be loth to speak like an ignorant fool in things that are before weighed and considered by men of more experience.

And for th' Old Base Town, methinketh it were good his Majesty resolved whether the same should be kept, or raised. If to be kept, the strangers that now only lodge in the same, as I told my Lord of Hertford and my Lord Admiral, being so few, and the place so are rather a prey to provoke th' enemy, and to put the citadel in danger, than for the surety of the same. If to be raised, to be then considered by his Majesty, whether the citadel may stand by itself: and if so, then the charge of the strangers to be alieved. I desired Rogers also at his last being with his Majesty, to move the same for a trench to be drawn for the Town Guyet to the bulwark of the citadel next the town. So to reduce th' old Base Town into a less room, for that so few men cannot suffice to keep the whole. For answer whereunto he declared to me at his return, that albeit his Majesty's pleasure was the strangers should be lodged there, there should yet be no such trench drawn.

And now touching Base Boulogne, I have not only declared my fantesy but the mind of Mr. Wyatt also, whom next to me the matter importeth most, as it shall appear by his letters sent unto you. And herewith you shall receive the whole numbers of the garrison of this town, which it shall please his Majesty to supply, as soon and in such sort as the same shall think good: mistrusting not but his Highness most prudently considereth that it were not meet the state of this jewel should depend upon the success of any other enterprize; but to be furnished of men and victuals of himself: which, how time, th' enemy, and the visitation of God may waste, the year past may serve you for a precedent: and to consider, that his Majesty's army at Ambleteuse, which only I hear of [by] Rogers, six miles distant from us, and divided by two rivers, can hardly prevent a puissant enemy (that hath his country at his back) to follow such attempts as he hath determined against this town. And if he begin now to assemble his army, as I hear, to fortify at Estaples, by likelihood he mindeth to lose nothing by prevention: assuring you, that by that I can gather by all intelligences he mindeth this year to shew his puissance.

This day we had with them of the fortress a great skirmish, if I shall call it so, but rather a charge; and now I see that the Frenchmen can run as fast away up the hill, as the Englishmen not long ago ran down. The leaders of the footmen was Salerne and Captain Arden, whose wise and hardy service, with the circumstance of the rest, I refer to the credit of this bearer, Sir Andrew Flammock; beseeching you that the two Colonels may, to encourage them, receive their thanks accordingly: and at the writing hereof, I wished that at your being here, when you desired to see a skirmish, I could have shewed you the like.

There was taken a vessel laden with spades and shovels; but all the pioneers embarked are arrived here without any letter of direction. Salerne most humbly contenteth himself with his Majesty's order, and desireth only his Majesty's letters to recover such soldiers as are embezzled hence by the new Captains.

I rejoice with you the taking of Courteney, and in the grace that God hath given our master, in that never yet attempt of treason against his Royal person took effect.

Finally, I recommend unto you poor Sir Andrew Flammock; whose service, as I observed in the town and field, hath been always of such sort as me thinketh he that well deserved to be defended from proverty now in his old days.

And thus wishing you that which your gentle heart most desireth, I bid you heartily well to fare. From boulogne, 15 March, 1546.

Your assured loving friend,

H. Surrey. [Nott, 220-224]

The Lane Letters

Following are a couple of letters from a larger collection first published in *Lady Jane Grey, an Historical Tale in 2 volumes*, printed for William Lane by the Minerva Press in 1791. That book contains one hundred and ninety-one pages with no mention of the source of the thirty-two "Lane" letters it contains. Lady Jane Grey is the main character in all thirty-two letters. Others mention Peter Carew and the two included here mention Thomas Wyatt the Younger. If the letters were genuine, it would represent a treasure indeed. However, the title calls the collection a "tale," inviting the interpretation that this amounts to a historical novel rather than a historical treatise. Still, there may be something we can learn from them.

My review of three of the five known copies of the book did not shed light on their source, as all three books are identical. However, there are records of the Minerva Press contained in *The Minerva Press 1790–1820* by Dorothy Blakey, PhD, 1939. Blakey reviewed all the known publications that the Minerva Press released and the sources used in those publications, but regarding *Lady Jane Grey an Historical Tale*, Blakey indicated, "no conjecture as to the authorship can be offered." Quite possibly William Lane purchased the original manuscript from an anonymous source while he was at the Minerva Press. This may be supported by this quote from *The Star* in the 26 June 1792 issue: "This may well be called the age of Novels, when Lane, at Minerva, Leadenhall-Street, has paid near two-thousand pounds for manuscripts."

The letters are controversial because the sources are unknown, and they might be said to resemble excerpts from a romance novel. It is probable they are fiction; this is why they have been separated from the main body of this work. However, there is a chance that the letters may in part be based on some obscure information otherwise lost in history. As well, they may add some shadings as we reconstruct in our imaginations the events and relations of the times. They have been included in this biography because they do contain interesting information and for the questions that they may prompt.

Letter 22 is as follows:

Again is this unhappy kingdom torn to pieces by a civil war. The Queen is about to form a Spanish alliance: the people are incensed at it, as Don Philip is a foreigner and a Catholic, and have been induced to take up arms: in many different counties are they shedding each other's blood with utmost violence. – How prophetic my fears, that we should not long enjoy the peaceful domestic pleasures which I described to you in my last letter.

The Duke of Suffolk has quitted us for some days past: we have a thousand apprehensions, lest he should be persuaded to join the insurgents. The Duchess has sent messengers every where, but cannot hear any tidings of him, where he usually resorted.

Both Lady Jane, and her Lord, most sincerely wish their father to forbear all pursuits of ambition, by which his family have suffered so much: he is not formed for them: in domestic life he is truly amiable; there he shines in every character; but he has never yet done so in a public one. We all, with the greatest impatience, wait the return of the messengers.

Since I wrote the above, the Earl of Devonshire has been here, and has confirmed our fears; informing us, that the Duke has indeed been prevailed on to join the male-contents. As soon as he heard of it, he flew to acquaint us with it, and prepare us for what might be the event. I cannot describe to you the grief of this family, and our suspense is almost intolerable.

Lord Guildford is very desirous of joining his father-in-law, but we all, with the greatest earnestness, entreat he will not. My father and uncle are with him, I find, which distracts me a thousand fears for their safety.

I will not conclude this letter, till I have further information; God grant it may be fortunate. Adieu.

CONTINUATION

Ah, my friend! new scenes of horror are preparing for us. My silence has been a long one, and the vicissitudes numerous, which have filled up the time since I began this letter. The consequent alarm, and anxious suspense in which it has kept my mind, would not permit me to finish it.

The Duke of Norfolk is taken, in endeavoring to raise the people of Warwick and Leicester, where his interest lay. He was pursued at the head of three hundred horse, obliged to disperse his followers, and fly to conceal himself; but his concealment was soon discovered, and he was carried prisoner to London.

As the Duke was encouraged to join the rebels by their promises to restore Lady Jane, if they succeeded, to the throne, you may imagine that the Queen's resentment is highly irritated against him and his family. The other male-contents are also subdued; and Sir Thomas Wyatt, the principle instigator of the rebellion, is condemned and executed. Four hundred persons are said to have suffered in this insurrection, and as many more were pardoned by the Queen, to whom they were conducted with ropes about their necks.

I have no hope remaining, that either the Duke of Suffolk, or his children, will be spared; and this afflicted, though innocent family, are now waiting, with painful suspense, the fate of their husband and father, and their own. - I also dread lest my father should share the same unhappy fate. I flew to enquire for him, but found he was not yet taken. - O, that he may escape!

And now, my dear Lady Laurana, prepare your heart; you have need also of fortitude, if you love the Earl of Devonshire: the vindictive Queen has again sent him into confinement, though perfectly innocent of the crime with which he is charged.

On the examination of Wyatt, he had accused the Lady Elizabeth, and the Earl of Devonshire, as accomplices; but on the scaffold, acquitted them, before the people, of having any share in his rebellion. However, on his first accusation of them, Mary immediately had her sister arrested, under a strong guard, and sent to the Tower; here, however, she did not stay long; the dying declaration of Wyatt, obliged the Queen to release her: but she soon after found a pretence to imprison her again, and sent her to Woodstock; and also confined the Earl, though equally innocent, in Fotheringay Castle. - What havoc does human passion cause in the world, unguided by wisdom and virtue!

I will write to you again, if I am able to do so, when the cup of fate is filled. - I cannot afford you any consolation at present, my friend; horrible images of death present themselves continually before my eyes.

How earnestly do I pray for the fortitude of Lady Jane. - How do I admire her noble steady mind, rising with a divine radiance, above the thick cloud of fate which hovers around her. - When will it break! When will the thunder burst from it, which thus oppresses us with its intolerable weight! - O God! prepare us for the event!

Anne Grey [Lane, Vol. II 74].

Letter 28 is as follows:

I was sitting one evening in my solitary apartment, in that kind of composed melancholy, which is cherished by those who have experienced deep afflictions, and which, so far from corroding the heart, softens it to benevolence and compassion, when a servant came to say, that a gentleman wanted to impart something of importance to me, and requested he might speak to me alone; I was surprised at the message, and hesitated, at first, if I had best comply with his request or not; however, I soon admitted him, and how still more surprised and delighted was I, to receive a letter from my father, who writ me, that he had found a safe retreat, at the time that my uncle Suffolk's party was obliged to disperse and hide themselves, and that he remained in it till the search of the Queen's troops was over; that then, by the disguise of a common sailor, he obtained a passage to France, where he then was, and meant to remain, till some happy revolution rendered his country more safe to him.

My father added, that he wanted the consolations of his beloved daughter's company, and was in daily apprehensions for her safety; while she remained in England; he therefore entreated me to commit myself to the care of the gentleman, who was the barer of his letter, and who would convey me safely to him, having a proper disguise, to prevent my being discovered.

Rejoiced as I was, to recover a father whom I had almost given up for lost, my thoughts, from this pleasing circumstance, reverted to my unfortunate friends in the Tower, whom I felt great regret to quit.

I, however, told the gentleman, I was greatly rejoiced to hear of my father's safety, and would prepare myself to attend him in two days. He respectfully urged me to set out immediately, lest it should, by any means, reach the Queen's ears, that my father had sent for me.

I told him, he need be under no apprehension, but that, if possible, I would go sooner: as the Queen had confiscated all the houses and estates of my father, I had been in a friend's house ever since the late troubles; I had therefore very little to take with me, besides some valuable jewels of my mother's and my own.

As soon as my father's messenger was gone, I was preparing myself to visit my friends in the Tower, and to take a final leave of them, which was a task almost too much for my resolution, when, who should I see enter my apartment, but the Earl of Devonshire.

On hearing his voice, I started from my reveries; yet, like one just awakened from a troublesome dream, could not believe my senses; nor that what I saw was real.

He at last convinced me it was himself, and told me, that the Queen's marriage, which I imagine you must have heard of, had occasioned his enlargement, from motives which he could not account for, unless it was the wish of popularity; Don Philip had set him at liberty.

We spent two or three hours together, in the painfully-pleasing employment, of conversing on the late melancholy fate of our friends; mixing joy with our tears, that they were now at liberty from Mary's tyranny, their parent's ambition, and all the ills that beset this mortal life.

He, almost at his entrance, asked impatiently if I had heard from you, whom he has so long been utterly excluded from by his confinement, as well as from writing to you.

You will not, I am sure, be angry, if I own I read some parts of your letters to him: he was delighted with them, lamented his hard fate, in being so long separated from you, and said, he was at length permitted to go abroad, as he has obtained the Queen's consent; that he would immediately go to Florence as he was impatient to see you, and as he would make you the offer of his hand; and, if you would consent to marry him, he would reside abroad, till it was more safe for him to reside in his own country.

I entreated him to give me some account of the reasons, that led Mary to suspect him of a passion for Elizabeth, and of their mutually conspiring against her. He said, he would relate the few incidents which had happened to him, since he parted from his dear Lady Laurana, and the unfortunate Lady Jane, at the Tower, which I will give you, as nearly as I can, in his own words.

"When I first came out into the world, and was introduced, by the Queen, to the young nobility at court, I felt so conscious of my want of those accomplishments suited to my rank, and which, the many years I had been immured in prison, had prevented my acquiring, that I was resolved to devote as much of my time as I could to attain them; in the mean time, the Queen's partiality for me, would not suffer me to enjoy so much retirement as I wished for, for that purpose, and which also my long habits of solitary life had rendered almost necessary to me; as well as my love for Lady Laurana, and my earnest desire to form myself, by my address and manners, more worthy of her.

"The reception I met with at Court, however, was too insinuating for a young man, who had been secluded so long from society.

"Not to have many charms, and the only thing that rendered it irksome to me, was my absence from Laurana, and the Queen's passion, which I both dreaded and detested, and which she had very early, after our first acquaintance, got me informed of.

"Her jealousy of the Lady Elizabeth, also, who is an amiable

Princess, had given me frequent cause of uneasiness; for her conversation, both engaging and instructive to a man like me, who has had so few opportunities of conversing with sensible and well-bred women, had induced me to attach myself a good deal to her, particularly as she showed me great attention.

"The Queen you know hates the Princess, and could not support the idea that I should slight her passion, and devote my time to her sister.

"In vain I assured her, on my honor, that I had never made the slightest effort to gain the Princess's affection.

"She could not believe that I would refuse her hand and crown, without the prospect of an equivalent at some future period.

"I entreated her Majesty to permit me to go abroad; expressed my earnest desire to see foreign courts, and to get a knowledge of the customs and manners of other nations, but she would by no means consent to it.

"As I generally informed Elizabeth of the Queen's threats concerning her, she thought it best to retire from court into the country, as she met with every instance of disrespect, that the Queen could show her in public.

"And not long after Wyatt's insurrection (which has been so fatal to the Duke of Suffolk's family) commenced, Elizabeth and myself were accused of being concerned in it, and both committed to different prisons.

"But as Wyatt, on his execution, entirely acquitted us of having the least concern in it, the Lady Elizabeth was tried by the Council, and vindicated her innocence so well, that the Queen was obliged to release her from confinement, as well as myself; at that time, more from the fear of the people than inclination.

"For she soon found another pretence of confining her again, which was by proposing an alliance for her with the Duke of Savoy; which, however, that Princess, in a submissive manner, begged leave to decline, saying, she wished to remain single. But this was construed into a confirmation of an engagement with me; and, in the resistance she made to her Majesty's pleasure, she found as she thought, a sufficient plea to confine her to Woodstock, and to send me to Fotheringay Castle.

"Here we remained till the Queen's marriage with Don Philip, and his affection for popularity induced him to release those of the Nobility which Mary had confined on suspicion, amongst the rest myself, and also to undertake the defense of the Princess Elizabeth from the malice of her sister.

"He, therefore, sat her at liberty, much to the disgust of the Queen, who, I believe, already perceives that Philip is more influenced by ambitious views than love to her.

"The Princess has not, however, since been at Court, but I received a message from her, soon after our enlargement, requesting to speak with me.

"I immediately visited her, and we met with expressions of that friendship, which a similarity of sentiments and dispositions had united us in.

"She told me, she had continually regretted that the Queen's unjust suspicions of me, on her account, should have been so injurious to me; and that she would willingly undertake any thing that might contribute to my happiness, and should rejoice to make any compensation for my past sufferings on her account. She said, there was something in my manner at times, which convinced her that some Lady had possession of my affections, though I dare not own it, on account of the Queen's partiality for me; but now her Majesty was married, she thought she had influence enough with Philip to engage him to promote the alliance; she, therefore besought me to consider her as my sincere friend, and to unfold to her my inclinations without reserve.

"I was struck with her goodness, but yet was at a loss what to do. Elizabeth, though possessed of eminent virtues, is vain, and fond of admiration.

"I had, on many occasions, observed, that she did not like that any Lady should have the preference to herself, not only in mine, but in the opinion of those Lords about her, whom she favored with any marks of attention.

"I thought too, that there was something in her manner confused, and as if she meant, by an appearance of generosity, to draw me into a declaration of particular attachment to herself; and if so, instead of extricating myself from the difficulties that lay in my way to the possession of Laurana, by my confidence in the Princess, I should only, perhaps, be involving myself in greater.

"What could I do? I had not seen enough of courts, and the deceits of them, to submit to the meanness of a lie. I was silent and confused; it was some time, before I could recollect myself sufficiently to thank her, for the interest she took in my happiness; to beg she would not urge me on a subject which I must ever be silent on, and to assure her, that the sense of her goodness would never be erased from my heart; and that, wherever my fate drove me, the Princess Elizabeth would ever possess the most sincere friendship of Devonshire.

"The Princess blushed, and I perceived that this speech flattered her vanity; she evidently imputed my confusion and reserve, to a passion for herself, which my respect for her, and the situation we were in, forbade my revealing.

"I was rejoiced, therefore, that I had not revealed my secret; and she did not urge me any more on the subject, but desired me to inform her if, in any thing, she could be serviceable to me with Don Philip.

"I told her, I thought myself very insecure in England, in my present situation, and had also a wish to improve myself by travel, and, if she would have the goodness to desire Don Philip to intercede with the Queen for that purpose, I should esteem myself infinitely obliged to her, though I should still regret the loss of her conversation, which had afforded me so many agreeable hours.

"The Princess took my compliment graciously, and promised to endeavor to obtain my desire, which she soon after effected.

"I went to court, to thank the Queen for this permission, but she would not see me, which I was no otherwise concerned at, than as it may affect the Princess's safety. I have seen Lady Elizabeth several times since, who has always shown me great attention, and friendly solicitude for my welfare.

"I am ready now to set out, and will, with pleasure, convey whatever letters, or message, you may have to your friend, my charming Laurana: the impatience which I suffer to behold her again cannot be equaled."

I informed the Earl, when he had ended his account, that my father was in safety, in France, and desired me to join him there; that he had sent a messenger to convey me to him, and that I should set out in two days.

He seemed quite rejoiced at the event; he said he would prepare himself to accompany me, and that when he had obtained his Laurana's hand, he would endeavor to prevail on her, to make mine the place of their residence.

Then, added he, I may hope for an amiable female companion for my wife, which will contribute to her happiness, and with *still* so many worthy friends about us, may I not flatter myself that, in spite of the past cruelty of my fate, I shall be one of the happiest of mortals?

I objected to his accompanying me as highly improper, since it would lay open my father's situation, and our affairs to the inspection of the Queen, in all probability; that he would go abroad in a manner suitable to his rank, but that I had a disguise provided for me, and should go in the most private manner that was possible.

He said, he could not prevail on himself to permit me to go, attended only by a stranger; that therefore, if I would pardon him, he would recommend to me to go in disguise, and attended by this gentleman, in his train, or, as passengers in the same vessel; that as soon as they were landed on the French shore, he would privately attend me, and commit me in safety to my father's arms.

I thanked him very sincerely, and said, I had no objection to his proposal, but the apprehension, least he should render himself liable to the Queen's displeasure, should we be discovered; or that, my father's asylum being found out, the consequences might be fatal to him; and those fears, I owned, were so great, that I should not enjoy a moment's peace during my voyage. I therefore declined his offer, and determined in the disguise prepared for me, and under the protection of the gentleman my father had sent, to commit myself to Providence, and take my voyage.

I went and took a sorrowful leave of my friends in the Tower, who expressed a great and generous pleasure in my father's safety, notwithstanding their own sad fate, and prayed that I might safely join my father.

They also found pleasure in the Earl's release, and prospect of happiness, and discovered those great and worthy minds, which, though under the chastening hand of Heaven themselves, can rejoice without envy at the felicity of their friends and fellow creatures.

Long we lingered before we could think of parting, and nothing but the approach of night could tear me from them; and, even then, I thought, was I to consult my own inclination, I had rather, at the time, have remained with them to console and entertain them, than forsake them in so bitter a fate. – But my father's will, and his want of an affectionate daughter, to render his exile more tolerable, enabled me to make a violent effort of resolution, and quit the place.

But adieu – perhaps forever! I could not say!

No sleep scarcely had I that night, but wept almost incessantly.

My father's messenger appeared in the morning, and brought with him my disguise – I told him I should be ready to attend him in the evening, and desired him to prepare every thing for me, and return early.

I had taken leave of my friend, in whose house I was, and was preparing to depart, when I was surprised by the appearance of the Earl, completely disguised as well as myself; who said he could not suffer me to set out without his protection; that, therefore, he had given orders that his suit should go in the vessel they were designed for, and told them and the captain, that he was obliged himself to sail in another ship.

Though much alarmed for his safety, he would hear none of my objections, and we went on board of the vessel provided for me.

As soon as we had sat down in the cabin, the Earl entered into an agreeable conversation, which a little dissipated my melancholy thoughts at quitting England, perhaps for ever, that recent scene of so much bloodshed, and so many horrors; but it was the recollection of my unhappy friends, that rendered my heart heavy; nor could I banish them from my idea, for in spite of his endeavors to awaken more pleasing and cheerful remembrances, our conversation adverted to them.

Yet, he still encouraged me to hope, that they would soon be released; that it would be of no consequence to the Queen to keep them confined, since their party was quelled entirely. He entreated me, therefore, to endeavor to banish sorrow from my heart, and to sympathize with him in his extreme joy, at the thoughts of seeing again his charming Lady Laurana.

I told him, I would endeavor to do it, in the hopes he had given me, that my captive friends would soon be at liberty. I began to look forward also, as the shore of France approached, to the pleasure of seeing again a father, for whom I had the sincerest duty and affection, preserved from the wreck of fate. I felt the most affecting gratitude to Heaven, for this consolation in my heavy afflictions; and for that goodness, which had not suffered me to sink under them, but preserved me to assist in supporting and comforting my exiled father.

Thus, I am persuaded, will all those, who listen to the divine lessons of resignation in their sorrows, have reason for gratitude in the midst of the severest fate; even though they cannot penetrate the veil of Providence, nor understand why they are thus severely dealt with.

I had began this letter before I received yours, which both delighted and shocked me. I was charmed to think that you had abjured the errors of popery; admired your sentiments on zeal and charity; but how was I shocked at the account of your impatience at the confinement of the Earl! – May Heaven preserve the reason of my friend, exclaimed I, with fervor! – O! may she be preserved from destroying herself! – from abruptly presenting a guilty soul, stained with suicide, before a pure and righteous God! – O! lay not on her more than her frail nature can support!

I congratulate you, my fair friend, on the happiness that awaits you. – Write to me at B-, where my father is. – I send this from the first inn we put up at in France. We remain here to-night, and in the morning, proceed on our journey to B-.

The Earl is resolved to accompany me; my father will rejoice to see him: his own ship and suite are not yet arrived; he has only one servant with him, in whom he can confide. – My father intends to meet me half way. With what delight shall I see him again, after so long an absence?

Farewell, my charming Laurana; you have with this a letter from the Earl.

Anne Grey [Lane 136].

APPENDIX VI. MAPS

Map 1. Where Wyatt's proclamations were issued

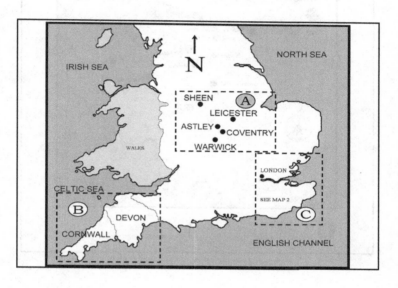

Main areas where Wyatt's proclamations against the queen were issued
[NOT TO SCALE]

    A: *The Duke of Suffolk in the North.*
    B: *Peter Carew in the counties of Devon and Cornwall.*
    C: *Thomas Wyatt in Kent and London.*

Map 2. Proclamations and Anti-Proclamations

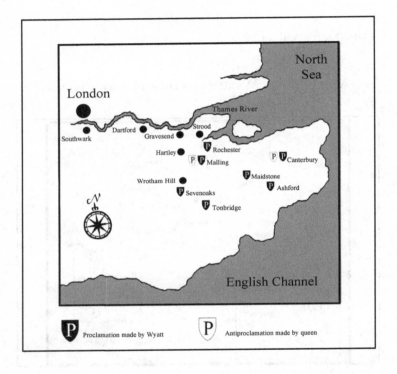

Map 3. Boulogne and Fort Chattilon

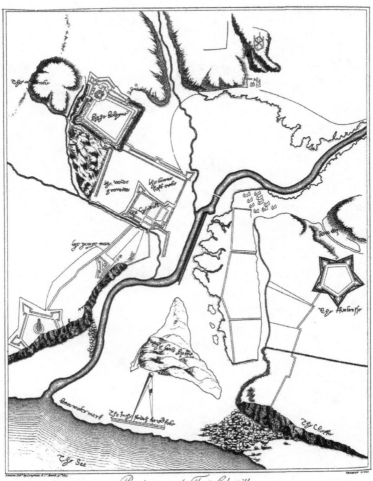

Boulogne, and Fort Chattillon.

From the Earl of Surrey's original Plan in the British Museum.

BIBLIOGRAPHY

Primary Sources

Aikin, Lucy. *Memoirs of The Court of Queen Elizabeth.* In two volumes. Long-man, Hurst, Rees, Orme and Brown. Paternoster Row London, 1818.

Arber, Edward. English Reprints, *Tottel's Miscellany, Songes and Sonnettes by Henry Howard, Earl of Surrey, Sir Thomas Wyatt the Elder.* A. Constable and Co. Westminster 1895.

Bayley, John Esq. F.S.A. *The History and Antiquities of the Tower of London.* In two volumes. London England: T. Cadell, 1821-25.

Brown, D. (printed for). *The History of the Life, Bloody Reign and Death of Queen Mary, eldest daughter to Henry VIII.* London England, 1682.

Calendar of Letters, Despatches, and State Papers relating to the negotiations between England the Spain. Royall Tyler. Longman, Green, Longman & Roberts,

    -Volume VIII Henry VIII 1545-1546. London 1900.

    -Volume XII Mary January-July, 1554. London 1949.

Churchyard, Thomas. *A Pleasant discourse of Court (and) of wars, with a repli-cation to them both, and a commendation of all those that truly serve Prince and Country,* written (in verse) by Thomas Churchyard, and called his Cherishing. By A. Hatfield for W. Holme, London, 1596.

Cruden, Robert Peirce. *The History of the Town of Gravesend in the County of Kent and of the Port of London.* W. Pickering, London 1843.

Ellis, Henry. *Original Letters relative to the English Reformation.* London England: R. Bentley, 3 series, 1825, 1827 and 1846.

Finch, Arah-Dean G. *The Wyatt Family of England and America with special reference to the descendants of John Wyatt of Morgan County Illinois.* 1929.

Hamilton, William Douglas. *A Chronicle of England, during the Reigns of the Tudors, from A.D. 1485 to 1559.* By Charles Wriothesley, Windsor Herald. London, 1877.

Holinshed, Raphael. *The First and Second Volumes of Chronicles, Comprising the Description and History of England, Ireland and Scotland.* London: Henry Denham, 1587.

Maclean, John Esq. *The Life and Times of Sir Peter Carew, Kt.* Bell and Daldy, London 1857.

Nichols, John Gough. *The Chronicle of Queen Jane and of Two Years of Queen Mary and especially of the Rebellion of Sir Thomas Wyat.* Camden Society, 1850.

Nott, George Frederick. *The Works of Henry Howard Earl of Surrey and of Sir Thomas Wyatt the elder.* Two volumes. London, 1816-18.

Pollard, A. F. *Tudor tracts 1532-1588.* Archiblad Constable and Co., Ltd. Westminster 1903.

Proctor, John. *The History of Wyates Rebellion.* London, 1554.

Stowe, John. *The Abridgement of the English Chronicle, First Collected by M. lohn Stow.* London 1611.

——*The Annales of England, Faithfully collected out of the most autenticall authors, records and other monuments of antiquitie.* London 1605.

Strype, John. *Historical Memorials, Ecclesiastical and Civil, of Events under the Reign of Queen Mary I. Volume III.* London. Printed by S. Richardson for John Wyat. 1721.

Wyatt, Thomas. *The Poetical Works of Sir Thomas Wyatt, with a Memoir.* Little, Brown & Co. 1854.

Secondary Sources

Abridgement of the History of England. Being a Summary of Mr. Rapin's History and Mr. Tindal's Continuation. Printed for John Paul Knapton, London 1747.

Adventures and Amours of the Marquis de Noailles and Mademoiselle Tencin. Printed in Ludgate Street, London 1746.

An excellent epitaffe of syr Thomas Wyat; with two other compendious ditties, wherein are touched, and set furth the state of mannes lyfe. London 1545.

Burghley, William Cecill, Lord. *A Collection of State Papers relating to Affairs in the Reigns of King Henry VIII, King Edward VI, Queen Mary, Queen*

Elizabeth. London, 1740.

Burnet, Gilbert. *The History of the Reformation of the Church of England in Two Parts.* London England: by J.D. for Richard Chiswell, 1691.

Calendar of Inquisitions Post Mortem and other Analogous Documents preserved in the Public Record Office.

-Volume III Henry VII London 1955.

Calendar of Letters, Despatches, and State Papers relating to the negotiations between England the Spain. Royall Tyler. Longman, Green, Longman & Roberts,

-Volume I Henry VII 1485-1509. London 1862.

-Volume VI Part 1, Henry VIII 1538-1542. London 1890.

-Volume VI Part II Henry VIII 1542-1543. London 1895.

-Volume X Edward VI 1550-1552. London 1932.

-Volume XI Edward VI and Mary, 1553. London, 1916.

-Volume XIII Philip and Mary, July 1554-November 1558. London 1954.

Calendar of the Patent Rolls preserved in the Public Record Office. Edward VI

-Volume 1, 1547-1548 His Majesty's Stationery Office 1924.

-Volume 2, 1548-1549 His Majesty's Stationery Office 1924.

-Volume 3, 1549-1551 His Majesty's Stationery Office 1925.

-Volume 4, 1550-1553 His Majesty's Stationery Office 1926.

-Volume 5, 1547-1553 His Majesty's Stationery Office 1926.

Calendar of the Patent Rolls. Philip and Mary.

-Volume 1, 1553-1554 Kraus-Thomson. Nendeln/Liechtenstein, 1970.

-Volume III, 1555-1557, London 1938.

-Volume IV, 1557-1558.

Cecill, William. *A Collection of State Papers relating to affairs in the reigns of King Henry VIII, King Edward VI, Queen Mary, Queen Elizabeth.* Lord Burghley London, 1760.

Chrimes, S.B. *Henry VII.* University of California Press, 1972.

Christopherson, John. *An Exhortation to all Menne to take hede of rebellion.* London, July 1554.

Cobbett's Complete Collection of State Trials and Proceeding for High Treason and other Crimes and Misdemeanors. London 1809.

Collins, Arthur. *Letters and Memorials of State, in the Reigns of Queen Mary, Queen Elizabeth, King James....* London England: T. Osborne, 1746.

Copland, W. The Copie of the publication of the trewse made between the most Cristien Kyne Henry Second. London 1555 or 1556.

Cox, Nicholas. Courtnay, Earl of Devon; or, the Trouble of the Princess Elizabeth, a Tragedy. London, 1707.

Days, John. The Second Volume of the Ecclesiasticall History, conteynyng the Actes and Monumentes of Martyrs. London, 1570.

Descriptive Catalogue of Ancient Deeds in the Public Record Office.

-Volume III, London 1900.

-*Volume V*, London 1906.

Dickens, A. G. *The English Reformation*. The Pennsylvania State University Press, University Park, Pennsylvania. 1964.

Foley, Stephen Merriam. *Sir Thomas Wyatt*. Twayne Publishers, Brown University 1990.

Foxwell, A. K. *The Poems of Sir Thomas Wiat*. Russell & Russell Inc. New York 1964.

Godwin, Francis. Annals of England: Containing the Reigns of Henry the Eighth, Edward the Sixth, Queen Mary. London England: by W.G. for T. Basset, 1675.

Godwyn, Morgan. Annals of England Containing the Reigns of Henry VIII, Edward VI and Queen Mary. Printed by W.G. 1675.

Grafton, Richard. An Abridgement of the Chronicles of England, gathered by Richard Grafton, Citizen of London. London 1563.

Harley, Robert, Earl of Oxford. Catalogue of the Harleian Collection of Manuscripts in the British Museum. London England: by D. Leach, 1759 edition.

Heylyn, Peter. Exam Historicum, or, a Discovery and examination of the Mistakes, Falsities and Defects in some Modern Historics. London, 1659.

Ecclesia Restaurata, or The History of the Reformation of the Church of England. An Appendex to the former book touching the Interposings made in Behalf of the Lady Jane Gray. London England: H. Twyford, 1661.

Howes, Edmund. Annales, or A Generall Chronicle of England. London, 1631

Impartial Account of Richard Duke of York's Treasons. Printed for Allen Banks, London, 1671.

Hume, David, Esq. *The History of England*. In 6 volumes. London England for A. Miller, 1762.

Jardine, David, Esq. Criminal Trials during the reigns of Queen Elizabeth and James I. Nattali and Bond, London, 1835.

King, J. *A Breviat Chronicle: containing al the kynes, from Brute to this daye.* 1554.

Lee, Sidney. *Elizabethan Sonnets Newly Arranged and Indexed.* Cooper Square Press, Inc. New York 1964.

Levy, Fred Jacob. *Tudor Historical Thought.* The Huntington Library, San Marino California, 1967.

Loach, Jennifer. *Edward VI.* New Haven Connecticut: Yale University Press, 1999.

Loades, D. M. *The Papers of George Wyatt Esquire of Boxley Abbey in the County of Kent.* University College London, London 1968.

John Dudley, Duke of Northumberland, 1504-1553. Oxford University Press, Oxford. 1996.

Lodge, Edmund, Esq. *Illustrations of British History, Biography, and Manners, in the Reigns of Henry VIII, Edward VI, Mary, Elizabeth, and James I.* London: J. Chidley, 1838.

Muir, Kenneth. *Life and Letters of Sir Thomas Wyatt.* Liverpool University Press. 1963.

Nicolas, Nicholas Harris. *The Literary Remains of Lady Jane Grey.* Harding, Triphook and Lepard. London 1825.

Nichols, John Gough. *The Diary of Henry Machyn, Citizen and Merchant Taylor of London from A.D. 1550 to A.D. 1563.* London 1848.

Nicholson, William. *The English Historical Library. Giving a Catalogue of the most of our Ecclesiastical Historians.* London, 1697.

Phillips, Thomas. *The History of the life of Reginald Pole.* London, 1767.

Pollard, A.F. *Tudor Tracts, 1532-1588.* Archiblad Constable and Co., LTD. Westminster 1903.

Pollard, Alfred W. *A Short-title Catalogue of books printed in England, Scotland and Ireland and of English book published abroad, 1475-1460.* London, 1926.

Rapin de Thoyras (Paul). *An Abridgement of the History of England. Being a summary of Mr. Rapin's Hisotry.* John and Paul Knapton, London 1747.

Rich, Barnabe. *Allarme to England: Foreshewing what perilles are procured.* Printed by Henrie Middleton, London, 1578.

Robinson, Rev. Hastings. *Original Letters Relative to the English Reformation, written during the Reigns of King Henry VIII, King Edward VI, and Queen Mary.* New York: Johnson Reprint Corp., 1846.

Sanford, Francis. *A Genealogical History of the Kings of England and Monarchs of Great Britain.* Thomas Newcomb. London 1677.

Scarisbrick, J. J. *Henry VIII.* University of California Press, 1968.

Schenk, Wilhelm. *Reginald Pole, Cardinal of England.* Longmans, Green. London, New York, 1950.

Simonds, William Edward. *Sir Thomas Wyatt and His Poems*. D.C Heath and Co, Boston 1889.

Smith, George. *The Dictionary of National Biography*. Oxford University Press, London 1922.

Starkey, David. *Six Wives, The Queens of Henry VIII*. Harper Collins, New York, 2003.

Strype, John. *Memorials of the Most Reverend Father in God, Thomas Cranmer, sometime Lord Archbishop of Canterbury. In three books*. London: R. Chiswell, 1694.

Thomas, F. S. *Historical Notes 1509-1714* Her Majesty's Stationery Office, London 1856.

Thurley, Dr. Simon. *The Royal Palaces of Tudor England*. New Haven: Yale University Press, 1993.

Ule, Louis. *A Map of London and Southwark, 1580-1620*. Rolling Hills, CA 1967. (Map reference)

Waley, John. *A Table collected of the yeres of our lord God, and of the yeres of the Kings of England*. London, 1567.

Woltmann, Alfred Friedrich Gottfried Albert. *Holbein and his Time*. R. Bentley and son, London, 1872.